Anonymus

Of the Origin and Progress of Language

Volume III.

Anonymus

Of the Origin and Progress of Language
Volume III.

ISBN/EAN: 9783742802064

Manufactured in Europe, USA, Canada, Australia, Japa

Cover: Foto ©Andreas Hilbeck / pixelio.de

Manufactured and distributed by brebook publishing software (www.brebook.com)

Anonymus

Of the Origin and Progress of Language

OF THE

ORIGIN AND PROGRESS

OF

LANGUAGE.

*Graiis ingenium, Graiis dedit ore rotundo
Mufa loqui.* ——— HORAT.

VOL. III.

THE SECOND EDITION.

LONDON:
PRINTED FOR T. CADELL, IN THE STRAND;
AND J. BALFOUR, EDINBURGH.
MDCCLXXXVI.

ADVERTISEMENT.

THE public demand has made a second edition proper, of this third volume of the Origin and Progress of Language, which completes the work; the firſt volume containing the Hiſtory of Language, its origin and progreſs among the barbarous nations—The ſecond, conſidering it as an art brought to perfection by nations more civilized, and explaining the ſcience and philoſophy of it—The third, ſhewing how words, the doctrine of which had been explained in the preceding part, are to be put together, ſo as to form what we call Style. Of theſe three parts the theory of language confifts: and, however defective the execution may be, I think I can venture to fay, that the plan is as complete and as comprehenfive as any that ever was executed, or even propofed upon the fubject.

The learned of this age, though they be fo much occupied with facts of natural hiftory, minerals, plants, flies, and reptiles, that they have no time to apply to the hiftory and philofophy of their own fpecies; yet I fhould think they would have fome curiofity about an art fo exceedingly ufeful, by which the whole bufinefs of human life is carried on; by which arts and fciences have been conveyed from man to man, and from nation to nation, and from the earlieft to the lateft ages; and without which they could not have been inftructed in the knowledge they value fo much: for

ADVERTISEMENT.

how elſe could they profit by the moſt accurate account of inſects, which Reaumur has given in ſix volumes in quarto, containing the hiſtory of flies with two wings, and flies with four wings, with a ſupplement to the hiſtory of flies with two wings; but which he very modeſtly intitles not a hiſtory, but only Memoires pour ſervir à l'Hiſtoire des Inſectes.

THE CONTENTS.

PART II.

BOOK IV.

                                Page

INTRODUCTION, - - - 1

Chap.

1. Divifion of ftyle into fingle words, and the compofition of thofe words—Each of thefe heads fubdivided—General plan of this part of the work, - - 10

2. Of changes made upon the found of words, for the greater beauty and variety of compofition—Examples of fuch changes in Greek—Much fewer in modern languages—Examples of fome in Englifh, - 15

3. Of proper words—Divifion of them into radical and derivative—Another divifion of them into fuch as are of the original ftock of the language, and fuch as are foreign—Thofe of Latin extraction moftly derived from corrupt Latinity—The reftoring them to their genuine fignification a beauty of ftyle, - - - - 23

CONTENTS.

Chap.   Page

4. Of Tropes, and the different kinds of them; particularly of metaphors—Metaphors used from necessity as well as for ornament—Observations on the use of metaphors,   -   -   -   31

5. Of the second part of style, viz. composition—This considered, first, with respect to sound—That diversified in the learned languages by musical tones and rhythms, which we have not—The sound, therefore, in our composition, can only be varied by the order of the words, and by periods—Each of these considered, and illustrated by examples,   -   -   45

6. Of figures of syntax—The Ellipsis—The Parenthesis—Repetition—Paronomasia—Like endings—Parisosis—Inconsequence—Foreign idioms—A figure of Milton without example—Transposition of words,   65

7. Recapitulation—Of the figures by which the sense is varied—These divided into three kinds—Of the first is Exclamation—Hyperbole—Epithet—Prosopopoeia—And Description,   -   -   106

8. Of the second kind of composition, figured with respect to the sense, viz. by the imi-

Chap. Page

tation of characters—The difference betwixt this kind of style and the pathetic—The difference betwixt describing and imitating a character—The Ethic style belongs both to Poetry and Rhetoric, but in different respects, - - 122

9. The great variety of composition illustrated by an example.—Of the third kind of figures of the sense—Some of these named, such as Interrogation—Antithesis—Simile—Allegory—Many more of such figures have no name—The use of them in composition—Examples of them from Virgil's Georgics, and Dr. Armstrong's Poem on Health—Praise of that Poem—Conclusion of what relates to the figures of speech—Apology for the Author's being so minute in explaining them, - - 137

10. An apology for the style of the author—The three general characters of style: The simple, the highly ornamented, and the middle between these two—Nature and use of the simple style—Lysias, the first who brought this style to perfection—Menander, and his translator, Terence, are perfect models of it—Among the moderns, Dean Swift, in his Gulliver's Travels, has excelled in it, - - 181

x   CONTENTS.

Chap.   Page
11. Of the ornamented ſtyle—This divided into
    two kinds, the auſtere and the florid—Of
    the firſt kind is the ſtyle of Thucydides—
    Character of that ſtyle—Of the ſtyle of
    Salluſt,   -   -   -   198

12. Of the ſtyle of Tacitus—That ſtyle conſi-
    dered by many as a model—Not an origi-
    nal ſtyle, but an imitation of Salluſt—Ge-
    neral obſervations upon it—Particular ex-
    amples—Of his unconnected compoſition
    —Of abrupt and harſh—Of obſcure brevi-
    ty—Of affectation in the expreſſion, and
    obſcurity thence ariſing—Compared in this
    reſpect with Julius Cæſar—Poetical dic-
    tion of Tacitus—Poetical deſcription—
    Quaintneſs and affectation of ſmartneſs—
    Praiſe of Tacitus as to his matter—Some
    things alſo in his ſtyle commendable—Effect
    that the imitation of him has had upon the
    ſtyle of modern writers—The beſt imitation
    of him is in Mr. Mallet's Life of Chancellor
    Bacon,   -   -   -   210

13. The ſtyle of Tacitus has the general charac-
    ter of the ſtyle of the age—The ſchools of
    declamation the cauſe of ſo general a cor-
    ruption of taſte among the Romans coming
    on ſo faſt—The beginning of thoſe ſchools

CONTENTS.

Chap.   Page

    at Rome, and the progress of them—The bad effects of them upon the taste of writing of all kinds—Some specimens of their style—Seneca the philosopher's style of the same kind - - - 250

14. Of the other kind of ornamented style, the gay and florid—Antient authors who have written in that style—Modern, such as my Lord Shaftsbury—Character of this style - - 282

15. Of the middle style—Examples of that style, antient and modern,   286

16. Of a fourth general character of style, the sublime—It consists chiefly of the matter—Examples of it—The counterpart of the sublime, or mock-heroic—Examples of this style, antient and modern—Improper use of it by Mr. Fielding, in his history of Tom Jones—Of a sixth general character of style, the ridiculous—The meaning of the word—The nature of the thing—The reason of the pleasure it gives us—General observations upon it—Vanity and affectation the proper subjects of it—Examples of a proper and an improper ridiculous character—Authors antient and modern that have excelled in the ridiculous—It does not belong to the greatest geniuses,   288

CONTENTS.

Chap.   Page

17. Of another general character of ſtyle, viz. the witty—Nature of wit, and the three things which it requires—Examples of this from the laconic apophthegms—from the ſayings of philoſophers, and from Cicero—Wit ariſes from the ambiguity of words, either ſingle or in compoſition—from metaphor—ſimile—antitheſis, - 315

18. The difference betwixt humour and a humouriſt—One ſpecies of humour is the imitation of the humouriſt—a general definition of it—Uſe of it in modern comedy—incompatible with wit, - - 342

19. Particular characters of ſtyle—Firſt, the ſtyle of cónverſation—quite different from that of public ſpeaking—The epiſtolary ſtyle—more conciſe than that of converſation—The didactic ſtyle—of two kinds—The different manner of the two didactic poems of Virgil and Lucretius—The hiſtorical ſtyle—It conſiſted of two parts among the antients—narrative and rhetorical—Is only narrative among the moderns—but the narrative often too rhetorical and poetical, 349

20. General obſervations—Compoſition an art as well as language—The Greeks our maſters both in that art and the other fine arts,

CONTENTS.

Chap.   Page

such as sculpture—The Romans likewise our masters, but at second-hand—only to be imitated in so far as they themselves imitated the Greeks—Praise of the style of Horace—Julius Cæsar—Cicero—Upon the revival of letters, the Greek writers most studied and imitated, particularly in England, - - - 370

21. The necessity of forming a style by imitation—The Greek authors the best models for imitation—Next to them the Latin—Who next to the Greek and Latin?—Not the writings of the French *Beaux Esprits* of this age—Examination of those French writers, both as to their matter and style—The imitation of our own authors, who have formed themselves upon the antient models, is best, next to the imitation of the Greek and Latin, - - 393

22. Composition not so difficult in English as in Greek and Latin—This arises from the want of rhythm and melody in our language, and the variety of structure of the antient languages—What is proper and suitable, essential in writing as well as in other arts—Art should not appear too much in composition—The practice of making different styles of the same words useful—Translation, and the use to be made of it, 403

CONTENTS.

Chap. Page

23. Of the sophistical style—Three several species of it—The pedantic—the florid—and the austere—The present style generally of the second kind—The antient authors who have written in this style—not approved of by the first restorers of learning—The causes that produce the sophistical style—Men of business the best writers, if not deficient in genius and learning—Sir John Checke's judgment in this matter, 413

24. A short account of the fate of antient learning in the several periods of the world—All the learning of Europe originally from Egypt—The first great blow to learning the destruction of the colleges of the Egyptian priests—The second, the destruction of the Pythagorean colleges in Italy—The third, the loss of the liberty of Greece, and the extinction of learning and good taste there—The fourth, the loss of liberty at Rome, and the corruption of taste there—The fifth, the conquests of the Saracens and Turks—The present state of antient learning in Europe—How the taste of it is to be revived, - - - 435

25. Conclusion of this part of the work—Two kinds of men will despise it—the avaricious and the luxurious—Something said to the first of these—more to the last—Leisure,

sure, which is thought so great a blessing, is the greatest source of human misery, if not well employed—Education only can enable men to employ leisure well—Bodily exercises formerly employed much time—These now laid aside—Arts and sciences now only remain to fill up leisure—By these only we have any advantages over savages—The Romans a striking example of the effect of Greek philosophy and arts—These preserved virtue among them in the most degenerate times—Another use of antient learning is to improve our luxury, and prevent, as far as possible, the bad effects of it—The want of it in this respect among us, and the fatal consequences of such want, - - - 445

PREFACE.

THE subject of this volume is *Style*, the next step in the progress of language after the grammatical part is completed—A subject of great importance, as it is by *style* only that language is made fit to answer the great purposes of life.

Now that I am so far advanced in this work, I begin to be sensible that it is not at all of a fashionable or popular kind. In the first part of it, which treats of the origin of language, I have been led, by my subject, to give an account of human nature, in what may be called its infantine state, such as will be thought by many highly derogatory from its dignity, and will therefore give great offence. My attempt also, to revive the old philosophy of Plato and Aristotle, will much displease those who think we have arrived to the summit of philosophy and science of every kind; and it will be thought by them a difgrace to this very learned age, that it fhould be propofed to us to go to fchool again, and return to thofe mafters once fo revered by our anceftors, but now almoft univerfally exploded.

It is for the honour of this antient philofophy, that there has been no example, as far as I know, of any man learned in it who was addicted to that *mad philofophy*, fo prevalent in our days, which excludes *mind* from the fyftem of the univerfe. The philofophers of this kind I have treated not only with indignation but contempt, as men of whom it may be truly faid, what Caligula the emperor faid moft falfely of Virgil the poet, that they are *nullius ingenii et minimae doctrinae*. To fuch men, whofe chief motive for publifhing doctrines fo pernicious to mankind is vanity, and an affectation of fuperior parts, I muft have given moft deadly offence.

In my firft volume, I may be faid to have attacked *human* vanity, by what I have faid of man in his natural ftate. And, in my fecond volume, I have fhocked the *national* vanity by the account I have given of our language and poetry, compared with thofe of the antients. But, in this volume, by what I have faid of *ftyle*, and of thofe great antient mafters of the writing art, the ftudy and imitation of whom can alone, in my judgment, form a good ftyle, I am afraid I have raifed up againft myfelf a more formidable fet of enemies than any I have hitherto mentioned ; I mean the fafhionable authors of this age, who have acquired great reputation as well as profit by their writings, and yet muft be confcious that it is not upon thofe models they have formed their ftyle. I am defirous of the praife of very few ; but I would not willingly give offence to any ; and, if thofe gentlemen will accept as an apology what follows, I fhall be glad of it. In the firft place, then, if they have really formed fo fine a ftyle and tafte of writing, as they and their admirers fuppofe, without the affiftance of learning, it is the greater praife of their genius and natural parts, and they may with juftice defpife me and others who grovel fo meanly after the antients, *adoring, at a diftance, thofe footfteps* in which we muft confefs ourfelves unable to tread. Nor have I said any thing of their writings in particular, though I have taken the liberty of animadverting pretty severely upon the style of some antient authors. They may, therefore, for me, admire themselves as much as ever; and their panegyrists may continue to set them up as standards for style and composition, and worthy to take the place of the old classics, when they shall be intirely neglected and forgot. Further, I acknowledge, that, if I had addressed this work to them, in which I have so much extolled authors that they do not read or understand, it would have been very ill-bred; but they should consider, that I write not for them, but chiefly for the scholars in England, and for the few that the prevalence of the French learning has left yet remaining in other parts of Europe. If this does not satisfy them, nothing remains but that they should continue to abuse me in Magazines and Reviews, by themselves or some nameless scribblers that they instigate, secure against any answers from me. For, though I think myself very much obliged to those who correct the many errors

PREFACE. xxi

I muſt have fallen into in the courſe of ſo long and ſo various a work, and am ready to acknowledge the obligation upon every occaſion, I am not ſo meanly vain as to value either the cenſure or applauſe of ignorance :

> Falſus honor juvat, aut mendax infamia terret,
> Quem niſi mendoſum aut mendacem.

But, whatever they may ſay of my knowledge of antient learning, they ſhould not, out of regard to the credit of the country, ſay any thing to the diſparagement of the learning itſelf, nor publiſh to the world, that a man in Scotland cannot be a good Greek and Latin ſcholar, without running the hazard of being eſteemed a man of no taſte or genius for ſcience *. For,

---

* In the Edinburgh Magazine and Review for the month of July 1775, there is a review of Mr Harris's Philoſophical Arrangements, which concludes in this manner :—' Upon the whole, Mr Harris, even in
' the preſent volume, with all its imperfections, has
' an elevation of ſentiment that riſes above the ordi-
' nary reach of mere claſſical ſcholars. He may be
' conſidered as a ſingular exception to a general and
' well-founded obſervation, that thoſe who have been

though it be true that antient literature is much declined among us, it is heartily regretted, not only by the scholar, but every man of sense and lover of his country, as the loss of what was once the greatest ornament of this country.

'remarkable for their skill in Greek and Latin, have 'seldom discovered a good taste, or any talents for 'philosophical disquisition.'

What would those scribblers be at? Would they put an end to the grammatical art, which is only learned by the study of these languages? Do they not know that a rude, imperfect language, such as ours, cannot be otherways improved than by the study of more perfect languages? Would they destroy all beauty, elegance, and even perspicuity of style? Would they have our learning and philosophy to speak a language as barbarous as the German metaphysics of Leibnitz, or the Swedish natural history of Linnaeus, which are not even intelligible, except to those who have made a particular study of their *lingos*? Ought not the public to resent such an attempt to put down our whole school, and a great part of our university education, and to render it impossible for our country ever to make again so conspicuous a figure in the great council of the nation as it does at present, by men who derive from *antient* learning, not only the ornaments of speech, but an elevation of spirit and sentiment which that learning, and that learning only, can bestow?

PREFACE. xxiii

Upon the whole, in an age in which the nomenclature of plants, and facts of natural history, are the chief study of those who pretend to learning; and, in the fashionable world, the foppery of modern languages and foreign wit (to use an expression of my Lord Shaftesbury) are reckoned the chief accomplishments, I cannot expect that a work of this kind should be much relished. Nevertheless, I am not sorry to have left, before I die, this memorial behind me, that the taste and knowledge of antient philosophy, and antient literature, was not, in the year 1776, wholly lost in Scotland, notwithstanding the endeavours of certain persons to discredit this kind of learning, merely from a consciousness that they themselves do not excel in it; for I aver, that there is no example of any man who truly understood the antient learning, and did not prefer it to every other.

OF THE
ORIGIN AND PROGRESS
OF
LANGUAGE.

PART II. BOOK IV.

OF STYLE.

INTRODUCTION.

LANGUAGE being formed in the manner I have defcribed in the preceeding volume, and completed both in fenfe and found; what remains is to apply it to the purpofe for which it was invented, that is, the communication of our thoughts to one another. This is done by compofing, either in fpeaking, or in writing. The composition I here mean is not that by which words are put together in syntax, or grammatical conſtruction; for that belongs to the grammatical art, and I have already treated of it; but I mean the *manner* of expreſſing our thoughts, and which is commonly known by another name, viz. *ſtyle*. For, in every compoſition of words, we muſt diſtinguiſh three things; the ſubject or matter of the compoſition; the order or method in which that ſubject is treated; and, *laſtly*, the ſtyle or manner of the expreſſion, which may be very different, the ſubject and method continuing the ſame.

As it is by ſtyle or compoſition that language produces its effect, and anſwers the purpoſe for which it was intended, the nature of this work, which is a general theory of language, requires that we ſhould treat of it as well as the grammatical part of language.

Compoſition, as I have ſaid, may be either in ſpeaking or in writing; but of theſe two, ſpeaking is ſo much the nobler art, by how much language is not only more antient, but of greater uſe, as well as more difficult invention, than the notation of it by characters of any kind, whether alphabetical, hieroglyphical, or, what is more antient than either, natural reprefentations of things. The affairs of life were conducted, and the counfels of men directed by fpeaking, long before the writing art was invented, nay, are at this day fo directed among the Indians of North-America, whom we are pleafed to call barbarous, but who deliberate and determine in matters of public concern with a fedatenefs, gravity, and attention to the fpeeches of their orators, which do not at all favour of barbarity: And in antient Greece and Rome, even after the invention of letters, their weightieft affairs, both in war and peace, were decided by fpeaking. And as to private and domeftic affairs, they are in all nations conducted chiefly by converfation or difcourfe. The fpeaking art has this great advantage too above writing, that, in it, the whole beauty of language is difplayed; for not only the *form* of it is fhewn, that is, the expreffion of our thoughts, but alfo the *matter* or found of it. For, in fpeaking, it is adorned with rhythms and accents, and all that can be called the music of language, besides the beauty which an agreeable articulation gives to language. And, when to these are added the proper changes of voice, such as the subject requires, and all the various tones of sentiment and passion, the ear is not only charmed, but the sense more forcibly conveyed. Speaking, therefore, may be said to be language *living*; whereas writing is nothing but the *dead* letter, and only a secondary art dependent upon speaking; for the best way of judging of the written style is to give it voice and pronounce it. Whoever, therefore, would excell in writing, should begin with forming his ear, and should be sure that he is a good judge of speaking; by which I do not mean that it is necessary he should be a good reader or speaker (for that depends upon natural organs, of which he may not be possessed); but he should be a judge of pronunciation, and know what will have a good or bad effect when it is spoken. If he want this knowledge, whatever other talents he may have as a writer, his composition will certainly be defective. This observation applies in a particular manner to all compositions in writing which are intended to be spoken, such as orations and dramatic poetry. The written orations of Demosthenes would not have had such an effect upon those that read them, as we are told by the antient critics they had [*], if he had not perfectly understood, as we know he did, the art of pronunciation; and our Shakespeare's scenes would not please so much, either in the reading or representation, if the poet himself had not been an actor, and so known what was proper for speaking on the stage. For though, as it is reported, he was a bad performer, yet he must certainly have been a judge of the art, otherwise he could not, by what he has written, have furnished to the player such opportunities of displaying his talents.

As, therefore, in composition the speaking art is principal, being that by which the merit of writing is to be judged, what we shall say of composition must be understood as chiefly applicable to speaking.

[*] Dionys. Halic. περὶ τῆς δεινότητος τῆ Δημοσθένης. cap. 22. *Edit. Hudson.*

In the beginning of this work, I said I was to treat my subject as a matter of science. Whether I have performed my promise or not, belongs not to me to judge. One thing is certain, that the subjects of which I have treated, particularly the nature and origin of our ideas, and what I have said of the grammatical art, are matters of science, however I may have handled them. But there are many who think, that the subject I am now upon does not belong to science, and that the merit of style and composition is to be determined by what they call *Taste*, a metaphorical expression borrowed from the sense well known by that name. And, if the metaphor be exactly just, this standard of judgment should be intirely from nature, and have nothing to do with art, any more than *taste*, properly so called. And if so, the common saying is certainly just, that there is no disputing about taste. And indeed in this way the subject appears to have been treated by almost all our modern writers, who entertain us with a great many words upon the subject, which import that they have some confused natural feelings of what is

Book IV. PROGRESS OF LANGUAGE. 7

beautiful or ftriking in compofition, but give us no *ideas*, at leaft none which they have thought proper to explain or define; and not being willing, or not able to inform us what the thing *is*, they have recourfe to metaphors and fimiles, and fo endeavour to make us conceive what it is *like*. Of this I am fure I could produce many examples from French and Englifh books; but, as I read not to cenfure, but to be inftructed, and admire, if I can, I have not noted the paffages, nor will I be at the difagreeable trouble of fearching for them and collecting them.

Thefe gentlemen are certainly fo far in the right, that, unlefs a man have a natural perception of what is beautiful in ftyle, or any other work of Art, and which may be called natural tafte, there is no art or fcience can give it him. Such a man may be a very good geometer, or he may be an excellent grammarian, and able to judge whether a ftyle be according to grammatical rules; but, *unlefs Melpomene has looked on his birth with placid afpect* *, and given

* Quem tu, Melpomene, feme)
Nafcentem placido lumine videris. Hor. *lib.* 4. *O.* 3.

him that natural taſte and genius, which is neceſſary for the critic as well as the compoſer, he never can be a true judge of the beauties of ſtyle and compoſition. Without that gift of Heaven, he is like the man who pretends to judge of the merit of a tragedy without being ſuſceptible of the paſſions of pity or terror. A critic of that kind might nibble at the diction, and ſhow that the particular words and phraſes were not proper; or, if he had a higher degree of underſtanding, he might find fault with the conduct of the piece, and prove that the unities were not obſerved, or that the events were not ſufficiently connected, and did not ariſe out of one another in a natural and probable manner. But he never could reliſh the true beauties of tragedy, nor reap the benefit which, according to Ariſtotle, ariſes from that poem, namely, correcting the exceſſes of thoſe paſſions of pity and terror, by exerciſing them on feigned ſubjects, and in that way leſſening the effects of them in real life, by making ſuch objects familiar to us.

Book IV. Progress of Language.

It appears, therefore, that in the critical, as in other arts, nature has done no more than furnish the materials, that is, the proper faculties of the mind, as, in this case, the natural sense of the beautiful in works of nature or art. In the same manner, in the matter of language, she has bestowed on us ideas, at least the capacity of forming them, and likewise the organs of pronunciation; and in music, she has given us throats capable of varying the voice, by different degrees of gravity and acuteness, and an ear that can perceive those differences. But these are no more than the raw materials, out of which the art is to be formed by the sagacity and industry of man; as here, out of the natural sense of beauty in style and composition, is to be formed an art, which corrects and improves that natural sense, by teaching us to distinguish accurately different styles and manners; to know what ornaments belong to each of them; and when these ornaments are properly used. This art is what is commonly called among us the *critical art;* and it is of it I am now to treat.

CHAP. I.

Division of style into single words, and the composition of those words.—Each of these heads subdivided.—General plan of this part of the work.

BY *style*, I do not mean every combination of words expressing some sense; but I mean such a combination, as, in regard either of the words, or the composition of these words, or both, is some way different from ordinary discourse *. It has a certain character by which we distinguish it, and denominate it the historical, the didactic, the poetic, the epistolary, and the like. Even dialogue writing, though it be in imitation of conversation, is

---

* When the *Burgeois Gentilhomme*, in *Moliere*, Act 2. sc. 4. asks his master in philosophy, whether, when he calls to his maid—*Nicole, apportez moi mes pantoufles, et me donnez mon bonnet de nuit*, it be prose or verse ? the philosopher answers, that it is *prose*; he might have further added, that, though it was *prose*, it was not *style*.

nevertheless different from ordinary conversation upon the common affairs of life [*].

Style consists of two parts; the choice of words, and the composition of those words [†]. And, as the last of these two is of greatest variety, and distinguishes most the several kinds of style from one another, we commonly, in English, denominate the whole

---

[*] Of this kind of style are the dialogues of Plato, and also the dialogue in our best comedies; which, though it be conversation, yet every reader of any taste will perceive it to be something above the style of ordinary conversation, as much as the tone and manner of the player who speaks it, is above that of ordinary conversation, though at the same time not altogether different from it, if the player has a just sense of decorum, and the propriety of the part which he acts.

[†] Omnis igitur oratio conficitur ex verbis; quorum primum nobis ratio simpliciter videnda est, deinde conjuncte. Nam est quidam ornatus orationis, qui ex singulis verbis est; alius, qui ex continuatis conjunctisque constat. *De Oratore, lib.* 3. *cap.* 37.

And, to the same purpose, the Halicarnassian, ἅπασα λέξις ᾗ ἡμεῖς μηνύομεν τὰ πράγματα, εἰς δύο τὰ πρῶτα διαιρεῖται, εἴς τε τὴν διάνοιαν τῶν ὀνομάτων, ὑφ᾽ ὧν δηλοῦται τὰ πράγματα, καὶ εἰς τὴν σύνθεσιν τῶν ἐλαττόνων τε καὶ μειζόνων μορίων.

De Thucyd. Judicium. p. 237. *Edit. Hudson.*

from that part, calling style, in general, by the name of *composition*.

Words taken singly are to be considered with respect either to their sound or their sense. As to the sound, they are varied in several different ways that have been observed by grammarians; but, with respect to the sense, or meaning, they are only either proper or tropical *.

As to the second part of style, or composition, it is more various; but all its variety may be reduced under three heads. *First*, the sound of words in composition; *secondly*, the different ways in which the composition may be varied by grammatical construction;

---

* In this division of single words, I have followed the Halicarnassian in the passage above quoted, where he says, ὁ ἐκλογὴ τῶν στοιχειωδῶν μορίων ὀνομαστικῶν λόγου καὶ ῥημάτων καὶ συνδέσμων, ἐκ τε τῶν κυρίων φράσιν διαιρεῖται, καὶ ἐκ τῶν τροπικῶν. *Ib.* Cicero, in the passage above quoted, cap. 39. mentions two other kinds of words, viz. *Old*, or *Obsolete* words, and *New*, that is, words made for the occasion. But these are only subdivisions of the division which I have given; for all words, whether old or new, are either proper or tropical. And I think it is fitter to mention that distinction of words, when we come to speak of the particular styles in which they may be properly used.

and, *laſtly*, the ſeveral changes which are made in the compoſition, by giving a different turn to the thought, and conſequently to the expreſſion. Theſe laſt are called, by critics, *figures of the ſenſe*, as the former are called *figures of conſtruction*.

Of theſe materials all ſtyle is made; for it is of theſe materials, differently uſed, that the didactic and the hiſtoric ſtyle are compoſed; the rhetorical and the poetic, the ſublime, the pathetic, the ethic, the familiar, the epiſtolary, the witty, the humorous, and whatever other difference of ſtyle can be imagined. All theſe may be called the *colours* of ſtyle; and of theſe I propoſe to treat, after having explained the materials above-mentioned, of which ſtyle is compoſed.

This is a ſhort ſummary of what is to be the ſubject of this book. The gentlemen above-mentioned, who think that nothing more is required to make a critic than genius and taſte, will, I know, deſpiſe this exactneſs of order and method. But I hold it to be as impoſſible to be a good critic, without ſcience, to which method is absolutely neceſſary, as to be a correct ſpeaker, or writer, without learning the grammatical art, or a good performer in muſic, without knowing the gamut. Mere practice will make one both a judge and a performer, to a certain degree, in any art; but it is only ſtudy, and the knowledge of the principles, that will make him excel in any.

I have only further to ſay, before I conclude this chapter, that I do not propoſe to write a full treatiſe of ſtyle and compoſition, any more than I have done of grammar. But my deſign is, *firſt*, to ſhew the whole extent of the ſubject, and to lay down a method, under which every thing that can be ſaid upon it may be brought; and, *ſecondly*, to explain ſome things relating to ſtyle, that have not been ſufficiently explained; and to correct ſome errors that, I think, have been fallen into.

Having premiſed ſo much concerning the plan of this part of my work, I begin with that part of ſtyle which relates to the choice of words; and, *firſt*, I conſider them with reſpect to their ſound.

CHAP. II.

Of changes made upon the sound of words, for the greater beauty and variety of composition.—Examples of such changes in Greek.—Much fewer in modern languages.—Examples of some in English.

I Have already, in the grammatical part of my work, said a great deal of the sound of language. What I am now to say on that subject will respect the changes which, in composition, it may be proper to make upon the sound of words, for the sake of the pleasure of the ear. What the sound of primitive words, in any language, ought naturally to be, is a matter, as we have seen*, of very difficult determination. But, with respect to compounded words, and such as are formed by derivation and flection, there are, in regular languages, certain rules by which we know what the sound of them ought to be; and what we are to consider

* Vol. ii. p. 194.

here, is, the changes or alterations of that found which they can admit of in compofition, for the purpofe of pleafing the ear.

The Greeks, in the formation of their language, ftudying the pleafure of the ear, no lefs than the fenfe, have made, as I have fhown elfewhere *, great alterations in their words, for the fake of a more agreeable found, by adding, taking away, changing, or tranfpofing letters. But it is not the formation of language, of which we are now fpeaking, but the changes which the words, after they are formed, will admit of. And, if we know by what rules the language is formed, we may know alfo how thefe rules may be varied, fo as to produce the defired effect in compofition, and yet the genius of the language be preferved: *e. g.* The Greeks, in order to make the found of their language fuller and ftronger, not contented with the found of fingle vowels, have joined together two of them, and made what we call diphthongs. Now, as vowels are thus joined together, fo as to

* Differt. 2. on the found of the Greek language, annexed to vol. ii.

make one found, they may be likewife feparated fo as to make two fyllables. Accordingly, we find the Greek poets, and particularly Homer, frequently do fo. And, it is evident, that it gives a great beauty and variety to their compofition, as well as facility to their verfe. The Latins too, ufe it with refpect to their diphthong *ai*, or *æ*, as it is commonly written; as when Lucretius fays, PATRIAÏ *tempore iniquo*; and, Virgil, AURAÏ *fimplicis ignem*; where we muft allow, that the change of the word is not only commodious for the verfe, but agreeable to the ear, and fuch as makes a pleafant variation in the compofition. In like manner, there are certain vowels in Greek, which, by the genius of the language, are contracted, that is, run together fo as to make a found different from both, and fometimes from either, not a found in which both are heard, as in the cafe of diphthongs. In this way the vowels αω, εω, οω, αο, εο, οο, are run together. Now, as in this way, the vowels are contracted, fo they may be likewife divided; and accordingly we fee they are frequently fo divided in

Homer; which, besides the beauty and variety it gives to his composition, assists him very much in making his verse. Again, we have seen * that, in the formation of the Greek language, there was a progress (and, indeed, it was impossible that a work of such art should have been at once completed), and particularly in the formation of the tenses of their verbs. Now, at the time that Homer wrote, it appears, that the old tenses were not out of fashion; so that he had the use of several forms of the same tense †. This gave him a liberty, as well

---

* Vol. ii. p. 516. & seqq.

† Thus, for example, he had for the infinitive three forms; for he uses τυπτημεναι, τυπτιμεν, or τυπτειν. All the past tenses he uses with or without the augment, except the preterperfect and pluperfect, which he always uses with the reduplication, or temporal augment. But I have observed, that Herodotus sometimes omits even these. Homer also adds the syllable θα to the second persons of his verbs, or φησθα and ιστωσθα; and to the third person subjunctive, he adds the syllable σι, as in ιλησι, and λαβησι; and the same syllable he adds to his datives, as in θυμω and υλησι; and to the same case he adds sometimes the syllable φι, as in βιηφι and οχεσφι. By these changes upon words, I think, Homer has sufficiently varied and enriched his composition, without supposing, as some

as a variety in compofition, which Virgil had not, in whofe time very few of the old forms of verbs, that had been in ufe among the Romans, were preferved. It is not, therefore, to be wondered, that Homer's verfe is fo much richer, and more various than Virgil's, notwithftanding all the pains which Virgil beftowed upon his; greater, I believe, than ever poet beftowed.

There is not, indeed, the fame liberty ufed with words, nor is it fit there fhould be, by the Greek profe writers as by the poets; but there is a good deal, which has been obferved by grammarians, and diftinguifhed by different names, fuch as *Profthefis, Epenthefis, Paragoge,* and others, which are to be found in the common grammars. Thefe, in a language in which rhythm and

critics do, that his language is a mixture of the different dialects then fpoken by the feveral tribes of Greeks. Such a mongrel dialect, I am perfuaded, was never written by any man; and the fact, I believe, was, that Homer wrote either the language that was fpoken in the country where he was born and educated, or that was ufed by the poets that had written before him, and was the eftablifhed language of poetry.

numbers were so much studied, are of great use, and therefore are much used by the Greek orators.

The modern languages admit few or no changes of this kind upon words; nor, indeed, is it possible that such changes in them could be made by any rules of art. For, as they are not original languages, but have grown out of other languages, such as the Gothic or Celtic, which are now obsolete, so that we do not know by what rules they were *formed;* we cannot therefore tell, as with respect to the Greek, by what rules they are to be *altered.* The modern composition therefore is, in this respect, as well as every other, much less various than the antient. In English, however, we make some few changes upon the sound of our words, as in the preterite tenses, and participles of our verbs; in place of *loved,* we say *lov'd,* a liberty which ought to be indulged to poets only, for the sake of their verse. For, by such abridgements, we add greatly to the number of monosyllables of our language, already too much crouded with them, besides making the found of our language still more harsh, by joining together, in the same syllable, so many consonants, which, without the elision of the vowel, would be separated into two syllables, as when we say *condemn'd* instead of *condemned*. Milton, in his verse, has used a much more judicious elision when he has run together two vowels, one ending the preceding word, and another beginning the subsequent, as in the following fine verses, expressing so well by the sound the idea they mean to convey:

> So he with difficulty' and labour hard,
> Moved on, with difficulty' and labour he.
> *Par. Lost*, book 2. v. 1021.

In these, and many such to be met with in this poem, Dr. Bentley, in his edition, has marked the elision by an apostrophe, as I have done; and he has observed, that in this Milton has chosen to follow the Latins, who only absorbed the vowel in the pronunciation, rather than the Greeks, who strike it out in writing.

Milton has, in other respects, used as much freedom with single words as the genius of the language would permit, and perhaps more. Thus, inſtead off *diſdain*, he has ſaid, *'ſdain*, cutting off the firſt ſyllable:

―――― Lifted up ſo high,
I 'ſdain'd ſubjection, and thought one ſtep higher
Would ſet me higheſt.   *Par. Loſt*, book 4. v. 50.

By a like liberty, from the word *impregnate*, he has cut off the laſt ſyllable, and made it *impregn*:

―――― As Jupiter
On Juno ſmiles, when he impregns the clouds
That ſhed May flowers.   Book 4. v. 500.

Whereas, according to the analogy of the language, it ſhould have been *impregnates*, as it is commonly uſed, being derived from the barbarous Latin verb *impregno* *; and ſometimes, inſtead of eliding letters and ſyllables, he has enlarged words, by adding ſyllables; as, for example, the corrupted word *hermit*, he has reſtored to its proper etymological orthography, and called it *eremite*, as in this line,

Embryos and idiots, eremites and friars.
Book 3. v. 574.

* See Du Cange's Gloſſary.

CHAP. III.

Of proper words.—Division of them into radical and derivative.—Another division of them into such as are of the original stock of the language, and such as are foreign.—Those of Latin extraction mostly derived from corrupt Latinity.—The restoring them to their genuine signification a beauty of style.

I Come now to consider single words, not as found merely, but as having a meaning. In this view I have already considered them with respect to the grammatical art; according to which they are divided into what is called the parts of speech, and have various accents belonging to them, which I have endeavoured to explain. But, with respect to style and composition, they are divided, as I have said, into *proper* and *tropical*, or figurative, as they are commonly called. By *proper*, I mean such as denote the things they stand for in their genuine and native signification, without any change or inverſion of the natural ſenſe of the word*. By *tropical*, I mean ſuch as are applied to ſignify ſomething different from what they ſignify in their proper ſenſe, and which, therefore, they may be ſaid to ſignify by change only, or tranſlation from one thing to another.

Proper words are either *radical* words of the language, or they are *derivatives*; under which I comprehend not only derivatives, properly ſo called, but compounded and inflected words. As to radicals, though, in defining what a *proper* word is, I have uſed the terms *genuine* and *native*, it is only in oppoſition to the inverted, or unnatural ſignification of words, as it may be called; for there is nothing, either in nature or the grammatical art, that determines the proper ſignification of a radical word. It is fixed by uſe alone; and, as that is variable in all living languages, it frequently happens that words change their ſignification. When that happens, the ſpeaker, or

---

* They are called in Greek κορα ὀνματα, which is literally tranſlated by Horace, *dominantia nomina.*
A. Poet. v. 234.

writer muſt ſubmit, and muſt uſe the word, if he have a mind to be intelligible, in the preſent ſenſe of it. For what Horace ſays of cuſtom is, in this reſpect, certainly true:

———uſus,
Quem penes, arbitrium, et jus, et norma loquendi.

It is, however, permitted to a poet to uſe a little freedom of this kind; and, accordingly, Milton has uſed many words in a ſenſe different from that which they denoted, I believe, even in his time. Thus the word *buxom*, in Engliſh, did antiently ſignify yielding, or obedient *; and therefore Milton has made it an epithet to the air †, tho', I am perſuaded, that in his days it had loſt that original ſignification, and was uſed to ſignify much the ſame thing that it now ſignifies, in which ſenſe it is uſed by Milton in other paſſages, as when he ſays of Euphroſyne, that ſhe is

So *buxom*, blyth, and debonair.

---

* See the word in Johnſon's Dictionary.
† Winnows the *buxom* air.

Vol. III   D

But, though proper words have no meaning but what custom gives them, it is otherwise with respect to derivatives; for they have what may be truly called a proper and natural signification, being such as is ascertained by grammatical rules; and, as it depends upon the etymology, it may be called the etymological signification. When such words lose this signification, and denote something else, not correspondent to their etymology, it is an abuse and corruption of language, but such as is very common in modern languages; to which, if it be once firmly established, we must submit, as well as to other abuses introduced by custom. But, if the word has not deviated very far from its proper meaning, or if the use of it, in another sense, is not fixed by constant and uniform custom, I hold it to be a propriety and beauty of style to use it in its true etymological signification.

There is another division of words in mixt languages, such as ours, that deserves, in this matter, to be attended to: It is into the native words of the language, such as those in English, which are derived from the Saxon, the original stock of the language, and foreign words, that is, those derived from other languages. In English, we have a great many words borrowed from the Latin, but a Latin much corrupted, in which the words were changed from their proper and classical signification. To restore them to that signification makes the style both proper and learned. Of this I shall give an example or two from our learned poet Milton. He describes Eve as going forth with a *pomp* of winning graces attendant on her, *book* 8. v. 61. Here the word *pomp* is used, not as it is at present, to signify *show* or *ostentation*, but in its proper and etymological sense, which is to denote *attendance* upon any one, either for honour or defence; or, as it is expressed by a French word, now used in English, *escorte**. Another example is, his use of the word *intend*, in that passage of Satan's

---

* Homer says, that Bellerophon went to Lycia,

θεῶν ὑπ' ἀμύμονι πομπῇ.   *Il.* ζ. v. 171.

that is, attended or conducted by the Gods. And, in imitation of him, Herodotus, speaking of the Persian conspirators that destroyed the *Magi*, says, that they went upon that enterprise θείῃ πομπῇ χρεώμενοι; lib. 3. cap. 77. This is the original and proper signification of

speech in the second book, where he desires the devils, while he was away on the adventure which he had undertaken, to *intend* at home, while that should be their home, what best might ease their present misery; where the word *intend* is used in its proper signification of bent or application to any thing; and in this sense the Latins say, *intendere animum*. Whereas, in corrupt Latinity, from which we have taken it, it signifies to design or project any thing*; and in this sense we now use the word *intend*, our words of Latin extraction being formed, as I have observed, mostly from such Latinity.

the word, being derived from the verb πεμπω. From thence it came naturally to signify what we call a *procession*, as *pompa funebris*, that is, the attendants upon a funeral, walking in such order as to make a show, and attract attention; and from thence again, by a corruption natural enough, it came to signify show, or ostentation of any kind. In this sense it is used, even by the Roman classic writers; but Milton, who forms his style upon the Greek originals, and not upon the Latin imitations of them, has restored the word to its proper and etymological signification. To trace, in this way, the progress of words through their several stages, makes a kind of history of language, curious and entertaining enough.

* See Du Cange's Glossary.

I shall give another example from the same author. It is the use of the word *observe*, which, in our common language, is a word of no force and emphasis; but, in good Latinity, it is a word of great significancy; and, in this classical sense, it is used by Milton in his first book, where, speaking of the host of fallen angels drawn up and reviewed by Satan, he says,

——— Thus far these beyond
Compare of mortal prowess, yet *observed*
Their dread commander.　v. 587.

where it denotes, as in Latin, *observed with particular attention;* or, as it is expressed by one native English word, *marked*.

The last example I shall give, is likewise from the same author, where, speaking of Helen, he calls her *Jove-born Helena*, in those beautiful lines in his Comus, where he makes the enchanter say to the lady, when he recommends his cup to her,

Not that Nepenthe, which the wife of Thon,
In Egypt gave to Jove-born Helena,
Was of such power to stir up joy as this,
To life so friendly, or so cool to thirst.

Here the English word *born*, which answers to the Latin word *natus*, he has used in the classical sense of *natus*; for the Romans said, *natus ex patre*, as well as *ex matre*; whereas, in common English, we say only, *born of the mother*.

In this way, I find Dr. Middleton, the author of the life of Cicero, has used a great many words, which gives a peculiar propriety and elegance to his style; and, I think, for that reason, as well as others, he may be reckoned among the most classical writers that we have had of late *.

* I will give some few examples from this author, among many that might be given. *Discipline*, in the common acceptation of the word, signifies the exaction of any thing with severity, and under the terror of punishment, and sometimes the punishment itself; but, in genuine Latinity, it signifies that study or exercise by which any thing is to be learnt; and, by an easy translation from this its proper and etymological signification, it is made to denote *what is* so learned; and, in general, any system of doctrines and institutions that have arisen from teaching and practice. In the first of these senses it is used by Dr. Middleton, where he says, ' Cicero had now ' run through all that course of *discipline*, which he lays ' down as necessary to form the complete orator ;' Life of Cicero, vol. 3. p. 36. edit. 3. And, in the other

CHAP. IV.

Of Tropes, and different kinds of them, particularly of Metaphors.—Metaphors used from necessity, as well as for ornament.—Observations on the use of Metaphors.

THE next kind of words of which I am to treat, according to the method I have laid down, is tropical or figurative

sense, it is frequently used by the Doctor, as in those passages where he speaks of the *discipline* of the state. In this last sense, the word is of common use when applied to military institutions; as when we say the *discipline* of the army.——The word *oppress*, in English, is commonly applied only to *persons*; but, according to the classical use, it is equally applicable to *things*. Thus they say in Latin, *Cæsar patriæ libertatem oppressit*, which the Doctor has translated when he has said, that ' Cæsar formed ' a design of *oppressing* the liberty of his country,' vol. 1. p. 34. Again, the word, in its common use in English, signifies only to press too hard, so as to hurt; but, in genuine Latinity, it signifies to press a thing so as to crush or destroy it altogether, the preposition *ob* having an intensive force in composition. Accordingly, when a man is killed by a house falling upon him, they say, *ruina*

words. Those which were the subject of the preceeding chapter are what Horace calls *inornata nomina et verba**, and make no more than plain speech; whereas these I am to speak of in this chapter make fine or ornamental language, and are treated of by all the writers upon rhetoric and poetry, to which they are thought chiefly to belong.

A trope, as I have already defined it, is a change of a word from its native and genuine signification to another that is different. This change is grounded upon some

---

adium oppressus est; and in this sense Doctor Middleton has commonly used the word.—In like manner, the word *reconcile*, in English, is applied only to friends, not to friendships; but, in Latin, they say *reconciliare amicitiam*, as well as *amicos*. The Doctor, therefore, has said, that ' a *friendship* cannot be said to be *reconciled*, which was never interrupted;' *Ib. p.* 248. In the same classical sense, he has used the words *perpetual, innocence, abstinence, piety*, &c. And, upon the whole, I think that, both for the choice of words, and the composition of them, the Doctor is to be numbered among the chief of the few classical writers of this age, though I know that his style has so much of the antient *simplicity*, and so little of the modern *brilliancy* (that I may use an Anglified French word, to express what we have chiefly learned from the French), as not to please the many.

* A. Poet. v. 234.

connection or relation betwixt the things signified by the two words; and the connection must be such as is well known, otherwise it will be an ænigma, or riddle, not a trope.

As the connections and relations of things are various, so also there are various kinds of tropes; for things are connected as genus and species, or as both specieses of the same genus. There is, therefore, a trope from the genus to the species, and *vice versa*, and from one species to another *. Things

---

* Tropes of this kind are comprehended under the general name of *synecdoche*. The transference is from the genus to the species, when Homer, instead of saying that a ship was moored, says, that she was fixed, or made to stand, νηα δε μοι ηδ ἑστηκε; for *mooring* is a species of the general idea of *fixing*: It is a very common figure, and easily understood by the thing to which it is applied, as in this instance to a ship; See *Arist. Poet. c.* 21. From the species to the genus, as when Homer says, μαρμαρῳ ὀκριοεντι βαλων; where marble, which is one species of stone, is put for the genus. From species to species, as when the same poet uses the word ταμιω for ἱρυσαι; and again, ἱρυσαι for ταμιω; as where he says, χαλκῳ απο ψυχην ἱρυσας, and ταμων ατηρι χαλκῳ; because both, says Aristotle, denote to *take away* something: *ib.* So that they are both specieses of the same genus, viz. *taking away.*

also are connected as whole and part; and hence arise two other kinds of tropes, one from the whole to the part, the other from the part to the whole*. Further, things have various accidents attending them; and, by these accidents, the things are denoted †. Again, there are circumstances which precede things, or are subsequent to them; and, from these also the things are denominated ‡. Again,

---

* From the whole to the part, as when Homer says, ὡδ' ἐστὶ ἀλλήλας ὀξεῖαν τυπτόν βοεσί; *Il.* 12. v. 105. where the *whole ox* is put for his *hide*, of which the shields were made. Again, from the part to the whole, when the same poet says, τειν δ' ἀν κεφαλὴν πολλοῖ, where the head is put for the whole man. Of the same kind is the common epithet he gives the Greeks, of ἱππογάσαις, which, from a single part of armour, denotes the whole. Both these tropes are likewise ranked under *synecdoche*.

† Thus Homer says of rowers, ἰζομενοι λευκαινον ὕδωρ; and of people travelling in chariots, he says, οἱ δε παῤῥιμφῶν σιων ζυγὸν; where, from the accident of *whitening the water*, rowing is denoted; and, from the *shaking of the yoke*, driving in a carriage. This trope is likewise called *synecdoche*, and is much used by the poets, because it paints the object, and, as it were, sets it before our eyes.

‡ From what precedes, as when Homer says, λυσι δε παρθενίην ζωνην, where the deflowering of a virgin is expressed by the preceding circumstance, of loosening the

Book IV. Progress of Language. 35

a man is connected with his father, with his country, or with any quality in him that is remarkable and distinguishing; and hence three kinds of tropes *. Another trope is, when a thing is denominated from another thing, or person, to which it refers †.

All these, and several more, are explained at large in treatises that have been written on rhetoric and poetry; but I do not know that they are any where better explained, and illustrated by examples from

---

virgin zone, or girdle. Again, the trope is from what follows to what goes before, as when he uses the word ἐναρίζειν, which signifies, *to spoil a dead man of his arms*, instead of φονεύω, to *kill him*; because the one, in those days, followed the other. This also is a species of the synecdoche, and is much used by poets.

* Thus we say *Pelides* for *Achilles*; the *Macedonian* or the *Stagirite*, for *Alexander* or for *Aristotle*; the *Orator* for *Demosthenes*; and the *Poet* for *Homer*. This trope is called *Antonomasia*.

† As when we say *Ceres* instead of *bread*; *Bacchus* instead of *wine*; *Vulcan* instead of *fire*. It is called Metonymy, a very general name, and which may be applied to all tropes.

Homer, than in the life of Homer, written, as some think, by Dionyſius the Halicarnaſſian, and publiſhed by Gale among the *Opuſcula Mythologica*.

There is a trope, commonly ſo called, which I mention, becauſe it is truly no trope, unleſs by the uſe of another trope called *abuſe*. The trope I mean is *Onomatopoeia*; by which the word is not changed in its ſignification, but created. Of this kind many inſtances are given from Homer, of words, which, it is ſaid, he formed from the ſound of the things expreſſed by them*. Whether he formed them or not, I hold to be very doubtful; and I rather incline to be of opinion that many of them, mentioned by the commentators, were original words in the language. For it is certain that there are many ſuch in every language, at leaſt

---

* The author, above quoted, of the life of Homer mentions the words ἄντα, ἀραβος, βομβος, and the verbs ῥοχθι and ἀπβρυχη. But why ſhould Homer have created theſe words, any more than other words he mentions, ſuch as φυω, *inflare*; ϝρζω, *ſecare*; μυκαοθαι, *mugire*; βροτω, *tonare*; which he acknowledges were names impoſed upon the things by the firſt formers of the language.

every language of art, and particularly in English, as, for example, the words *roar, crack, grunt, gurgle*, &c. which certainly are not the creation of any particular author, but as old as the language.

I shall conclude what I have to say of tropes by some observations on the metaphor, the most common of all tropes, being used in common conversation, and often from necessity, as well as for ornament. The word, in its proper and etymological signification, will apply to every kind of trope; for it denotes a change or transference, and accordingly it is rendered into Latin by the word *translatio* *. And it is defined by Aristotle in such a manner as to comprehend several of the tropes that I have before mentioned†; but, according to the common

---

* See Cicero *de Oratore*, lib. 3. c. 38. where he calls every figurative, or tropical word, *verbum translatum*; and speaks of the *modus transferendi verbi*, as applicable to every way of using a word, except in its proper signification.

† Μιταφορα δι ιςιν ονοματος αλλοτριυ ιπιφορα, η απο γινυς ιπι ιδος, η απο ιιδυς ιπι γινος, η απο ιδυς ιπι ιδος, η κατα το αναλογον; *cap.* 21. *Poet*. This definition comprehends

use of the word, it is that kind of trope which is taken from the resemblance, similitude, or analogy, that one thing has to another*. It may be called the *witty* trope; for it is in it that wit chiefly consists; and it is, as Aristotle has observed, the sign of good natural parts. For it shews a comprehensive mind, that can collect together

---

several speciefes of the synecdoche above-mentioned; but it is only the last part of it, viz. κατα τὸ αναλογον, which makes what is commonly called a *metaphor*, in contradistinction to other tropes.

* It is thus defined by the author above-mentioned of the life of Homer, Μεταφορα ἐστιν απο τȣ κυριȣ ἐπι αλλο μὲν πραγματος ἐφ᾽ ἑτερον μετηνεγμενη, μετα της ἀμφοιν αναλογȣ ὁμοιοτητος. This definition perfectly coincides with the last part of the definition from Aristotle, mentioned in the preceding note; and the examples he gives of it agree perfectly with those given by Aristotle. For example, he says that Homer calls the top of a mountain the head; for, says he, what the head is to a man, the same the top of a mountain is to the mountain, ὁ γαρ λογος ἐχει κορυφη προς ανθρωπον, τȣτον και ἡ ακρωρεια προς το ορος. And of the same kind is the instance given by Aristotle of the expression of the evening of life for old age; for, says he, what the evening is to the day, old age is to life; *cap.* 21.

Book IV. Progress of Language. 39

different things under one resemblance or likeness *.

I have said, that it is the trope most used in conversation; therefore Aristotle says, that it is the fittest for Iambics, that is, the verse of dramatic poetry; because that poetry is the imitation of discourse or conversation †. And, accordingly, the style of the Greek tragedy is very metaphorical.

I have also observed, that we often use metaphorical words, not by way of ornament, but for want of proper terms; as when we say the FOOT *of a bill*, or of a *chair*, or a *table*, with many like expressions ‡. And there is a set of words, I believe, in all languages, which are metapho-

---

* ἰσχνῶς ἐστι σημεῖον, τὸ γὰρ ἐν μεταφέρειν τὸ ὅμοιον θεωρεῖν ἐστι; cap. 22.

† Poet. cap. 22.

‡ This is observed by Cicero. 'Tertius ille modus 'transferendi verbi late patet, quem necessitas genuit, 'inopia coacta, et angustiis; post autem delectatio ju- 'cunditasque celebravit. Nam, ut vestis frigoris depel- 'lendi causa reperta primo, post adhiberi cœpta est ad 'ornatum etiam corporis, et dignitatem; sic verbi

rical, but, for want of other words, are constantly used as proper, so that the metaphor is entirely overlooked. The words I mean are those expressing the operations of mind, which are commonly translations from bodily operations. Such are the words *reflect, ponder, ruminate*, and the like.

It is, I believe, for this reason that barbarous languages are observed to be figura-

---

* translatio instituta est inopiæ causa, frequentata delec-
‘ tationis;' *De Oratore, lib.* 3. *cap.* 38. And he proceeds to give very proper examples from his own language of this figure being used from necessity: *Nam gemmare, vitres, luxuriem esse in herbis, latas segetes,* etiam rustici dicunt; *ib.* Here we may observe, that it is no impeachment of the simplicity of Virgil's exordium of the Georgics, that he has used the expression *latas segetes,* which, it seems, was commonly used by the farmers. Nor is his denoting the time of plowing by the stars to be considered as figurative, since the farmers in those days regulated their plowings and sowings by the rising and setting of certain stars, as we do by the days of our calendar months. The expression, therefore, among us, would be highly figurative, so as not to be intelligible, except to the learned reader; whereas, among the Romans, it was a simple and common phrase. This shews the necessity of understanding exactly both the language of a people, and their customs and manners, in order to be able to judge certainly of the style of their authors.

tive, which by many is thought to be a sign of their richnefs; whereas I hold it to be a proof of their poverty. For, not being able to exprefs a thing by its proper name, they are naturally driven to tell what it is like. The moſt perfect language is, therefore, that which has proper names for every thing, and ufes figurative words only by way of ornament.

Another obfervation proper to be made is, that we cannot underſtand perfectly a metaphorical expreſſion, unlefs we know the proper meaning of the word; for we cannot tell whether two things be like or not, if we do not know them both. Whoever, therefore, borrows a metaphor from a thing that he does not underſtand, will be apt to apply it very improperly. And, as the whole beauty and elegance of the tropical or figurative ſtyle depends upon this knowledge, every dictionary, or other book explaining words, ſhould diſtinguiſh accurately betwixt the proper and figurative meaning of a word; and, beginning with the proper, ſhould from thence deduce the metaphorical ufe. And I will take it upon me to fay, that a dictionary, which only gives you different fignifications, without diftinguifhing what is proper from what is figurative, is imperfect in its kind. The moft perfect dictionary, in this refpect, I have ever feen, is that which the French Academy have given of their language, where there is another diftinction made of words, which, I think, is alfo proper, between thofe that are of low and vulgar ufe, and thofe that are proper for the high or grave ftyle. And, upon the whole, I think it is, in every refpect, a moft complète dictionary, fuch as does much honour to that learned body.

Another obfervation I fhall make is, that it is a great fault in ftyle when the metaphors are too much crouded; for, if they are not clear, it becomes a riddle; or, tho' they be, the compofition is difagreeable, becaufe it is the affectation of wit; and fuch a ftyle puts me in mind of a kind of game that I remember to have played at, called *what is it like?* This excefs is avoided by all the great writers of antiquity; and if, at any time, any of them fall into it, they do not escape the censure of the critic: And Plato particularly is, on that account, found fault with by the Halicarnassian. But there was one kind of composition among them, which was professedly figurative to such a degree, as to be almost ænigmatical. This was the chorus of the antient tragedy, of which I shall have occasion to say more afterwards.

My last observation upon this trope is, that, as it requires, according to Aristotle's observation, genius and fancy; so it requires also a great deal of knowledge of different arts and sciences, and likewise of the common affairs of life, if we have a mind to adorn our style much in this way. For these are the materials of which metaphors are made; and, besides those requisites, there must be a correct taste, by which we are taught to know what is proper and becoming, and suitable to the genius of our work. This is only to be acquired by the study of rules, and by the forming our style upon the best models. And, in general, there are three things absolutely necessary for fine writing. *First*, Natural genius, without which nothing truly excellent can be performed in any art. *Secondly*, Various knowledge, which furnishes the materials to work upon. And, *thirdly*, The knowledge of the rules of the art. Those, therefore, who think that genius alone is sufficient to make a fine writer, or good artist of any kind, have but a very imperfect knowledge of the extent of the art, or rather do not know that it is at all an art, or, being an art, that it requires materials to work upon.

CHAP. V.

*Of the second part of style, viz. Composition.
—This considered, first, with respect to sound.—That diversified in the learned languages by musical tones and rhythms, which we have not.—The sound, therefore, in our composition, can only be varied by the order of the words, and by periods.—Each of these considered, and illustrated by examples.*

I Come now to speak of the second part of style, viz. composition, of so much greater power and influence than single words, that the whole, as I have observed, is not improperly denominated from it. For, by different composition, we make different style of the same words; and, in the same style, it gives a variety, which it is impossible any choice of words can give. Now, in all arts, and in the art of composition, no less than in any other, there can be no pleasure or true beauty, without variety. For, though the composition were in itself ever so perfect; yet, if it be not agreeably varied, it will soon disgust and offend. Dionysius the Halicarnassian has written a treatise of composition, very often quoted in the course of this work, in which, though he has only treated of one third part of it according to my division, viz. the sound[*]; yet, even this he makes of such importance, that he compares it to the rod of Minerva in Homer, which could transform a beggar into a king, or hero, or *vice versa*. In like manner, says he, of common, or even mean words, a certain composition will make fine poetry or prose; and, contrariwise, bad composition will disgrace the best words; and he gives examples of both[†].

---

[*] The name in Greek for this part of composition is, συνθεσις; and therefore the work of Dionysius is entitled περι ονοματων συνθεσεως. This we must distinguish from the grammatical construction of words, called in Greek συνταξις, from whence our English word *syntax*. The name the Greeks gave to what we call style or composition is λεξις, which, by its etymology, shews that the Greeks thought *speaking* the principal work of composition.

[†] See περι συνθεσεως, § 4. and what is said upon this subject in the beginning of my third dissertation, annexed to vol. 2.

It is this part of composition that I am now to treat of; for the reader will remember, that I have said composition was varied in three ways; by sound, by figures of construction, and, *lastly*, by figures of the sense.

As to the sound, or material part of language, as I call it, I have treated of it very fully in the preceeding volume. I there divided it into three parts, articulation, accent, and rhythm, and endeavoured to shew the effects of all the three in composition. The articulation of our modern languages, according to the account there given of it, is rude and barbarous, compared with that of the learned languages; neither is it softened by the music which belonged to those languages, consisting of their accents, which were musical tones, and their rhythms, which were compositions of long and short syllables, and made what may be called the *time* of their speech. We cannot, therefore, have any thing in our language like the numbers or melody of the Greek and Latin; so that we want what the Halicarnassian reckoned so great a beauty in the Greek composition; and there remain to us only two things, by which our style can be varied, and made agreeable to the ear, viz. the order or arrangement of the words; and, *secondly*, composition in periods of different lengths, and consisting of more or fewer members; likewise of different lengths*.

As to the order of the words, I have shewn, in the preceeding volume, book 3. c. 10. &c. how much the antients excelled us likewise in that. It was by the liberty of arrangement, which the genius of their language allowed, that they produced those

---

* Cicero, in his *Orator ad M. Brutum*, c. 44. mentions three things relative to the sound of composition. His words are, ' collocabuntur igitur verba, aut ut inter ' se quam aptissime cohaereant extrema cum primis; eaque ' sint quam suavissimis vocibus; aut ut forma ipsa concin- ' nitasque verborum conficiat orbem suum; aut ut com- ' prehensio numerose et apte cadat.' The *first* is, what I call the order or arrangement of the words; the *second* is the period; the *third* is the numbers or rhythms. And as to the accents, which made the melody of the Greek language, It seems Cicero did not think them of such consequence in the Latin composition as to mention them. The two first beauties of composition we may have, as I have said, in our language; the other two we cannot have. 9.

numbers, which were thought so essential to all fine composition, and particularly to the oratorial. And I have further shewn, that this liberty of arrangement, as used by the great authors of antiquity, did not only not impair or obscure the sense, but inforced it *. However, though we cannot, even in this single article of arrangement, come up to the beauty of antient composition, we may do a great deal by it, more than is commonly believed.

And, in the first place, by mixing our words properly, joining those of harsh sound with those of better, and polysyllables, where we can find them, with monosyllables, we may soften, in some degree, the native rudeness of our northern dialect; and I am not sure but that something may be made of the variety of our accents, such as they are, even in our prose composition. I have shewn that our verse is made by them; and, if so, I do not see why our prose composition may not be agreeably diversified, by a judicious mixture of accented and unaccented, or, to speak more pro-

* Differt. 3. annexed to vol. 2. p. 571. & seq.

perly, loud and soft syllables; (for the reader must always remember, that I do not use accent, in the classical sense of the word, to denote a variation of tone upon the syllable;) but we must take care not to make verse of it, nor bring it even near to verse. This is as great a fault in our composition as it was reckoned in the antient; for our accents, like their quantities, must be so mixt in the composition, and so little astricted to rule, that, though the effect of them be felt even by the vulgar, they are not perceived, except by the critic. I must therefore take upon me to condemn all that has been written of late in the rhapsody style, or measured prose, as it is called by some, where the numbers are so apparent, that they are perceived by every body. It is a style hobbling between verse and prose, of which I do not approve; at the same time, I cannot help thinking, but that those accents which make our verse would have some effect upon our prose, if properly used, though I do not know that it has been attended to by any body.

But, setting aside all consideration of the accents, the arrangement of the words is

what gives a turn to a sentence, that is either pleasing to the ear, or uncouth and disagreeable. That this is the case in high composition, must be evident to any one who will take the trouble to put the words out of the order in which the author has placed them, and take down the sentence in the manner I have taken down that fine period of Milton, in the beginning of the second book of Paradise Lost*; by which not only the pleasure of the ear is lost, but the sense and spirit of the composition flattened and enervated. I will give another example from the prose writings of the same author: It is the period with which he begins his *Eiconoclastes*, or answer to King Charles's Εικων Βασιλικη. It runs thus:—'To
' descant on the misfortunes of a person
' fallen from so high a dignity, who hath
' also paid his final debt both to nature and
' his faults, is neither of itself a thing com-
' mendable, nor the intention of this dis-
' course †.' Now, let the order of the words

---

* See vol. 2. p. 358.

† I will here add the sequel of this passage:—
' Neither was it fond ambition, or the vanity to get a
' name, present, or with posterity, by writing against a
' king. I never was so thirsty after fame, nor so desti-
' tute of other hopes and means, better and more cer-

be altered in this manner: 'It is not in it-
'self a thing commendable, nor is it the
'intention of this discourse, to descant on the
'misfortunes of a person fallen from so

'tain to attain it; for kings have gained glorious titles
'from their favourers by writing against private men,
'as Henry VIII. did against Luther: But no man ever
'gained much honour by writing against a king, as
'not usually meeting with that force of argument in
'such courtly antagonists, which to convince might
'add to his reputation. Kings most commonly, tho'
'strong in legions, are but weak at arguments; as they
'who ever have been accustomed, from the cradle, to use their
'will only as their right hand, their reason only as their
'left; whence, unexpectedly constrained to that kind
'of combat, they prove but weak and puny adversaries.
'Nevertheless, for their sakes, who, through custom,
'simplicity, or want of better teaching, have not more
'seriously considered kings, than in the gaudy name of
'majesty, and admire them and their doings, as if they
'breathed not the same breath with other mortal men,
'I shall make no scruple to take up (for it seems to be
'the challenge both of him and all his party) this gaunt-
'let, though a king's, in the behalf of liberty and the
'commonwealth.'

This, I think, is a specimen of noble and manly eloquence. For, not to mention the weight of matter that it
contains, and the high republican spirit which animates
it, I ask those gentlemen, who despise the Greek and
Roman learning, and admire only the French authors,
or some later English writers, that they are pleased to
set up as models (for Milton, I know, they think uncouth, harsh, and pedantic), whether they can produce

' high a dignity, who hath also paid his
' final debt both to nature and his faults.'
Here the words are not only the same, but
the order likewise is preserved, except that
the first and last members of the sentence
have changed their places. The period also is preserved; and yet what a change
there is in the composition! How flat, insipid, and, as it were, supine it becomes,
instead of flowing, rounded, and spirited!
If we were to change the order further, it
would become harsh and uncouth, as well
as flat and spiritless. Suppose, for example,
we were to give it this turn; ' It is not in
' itself a commendable thing, nor is it of
' this discourse the intention, the misfortunes
' to descant on of a person from so high a
' dignity fallen, who to nature and his
' faults hath also paid his final debt.' This
is English, and sufficiently intelligible; but
it is a composition that will offend every

any thing themselves, or find any thing in their favourite authors, which they can set against this passage in Milton, either for the choice of the words, or the beauty and variety of the composition? It may be considered as a *gauntlet* that Milton, for the honour of antient literature, has thrown down to those gentlemen, which he must be a bold man among them who will venture to take up.

body*. Yet we have seen, in our time, a whole work in a taste of composition very little better; I mean Gordon's translation of Tacitus, a work which had once a high

---

* Cicero, in his *Orator ad M. Brutum*, has given us examples, from orations of his time, and in his language, to shew how much the finest composition may be spoiled by a slight change of the order of the words. The passage is long; but it is so much to our present purpose, that I will here insert it:—" Quantum autem sit apte dicere, experiri licet, si aut compositi oratoris bene structam collocationem dissolvas permutatione verborum. Corrumpatur enim tota res, ut et hæc nostra in Corneliana, et deinceps omnia, *Neque me divitiæ movent, quibus omnis Africanos et Lælios multi venalitii mercatoresque superarunt.* Immuta paulum, ut sit, *multi superarunt mercatores venalitiique,* perierit tota res: Et quæ sequuntur, *Neque vestis, aut cælatum aurum, et argentum, quo nostros veteres Marcellos Maximosque multi eunuchi å Syriâ Ægyptoque viterunt.* Verba permuta sic, ut sit, *Vicerunt eunuchi à Syriâ Ægyptoque.* Adde tertium, *Neque vero ornamenta ista villorum, quibus Paullum & L. Mummium, qui rebus his urbem, Italiamque omnem, referserunt, ab aliquo video perfacile Deliaco aut Syro potuisse superari.* Fac ite, *potuisse superari ab aliquo Syro aut Deliaco:* Videsne ut, ordine verborum paulum commutato, iisdem verbis, stante sententia, ad nihilum omnia recidant, cum sint ex aptis dissoluta? Aut si alicujus inconditi arripias dissipatam aliquam sententiam, eamque, ordine verborum paullum commutato, in quadrum redigas, efficiatur aptum illud, quod fuerit antea diffluens, ac solutum. Age, summe de Gracchi apud Censores illud, *Abesse non potest, quin ejus-*

reputation, but, I think, is now admired by no body. This tranflator wanted to imitate the manner of his author, by making him fpeak Englifh fo uncouth; but it is plain that he did not know the peculiarities of Tacitus's ftyle, which are—a fhort disjointed compofition, fuch as that of Seneca, which Caligula, wittily enough, compared to fand without lime *; an affectation of brevity, and of expreffing common things in an uncommon way; and, *laftly*, a certain point and turn, very different from the noble fimplicity of the great writers of antiquity. But his ftyle, as far as concerns the arrangement, is claffical enough; whereas, a ftrange uncouth order of the words is the diftinguifhing mark of his tranflator's ftyle.

And not only is the high ftyle disfigured by an improper arrangement, but common difcourfe. For if, inftead of faying, *give*

dem hominis fit probos improbare, qui improbos probet. Quanto aptius, fi ita dixiffet, *Quin ejufdem hominis fit, qui improbos probet, probos improbare?* Hoc modo dicere nemo unquam noluit; nemoque potuit, quin dixerit; qui autem aliter dixerunt, hoc affequi non potuerunt; *cap.* 70.

* Suet. in *Calig.*

me bread, I say, *bread give me;* or if, instead of *give me small beer*, I say, *small beer*, or, *beer small, give me*, such an order of words makes the composition of ill sound, affected, and ridiculous.

Such an arrangement is undoubtedly bad. But what is the right arrangement in English? For this it would not be easy to give particular rules; nor, indeed, would it be worth the while to attempt it, as a good natural taste, without which nothing good can be done in any art, and the study of the best authors, will sufficiently direct us. But some general rules may be given. And, *first*, our arrangement must be such as the nature of the language will admit, without obscurity or ambiguity; for we cannot pretend to that liberty of arrangement which the Greek and Latin authors use. *Secondly*, We must have regard not only to the grammar of the language, but to custom; for we will not endure, in favour of any author, to have our ears violated by a composition altogether strange and unusual. But custom allows a considerable latitude in English, much more than in French, and more

Book IV. Progress of Language.

in poetry than in prose, that being one way in which our poetic style is not improperly distinguished from prose composition. Further, it must be as agreeable to the ear as it can be made of such rough materials as we have to work upon. *Lastly*, and what is principal, it should be such as to convey the meaning as clearly and forcibly as possible.

The second thing I mentioned, by which we can vary the sound of our composition in English, is, by making periods. A period may be defined to be a certain comprehension and circumscription of words, in which the ear perceives number and measure, and a certain roundness and compactness, so as to appear to have nothing redundant, or nothing wanting*. As every thing

---

* Cicero has not defined a period, but has translated the word into Latin by many synonymous terms. He calls it ' circuitus ille orationis, quem Græci περιοδον, nos ' tum ambitum, tum circuitum, tum comprehensionem, ' aut continuationem, aut circumscriptionem, dicimus;' *Orator ad M. Brutum, c.* 61.

The description I have given is a paraphrase of Aristotle's definition of it, which is in the following words: λεγω δε περιοδον, λεξιν εχουσαν αρχην και τελευτην, αυτην καθ᾿ αυτην, και μεγεθος ευσυνοπτον; *a period is a composition of words,*

is best illustrated by its contrary, I would advise a man, who desires to know exactly what a period is, to study the author I mentioned above, I mean Tacitus. For there, instead of roundness and compactness, leaving nothing to be desiderated, he will find short sentences, with abrupt cadences, which cheat the ear; then let him compare either this harshness of Tacitus, or the sand without lime of Seneca, with the flowing composition of a Cicero or Demosthenes, and he will understand the definition I have gi-

---

having a beginning and end in itself, and an extent such as can be comprehended in one view; Rhetoric. lib. 3. c. 9. The opposite to a period is what he calls Λέξις εἰρομένη, which has neither beginning nor end in itself, but is only terminated by the sense. In this kind of composition, the words are so put together, as that the ear expects no conclusion; and, consequently, is surprised when the conclusion comes; whereas, in a period, the ear foresees, as it were, the end, and is not cheated by its coming, either too soon, or too late. This gives the mind a certain perception of number, measure, and aptness of parts, which pleases very much.—The whole chapter is well worth reading, as it shews very plainly the difference betwixt a philosopher who knows, and can explain the reasons of things, and an orator, who knows indeed the practice of the art, but, not being able to define or explain like a philosopher, contents himself with giving us many words for the same thing.

ven. Or, if my reader is not learned, let him have recourse to Milton, and study the speeches in the *Paradise Lost*, particularly those in the second book; there he will find that fine period, in the beginning of Satan's first speech, which I have elsewhere quoted and commented upon*. And there is another in the beginning of Belial's speech in the same book, also worthy of his attention. It runs thus:

> I should be much for open war, O peers!
> As not behind in hate, if what was urged,
> Main reason to persuade immediate war,
> Did not dissuade me most.

And, if he further wants an example of a good period in prose, I think the one I have given above, from Milton's Eiconoclastes, may suffice. And if he would desire to have here likewise a contrast, he may go to some of the fashionable productions of this age, where he will find a short, smart cut of style, imitated from Tacitus; or, if the imitator is not learned enough to understand him, from some late French writers, very different from the composition of Milton, and other good writers in English.

* Vol. 2. p. 356.

Periods are commonly divided into members, which, if properly done, adds greatly to their beauty, becauſe it makes the variety greater. For every combination, if the parts are proper, and properly put together, is more beautiful than any ſimple thing. A long period, therefore, conſiſting of ſeveral members, if it be not immoderately long, ſo as not to be eaſily ſpoken in one breath; and if the members are aptly joined, and have each in itſelf a certain roundneſs and compactneſs; and, *laſtly*, if the ſenſe be clear, and more forcibly conveyed than it would be in detached ſentences, the matter being connected as well as the words; is more beautiful than a ſhort period. For inſtances of ſuch periods, I refer the learned reader to two, quoted in the note below, one from Demoſthenes, and the other from Cicero *. And the reader, if he be not learned, may be ſatisfied with thoſe that I have already quoted from Mil-

---

* Demoſthenes begins his third Philippic thus:— Πολλων, ω Ανδρες Αθηναιοι, λογων γιγνομενων, ολιγα δων καθ' ἑκαστην εκκλησιαν, περι ὡν Φιλιππος, αφ' ἡ την ειρηνην εποιησατο, ε μονον ὑμας, αλλα και τως αλλως Ἑλληνας, αδικει· και παντως, ευ οιδ' ὁτι, φησαιεν γε αν (ει και μη ποιωσι τετο) και λεγειν δειν, και πραττειν ἁπαντα προσηκειν, ὁπως

ton; or, if he defires longer ones, he will find great plenty of such in his controverfial profe writings.

μιμος παυονται της ύβρεως, και έαν δοτις εις τοτο υπαγμιια παντα τα πραγματα, και πξιωματα, ιξω εστι διδαεαι, μη, βλασφημαν μει ηπτω, αληθες δε ε' τε και λεγω απαντες εβελοντε ι παρεντες, και χειροτωαιν ύμει, εξ ων ας φανλοτατα ιμιλλε τα πραγματα εξειν με αι ηγεμαι, δυνοσθαι χειρω, η και, διατιθεσαι.

Cicero begins his oration for Archias the poet, in this manner:—' Si quid est in me ingenii, Judices, quod sentio quam sit exiguum; aut si qua exercitatio dicendi, in qua me non inficior mediocriter esse versatum; aut si hujusce rei ratio aliqua ab optimarum artium studiis, et disciplina, profecta, a qua ego nullum confiteor aetatis meae tempus abhorruisse; earum rerum omnium, vel in primis, hic A. Licinius fructum a me repetere prope suo jure debet.'

Cicero's composition in this exordium is, no doubt, very good; but it has neither the compass nor variety of Demosthenes's period, which contains a great deal of more matter, and has more members, and these more diversified by hyperbatons and parentheses. The connection too of the several members is more artificially varied; for those of Cicero's period, all except one, begin with *si*, or *aut si*. The Halicarnassian, § 9. *περι της δεινοτητος του Δημοσθενες,* gives it as an example of the manner of Thucydides, imitated by Demosthenes. But, tho' Thucydides be the most obscure of all authors of any value, and though the composition here has, no doubt, a great deal of the character of Thucydides; yet there is not the least obscurity in it, to a man who understands the lan-

But all periods muſt not be of the ſame kind, but different in different ſtyles. The hiſtoric period, for example, muſt flow more looſely than the oratorial, which ſhould be more aſtricted, and, as it were, contorted. For, as the tone of the voice and pronunciation in argument and contention is different from what it is in plain narrative, ſo muſt the compoſition be. Theſe differences are obſerved and explained by the antient critics, and particularly by the Halicarnaſſian; and to them I refer for further information on this head *.

guage. And, I am convinced, that, as it was ſpoken by Demoſthenes, it not only filled and pleaſed the ears of the hearers, but conveyed to them the ſentiment which concludes it with very much more force than it could have done, if it had been frittered and broken down into ſhort ſentences, after the manner of Tacitus and Seneca. I ſhall only further obſerve, upon this fine period, that there is not one metaphor or other trope in it; nothing ſhining or ſplendid of any kind in the words, but all of them common, and of ordinary uſe—no *purple patches*; not even a ſingle *verbum decorum*, to uſe an expreſſion of Horace; yet the compoſition moſt beautiful, and the fartheſt in the world from being vulgar or trivial—*Tantum ſeries juncturaque pollet.*

* See Dionyſius's Treatiſes on *Thucydides* and *Demoſthenes*.

Further: In some kinds of composition periods are not at all proper; as in the epistolary and the familiar style, where the best composed periods would offend a man of correct taste. And in no kind of composition must all be periodized; for that would make the style too uniform, wanting that variety which, as I have said, is the chief beauty of all the works of art; and, besides, the sense might often be injured by it. There should therefore, be thrown in among the periods, now and then, some short *commatic* sentences, as the Greek masters of the art call them, such as interrogations, to raise the attention of the reader or the hearer; or even some things in the argument or narrative, which may have a better effect standing by themselves, than thrown into a period with other things; for this is a matter of taste and judgment, which cannot be directed by any rule.

And thus I have finished what I have to say of composition, with respect to the sound, and the pleasure of the ear, which no good composer will neglect; for, through the ear, the mind is not a little affected, even of the beſt judges. And, as to the people, they may be ſaid to be *led by the ears*. And, accordingly, the ſtatue of the Galic Hercules, who, it ſeems, was their god of eloquence, was repreſented, as Lucian deſcribes him, drawing the multitude after him by a chain, which reached from his mouth to their ears*.—In the next chapter, I am to treat of the ſecond way, according to my diviſion, by which compoſition is varied, viz. figured conſtruction.

* Lucian's Treatiſe of the Galic Hercules.

CHAP. VI.

Of figures of syntax.—The Ellipsis.—The Parenthesis.——Repetition.——Paronomasia.— Like endings.--Parisosis.—In consequence.— Foreign idioms.—A figure of Milton without example.—Tranposition of words.

THE ornaments of speech, of which I am now to treat, are, in the language of antient criticism, called *figures*, in contradistinction to tropes, which are immutations of single words. But we, who do not distinguish so nicely, call by the name of *figure* every mode of expression different from the common, whether relative to single words, or the composition of them.

The figures of construction, which are the subject of this chapter, although they be treated of in our common grammars, do not properly belong to the grammatical art, not being neceffary to language, but ornamental, like every thing elfe we call figures of fpeech; and many of them are fo far from being according to the grammatical rules of fyntax, that they are exceptions or deviations from thofe rules; and all of them are ways of fpeaking unufual and different from plain grammatical fpeech.

In languages, fuch as the Greek and Latin, fo much more artificial than ours, it is evident that there muft be many more figures of this kind. For the rules of their fyntax being more various, muft neceffarily admit of more exceptions, and more ways of throwing the ftyle out of common idiom; fo that in this refpect, as well as in every other, they could diverfify and adorn their ftyle more than we can do *. But, as I do not intend to treat of ornaments of fpeech,

---

* I will give but one example of this, taken from the ufe of genders, which the Greeks have, and we have not. By changing thefe, they varied their compofition, without in the leaft obfcuring the fenfe. Thus, when Helen fays to Telemachus in the Odyffey,

Δωρον τοι και εγω, τεκνον φιλε, τουτο διδωμι,

Book IV. PROGRESS OF LANGUAGE. 67

that will apply to the learned languages alone, I shall mention only such figures of this kind as will apply equally to those languages and to ours; and I will begin with a well known one, viz. *ellipsis*, which

she changes the gender from the word to the person, which makes a composition very different from the common; and yet the sense is not at all obscure or ambiguous, but rather more perspicuous, by shewing that the child was a male. Of the same kind is what Dione says to Venus, in the Iliad,

Τετλαθι, τεκνον εμον, και ανασχεο, κηδομενη περ.

Likewise what is said of the ghost of Tiresias in the Odyssey,

———— ηλθ δ' επι ψυχη Θηβαιου Τειρεσιαο,
Σκηπτρω εχων.

And there is a passage in the second Iliad, where Homer twice changes the gender. It is that fine simile of the birds, to which he compares the Grecian host, when they crowded from their ships to be drawn up in battle against the Trojans:

Των δ', ωσ τ', ορνιθων πετεηνων εθνεα πολλα
Χηνων, η γερανων, η κυκνων δουλιχοδειρων
Ασιω εν λειμωνι, Καυστριου αμφι ρεεθρα,
Ενθα και ενθα ποτωνται αγαλλομεναι πτερυγεσσι,
Κλαγγηδον προκαθιζοντων, σμαραγει δε τε λειμων.

where, from the neuter word εθνεα, he goes to the feminine αγαλλομεναι, agreeing with ορνεις, and returns again to the neuter, in the participle προκαθιζοντων.

is, when one or more words are wanting, that, by the rules of grammar, are required to complete the fenfe. Examples of it are fo common in Greek and Latin, that I need not quote them. It is not fo common in our language, any more than in other modern languages. But I will give one or two examples of it from our great Milton, who wrote at a time when there was no imitation of French authors among us, nor of any other, except the great antient authors, and of the Greek more than the Roman, who were themfelves confidered only as imitators. The authors, therefore, of that age endeavoured to bring our language as near to this claffical ftandard as poffible, and particularly Milton, from whom I am to take my examples[*]. There is one paffage that

---

[*] This author I have frequently mentioned before, and fhall, in the fequel, quote him oftener than any other Englifh writer, becaufe I confider him as the beft ftandard for ftyle, and all the ornaments of fpeech, that we have in our language. He was a fingular man in this refpect, that he had as much original genius as any man, and, at the fame time, more learning than perhaps any, even of that learned age in which he lived. For, it appears from his writings, both in profe and verfe, and particularly from his little treatife upon

furnishes two examples of the ellipsis. It is where Adam, taking leave of the angel, says,

——Since to part,
Go heavenly guest, ætherial messenger,
Sent from whose sovereign goodness I adore.
book 8. v. 645.

education, that his course of study had taken in the whole circle of human knowledge. His poetic genius appeared very early, both in Latin and English; and there is an elegiac epistle of his in Latin, written, as it is supposed, when he was about seventeen or eighteen years old, to his companion Carolus Diodati, who, it seems, had pressed him much to leave London, where he was then residing, and return to the university of Cambridge, where he had been educated, which I will venture to set against any thing of the elegiac kind to be found in Ovid, or even in Tibullus. I shall only quote four verses of it, which will give the reader some taste of the whole. It is where he speaks of his residence in London, the place of his birth:

Me tenet urbs, reflua quam Tamesis alluit unda;
Meque, nec invitum, patria dulcis habet.
O utinam vates nunquam graviora tulisset,
Ille Tomitano flebilis exul agro!

There can be nothing, I think, finer of the elegiac kind than in these lines. In the first, London is most beautifully and poetically described, by the circumstance of its being washed by the refluent water of the Thames. The second line has the proper cadence, as well as turn of expression of this kind of verse; and the two last lines, for the elegance of the composition, and the sweetness of the versification, are hardly to be matched in Latin,

In the first we must supply, *it is necessary;* so that the full phrase is, *since to part is necessary.* This is an ellipsis common enough in Greek, where the word δει, signifying *it must be,* is understood. The other is the ellipsis of the pronoun *him;* so that the complete phrase is, *sent from him, whose goodness I adore.* There is another of the same kind, where he says, speaking to his muse,

or in any other language. It is pleasant, I think, to observe this great genius ' teneris juvenescens versibus,' to use an expression of Horace, wantoning in the soft elegiac, playing with fable and mythology, as he does in those Latin poems; and, by this exercise of his young muse, preluding to his great work, which he executed in the full maturity of his age,

' Long chusing and beginning late;'

I mean his *Paradise Lost.* To his other accomplishments, he joined the advantage of travelling, and in a country which was then the seat of arts and sciences; I mean Italy, where it appears that he applied himself much to the study of the Italian authors, particularly the poets. And his muse exercised herself in that language, as well as in Greek, Latin, and English. And though his genius was so early, and even what may be called premature; yet it did not, like other things that grow hastily, decline soon. For, at the age of sixty-two, when, besides his blindness, and the infirmities accompanying so advanced a period of

Book IV. PROGRESS OF LANGUAGE. 71

> So fail not thou, who thee implores. B. 7. v. 38.

It is like that of the word *illa* in Virgil, where he says,

> Canto quæ folitus, fi quando armenta vocaret. *Ecl.* 2.

Milton has fometimes left out the fign of the infinitive mood, viz. the particle *to*, where he thought it would occafion no ambiguity; as where he makes Beelzebub fay, in the council of the devils, that, by getting poffeffion of this earth, they would be lifted up nearer to their antient feat:

> ——————Perhaps in view
> Of thofe bright confines, whence, with neighbouring
>   arms,
> In opportune excurfion, we may chance
> Re-enter heaven.———

unlefs we fhould chufe to underftand *chance* there as an adverb, of the fame fignification with *perhaps*.

life, he was involved in the ruin of his party, and, as he himfelf has faid,

> ———Fallen on evil days, and evil tongues;
> With dangers and with darknefs compafs'd round,
> And folitude.

He wrote the *Sampfon Agonifies*, the laft and the moft faultlefs, in my judgment, of all his poetical works, if

But there is another example where there can be no doubt of the ellipsis. It is where he says,

>   ——— Champions bold
> Wont ride in armed ———   Book 1. v. 764.

in place of *wont to ride*.

Another ellipsis, in the same author, is to be found, book 10. v. 157.

> So having said, he thus to Eve in *few* —

where *words* are understood; an ellipsis very common both in Greek and Latin.

There is another figure of construction, very common in antient authors, which we call *parenthesis*, by which a whole member of a sentence often is thrown in, that is not construed with the rest of the sentence; so that it might be left out, and yet the sense and syntax be complete. Some of our

not the finest. And his poetic genius was as extensive as it was lasting; for it is difficult to say whether he excels most in the heroic, the tragic, the elegiac, the lyric, the pastoral, or the anacreontic. Of this last kind is a great part of the Comus, which is not to be equalled for scenes of festivity, jollity and riotous mirth, as well as for the noblest sentiments of virtue.

Book IV. Progress of Language. 73

modern smatterers in criticism condemn this figure, as interrupting the connection, and obscuring the sense. But the great antient writers judged otherwise. I took occasion, in the preceeding volume *, to quote a remarkable one of Virgil, in the first Georgic, beginning with this verse,

Quicquid eris (nam te nec sperent Tartara regem, &c.)

There is one in Homer, which may be seen at the bottom of the page †. Horace begins an ode with one of them; it is the eleventh of the third book.

Mercuri, (nam te docilis magistro
Movit Amphion lapides canendo)
Tuque, Testudo, resonare septem
    Callida nervis.

And there is one in the fourth ode of the fourth book so long, that it may be called a digression. And, that we may not think this a poetical licence, the prose writers use this figure as often as the poets, and parti-

---

* See Dissert. 3. annexed to vol. 2. p. 561, and 562.

† ———— Ἀργεῖοι δὲ μέγ' ἴαχον (ἀμφὶ δὲ νῆες Σμερδαλέον κοναβησαν ἀϋσάντων ὑπ' Ἀχαιῶν) Μῦθον ἐπαινησαντες Ὀδυσσῆος θείοιο. Il. 2. v. 333.

cularly Demosthenes is full of it, having sometimes parentheses within parentheses *, which, by his great art of pronunciation, he had, no doubt, the skill to make not only intelligible, but even agreeable to his hearers.

Milton in this, as in other things, followed the taste and judgment of the antients, thinking that he could not vary his composition sufficiently, nor sometimes convey the sense so forcibly as he would wish, without the use of this figure. Accordingly, he has used it very much, more than, I believe, has been commonly observed, of

---

* The Halicarnassian in his Treatise, περὶ τῆς λεκτικῆς Δημοσθένους δεινότητος, cap. 9. p. 275. has given, from the oration against Midias, an example of this, which he has explained at great length. The words of Demosthenes are, ἐμοὶ δ᾽ ὃς (ἔστι τις, ὦ Ἀθηναῖοι, βούλεται ἰσμύσαι μάλιστα (μάλιστα γὰρ ἴσως ἐστὶν ὑπὲρ δύναμιν τὶ ποιεῖν) ὅτι καὶ φιλοτιμίας χάριτος ὑπέστην. This is as remote from what the Halicarnassian calls ἰσθμία ἑρμηνεία, or plain speech, and as much ἐξηλλαγμένη and πολυπλόκος as almost any thing to be found in Thucydides; and yet I can very well conceive, how his pronunciation might make it not only intelligible, but agreeable to the ears of his hearers, and perhaps convey the meaning more forcibly than he could have done otherwise.

which I have elsewhere * given an instance, in that fine passage of the second book, where he describes Belial rising to speak. And, as Horace begins an ode with a parenthesis, so he begins Satan's speech, in the beginning of the second book, with one, and a very long one too, in this manner:

> Powers and dominions, Deities of heaven!
> (For since no deep within her gulph can hold
> Immortal vigour, tho' oppress'd and fallen,
> I give not heaven for lost : From this descent
> Celestial virtues rising, will appear
> More glorious and more dread than from no fall,
> And trust themselves to fear no second fate)
> Me tho' just right, and the fixt laws of heaven, &c.

I will give one other instance from Milton of a parenthesis, which I think very beautiful. It is in the Comus, where the younger brother, speaking of the situation of his sister, says,

> I do not think my sister so to seek,
> Or so unprincipled in virtue's book,
> And the sweet peace that goodness bosoms ever,
> As that the single want of light or noise
> (Not being in danger, as I trust she is not)
> Should stir the constant mood of her calm thoughts,
> And put them into misbecoming plight.

* See Dissert. 3. vol. 2. p. 561.

The whole paſſage is exceedingly beautiful; but what I praiſe in the parentheſis is, the pathos and concern for his ſiſter that it expreſſes. For every parentheſis ſhould contain matter of weight; and, if it throws in ſome paſſion or feeling into the diſcourſe, it is ſo much the better, becauſe it furniſhes the ſpeaker with a proper occaſion to vary the tone of his voice, which ought always to be done in ſpeaking a parentheſis, but is never more properly done than when ſome paſſion is to be expreſſed. And we may obſerve here, that there ought to be two variations of the voice in ſpeaking this parentheſis. The firſt is that tone which we uſe when we mean to qualify or reſtrict any thing that we have ſaid before. With this tone ſhould be pronounced, *not being in danger*; and the ſecond member, *as I truſt ſhe is not*, ſhould be pronounced with that pathetic tone in which we earneſtly hope or pray for any thing. The parentheſis in Demoſthenes, quoted in the preceding note, though it be, as I have ſaid, a parentheſis within a parentheſis, which is a mode of composition that is generally very much condemned; yet, if pronounced with such proper variations of tone, as the sense not only admits, but requires, it would convey the meaning both clearly and emphatically, and would, at the same time, very much please the ear. But, though such variations of the voice be very agreeable, I hold it to be a great fault in speaking, and a common player-trick, to vary the voice for the pleasure of the ear merely, without the sense requiring it. The common reason given for it is, to avoid monotony; but, if the composition be good, there will be variety enough in the matter to furnish occasion for a sufficient variation of the voice. And, if ever there should be a monotony continued for some time, it would offend a good judge less than an affected change of the voice.

Though composition, in order to be beautiful, must be various, it ought not to be like Mr. Bayes's play, where no one thing was to be like another *; but there

---

* ' Because I would not,' says Mr. Bayes, ' have any one
' thing in this play like another; as I began the last act
' with a funeral, I begin this with a dance.' *Rehearsal.*

should be similarity, as well as diversity. There are, therefore, certain figures, the beauty of which consists in the words having a resemblance to one another. The first of this kind I shall mention, is *repetition*, of which there is a remarkable instance in Homer, where he mentions Nireus in his catalogue. This Nireus was but a poor warrior. He brought to Troy no more than three ships, the smallest number that followed any of the Greek leaders.

I do not know any piece, antient or modern, in which a false taste of writing is better ridiculed than in the Rehearsal. It is a piece that, I believe, is *singular* of the kind; for, though the ridicule of the bombast of tragedy was a species of wit much in use among the antient comic writers, yet I do not know that a whole piece of that sort was written by any of them; at least, no such piece has come down to us. But, if such a piece had been preserved, there is a humorous circumstance in the Rehearsal, which, I am persuaded, is the invention of the author. The circumstance I mean is, that of making Mr. Bayes the spectator of his own play, with two other spectators, one of whom flatters him, and the other contradicts and finds fault with him;—the way, of all others, the most proper to make a fool show himself. As false taste never can be truly ridiculed but by one who has himself a good taste, the Duke of Buckingham, in this piece, has shewn that he was as good a critic, and had as correct a taste in writing, as perhaps any man that ever was in England.

But, as he was a very handsome man, and the exactness of Homer's catalogue, which, I am perfuaded, was taken from some written monument then extant, required that he should be mentioned among the other commanders; in order to give him some kind of heroic dignity, and, at the same time, to adorn his verse, he has named him thrice in three verses, and in the same place, viz. at the head of each verse *, which makes the figure assume the name of ἐπαναφορα in Greek †. This is a common figure in all languages, and in all kinds of composition. It gives not only a beauty to the style, when discreetly and properly used, but a great pathos, as in these fine lines of Virgil:

> Te, dulcis conjux, te solo in littore secum,
> Te veniente die, te decedente canebat.

And I remember a passage in Milton where it has the same effect. It is in the second

---

* Νιρευς δ' αὐ συμηθεν ἀγεν τρεις νηας ἰσας,
Νιρευς Αγλαΐης υἱος, Χαροπου τ' ἀνακτος.
Νιρευς, ὁς καλλιστος ἀνηρ ὑπο Ιλιον ἠλθε,
Των ἀλλων Δαναων, μετ' ἀμυμονα Πηλειωνα.   v. 671.

† See the life of Homer above quoted.

book, where Beelzebub, speaking of the disturbance that the fall of man would give to the Almighty, says,

——— his darling sons
Hurled headlong to partake with us, shall curse
Their frail original, and faded bliss,
Faded so soon.———

And there is another passage in the seventh book, where the repetition is of more words, and the pathos still greater:

——— Tho' fallen on evil days,
On evil days tho' fallen, and evil tongues,
In darkness, and with dangers compass'd round,
And solitude, &c. v. 25.

Besides pathos, it expresses also vehemence of contention, and is properly used when we want to inforce any thing very strongly. It is, therefore, a figure very proper for rhetorical composition; and, accordingly, it is much used by the orators, and particularly by Cicero; but he sometimes uses it, as well as other figures, intemperately, as in the oration *pro Archia poëta, c.* 6. where there is this passage: ' Quare quis tandem
' me reprehendat, aut quis mihi jure fuc-
' censeat, si, quantum cæteris ad suas res
' obeundas, quantum ad festos dies ludo-

Book IV. Progress of Language. 81

' rum celebrandos; quantum ad alias vo-
' luptates, et ad ipsam requiem animi et
' corporis conceditur temporis; quantum
' alii tribuunt tempeſtivis conviviis; quan-
' tum denique aleæ, quantum pilæ; tan-
' tum mihi egomet ad hæc ſtudia recolen-
' da ſumpſero.' Here he dwells much too long upon the word *quantum*, even though there were any pathos to be expreſſed, or vehemence of contention. But the ſubject admits of neither. For he is talking of his own application to ſtudy, very commendable indeed, but which had no relation to the queſtion in hand, whether or not Archias was a Roman citizen; and it is one of thoſe digreſſions of vanity, in which Cicero indulges himſelf much too often in his orations, and, indeed, in almoſt all his writings. Demoſthenes uſes this figure too, but much more ſparingly, and never but with a ſtrict regard to decorum and propriety. And, I think, I may venture to affirm, that there is not, in any of his orations, one example of ſuch a tedious and unmeaning repetition. I doubt not, however, but that Cicero would be much applauded and clapped (ſo the Ro-

mans praised their orators) for this whole sentence, divided into members, all beginning with the same word, and the greatest part of the same length, and of the same structure and form of composition. This kind of concinnity, or prettiness, as we may call it, would be very much admired by men who had formed their taste of speaking upon the practice of the schools of declamation then in Rome, in which Latin rhetoricians were the teachers, who, as Cicero himself confesses*, were not comparable to the Greek masters: But, I am persuaded, it would not have been tolerated in Athens, not even in an epidictic oration, spoken merely for the pleasure and entertainment of the hearers; much less in a pleading, or speech of business.

A-kin to this figure, is one called in Greek παρονομασια, by which words of like sound, and sometimes the same word repeated, are thrown together, so as to make a jingle, not unpleasant to the ear, if sparingly and properly used: For it ought not to be used without a reason; and the reason

* Brut. p. 357. 432. *Edit. Lambini.*

commonly is to affirm or deny a thing strongly. Thus Homer says,

Οὐδὲ γὰρ οὐδὲ Δρύαντος υἱὸς, κρατερὸς Λυκόυργος *, &c.

meaning to affirm strongly that this Lycurgus did not live long after contending with the gods. Plato has used it often, but sometimes, I think, intemperately†. In English it has a good effect both in prose and verse, when it falls in naturally, and does not appear to be studiously sought; it is called, I observe, *alliteration* by some English critics; and it no doubt pleases the ear, by making the words run glibly, or, as Shakespeare expresses it, *trippingly* off the tongue.

There is another figure of likeness or similarity, well known, and but too much

---

* Iliad 6. v. 30.

† The Halicarnassian has taken notice of one passage of this kind in his ἐπιταφιος λογος. It is in these words: ἐν ἴσα, καὶ πρώτω, καὶ ὁρατὸν, καὶ ἐν παντὶ, πᾶσαν παντὸς κρείττων παρασκευὴν ἔχων; *Dion. Halic. περὶ τῆς δυνάμεως τῆς Δημοσθένους; c.* 26. *Edit. Hudson.* And, even in his philosophical reasonings, there is often too much of this kind of jingle.

practised among us; I mean the figure of like endings, by which verses or half verses, sentences, or members of sentences, are terminated by the same syllables, one or more. This figure is sometimes used by Homer, and often by the Greek orators, especially in their epidictic orations; and, when sparingly and properly used, is no doubt an ornament of style *. We always avoid

* Homer, I observe, uses it, when he has a mind to make his verse very sweet and flowing, as in his similies, which are the most ornamented parts of his poem. Thus, in the first simile of the Iliad, he has even double rhymes concluding the verse.

Ἠΰτε ἔθνεα εἶσι μελισσάων ἁδινάων,
Πέτρης ἐκ γλαφυρῆς αἰεὶ νέον ἐρχομενάων.   Il. 2. v. 87.

But the rhymes of his hemistichs are more common, as in the simile of the nightingale in the Odyssey,

Ὡς δ' ὅτε Πανδαρέου κούρη χλωρηῒς ἀηδὼν
Καλὸν ἀείδῃσιν, ἔαρος νέον ἱσταμένοιο,
Δενδρέων ἐν πετάλοισι καθεζομένη πυκινοῖσιν.

And, in his description of heaven, in the same work,

Οὔλυμπόνδ', ὅθι φασὶ θεῶν ἕδος ἀσφαλὲς αἰεὶ
Ἔμμεναι, οὔτ' ἀνέμοισι τινάσσεται, οὔτε ποτ' ὄμβρῳ
Δεύεται, οὔτε χιὼν ἐπιπίλναται, ἀλλὰ μάλ' αἴθρη
Πέπταται ἀννέφελος, λευκὴ δ' ἐπιδέδρομεν αἴγλη.

But, in other places, where there is neither simile nor description, he has avoided such rhymes, as his commentators have observed, when he might have had them. As the Latins have not such sweet terminations, they do it in profe, having got, as it would feem, a furfeit of it in verfe.

Another of this kind is what is called in Greek παρισωσις, when the words in different fentences, or different members of the fame fentence, anfwer exactly to one another, being the fame parts of fpeech, in the fame cafe or tenfe, if declineable, and occupying the fame place in the fentence. And, in general, I comprehend under this figure every fimilarity in the compofition, by which like is referred to like, oppofite to oppofite, and the cadence of different fentences, or different members of the fame fentence, is made the fame. This alfo pleafes the ear, if not ufed to fatiety; and it is a beauty of diction likewife not unknown

not ufe this ornament in their verfe; for their *orum* and *arum* have but a difagreeable found, compared with the ων or αων, the οιο or the των of the Greeks. I hold, therefore, fuch rhymes to be a fault in Latin verfe, as in that of Horace,

'Atque alii quorum comœdia prifca virorum,'

which, I am perfuaded, was not ftudied by Horace; but he let it pafs, rather than take the trouble to follow his own precept, and

——— ' incudi reddere verfum.

to Homer *. It is frequently used by the Greek orators, and more still by Cicero. In his oration *pro Sexto Roscio Amerino,* speaking of the punishment of parri-

---

* He says,

Ἀιδεῖσθαι μὲν ἀνήνασθαι, δοῦναι δ' ὑποδέχθαι. Il. ϰ, v. 93.

And again,

Μενοίμω μὲν ἀπερρίψαι, φιλότητα δ' ἑλέσθαι.

The mere modern reader, if I shall have any such, will be surprised to find, that I have quoted Homer so often for examples of the ornaments of speech; and he will be still more surprised when I tell him, that there is not a beauty of language, of any kind, that is known in this learned and refined age (to speak in the fashionable style) but what is practised by Homer, who lived in a barbarous age and nation, as is commonly thought. And I think I may venture to add, that no ornament of speech can be devised that is not to be found in him. But the learned know, that, in Homer's time, and before him, in the age of the Trojan war, speaking was become an art, which distinguished men as much as fighting. Phoenix tells Achilles that he received him from his father,

Νήπιον, οὔπω εἰδόθ' ὁμοιίου πολέμοιο,
Οὐδ' ἀγορέων, ἵνα τ' ἄνδρες ἀριπρεπέες τελέθουσι. Il. 9. v. 440.

but he taught him

Μύθων τε ῥητῆρ' ἔμεναι, πρηκτῆρά τε ἔργων. Ib. v. 244.

Even at this day, the nations of North-America have an art of speaking; and it is well known to those that have been among them, that their orators are in high estimation, and that they are as attentive to preserve the purity and elegance of their language as the most civilized nations

Book IV. Progress of Language. 87

cide among the Romans, he has thefe words: 'Etenim quid tam eſt commune, quam ſpiritus vivis, terra mortuis, mare fluctuantibus, littus ejectis? Ita vivunt, dum poſſunt, ut ducere animam de coelo non queant: Ita moriunter, ut eorum oſſa terra non tangat: ita jactantur fluctibus, ut nunquam abluantur: Ita poſtremo ejiciuntur, ut ne ad ſaxa quidem mortui conquieſcant.' Here there is a great deal too much of this artifice of compoſition; and, accordingly, he himſelf finds fault with it, and pleads for his excuſe, that this oration was a juvenile performance. But, I think, there is too much of it, even in that famous oration which he ſpoke for Milo, when he was in the fulneſs of years and of glory, though, from what he ſays of it in his *Orator ad M. Brut. c.* 49. written when his judgment

in Europe. Yet they are no better than abſolute barbarians, and are truly what we call them, *ſavages*, compared with the Greeks in the days of Homer, or the Trojan war. For, beſides the many neceſſary arts of life, as we think them, which they want, and the Greeks then had, ſuch as agriculture and paſturage, and all the ſeveral arts of Vulcan and Minerva, they have no poetry, which was an art, as we ſee, perfectly well underſtood in the days of Homer, and which contributes ſo much to improve language, and, by conſequence, the oratorial art.

was still more mature by age, he seems to be pleased with it: 'Est enim, judices, hæc 'non scripta, sed nata lex: Quam non di- 'dicimus, accepimus, legimus; verum ex 'natura ipsa arripuimus, hausimus, expres- 'simus: Ad quam, non docti, sed facti: 'Non instituti, sed imbuti sumus.' But, though the excess be blameable, it cannot be denied that it is a figure which gives a concinnity to an oration that is very agreeable; and I think we are obliged to Gorgias the sophist, who first invented it, as Cicero tells us, a little after the passage above quoted in his Orator, c. 52. And, if we can believe Cicero, till the time of Isocrates, there were no other numbers known in prose, except such as were formed by this correspondence of words to one another. For he tells us*, that Isocrates first discovered there might be numbers in prose, without run-

---

* 'Itaque si quæ veteres illi (Herodotum dico, et Thu- 'cydidem, totamque illam ætatem) apte numeroseque 'dixerunt, ea non numero quæsito, sed verborum collo- 'catione ceciderunt. Formae vero quaedam sunt ora- 'tionis, in quibus ea concinnitas inest, ut sequatur nu- 'merus necessario. Nam cum aut par pari refertur, aut 'contrarium contrario opponitur, aut quæ similiter ca- 'dunt verba verbis comparantur. Quidquid ita conclu- 'ditor, plerumque fit ut numerose cadat;' *Orator ad M. Brutum,* c. 65. *See also* c. 55. But, as I have elsewhere

ning it into verse. But, before his time, every thing that could be called numerous in prose composition, was owing to the order of the words, by which like was referred to like, contrary opposed to contrary, and words ending in the same manner were set against one another*. In English, and in every other language, it must produce a very good effect, when sparingly, and not affectedly used. But I would advise the English orator to use it as Demosthenes and the other great orators of Greece have used it, not so intemperately as, I think, Cicero

observed, the Halicarnassian is of a different opinion, and thinks that the great prose-authors, even before Isocrates, studied numbers, properly so called, that is, such as arise from the mixture of short and long syllables; and I confess I pay more regard to the opinion of the Halicarnassian than to that of Cicero, especially in his judgment of the authors of his own country; nor do I think that it is possible for any man of taste to read Herodotus with attention, and not be convinced that he studied these numbers, even more than the numbers of which Cicero speaks, and which, as I shall observe presently, were much more practised by him than by any Greek writer.

* De Clar. Orator. cap. 8.

has done. For the moſt admired paſſages of that kind in this author, ſuch as that above quoted from the oration *pro Milone*, and another in the oration *pro Archia Poëta**, which is in the mouth of almoſt every ſcholar, I would not recommend to the imitation of any writer or ſpeaker.

Under the *pariſoſis*, according to the definition I have given of it, is comprehended the well-known figure of *antitheſis*; ſo well known, and ſo much practiſed in all kinds of compoſition, both antient and modern, that it would be ſuperfluous to give examples of it;

---

* ' Hæc ſtudia adoleſcentiam alunt, ſenectutem oblec-
' tant, ſecundas res ornant, adverſis perfugium ac ſola-
' tium præbent, delectant domi, non impediunt foris,
' pernoctant nobiſcum, peregrinantur, ruſticantur.'

If this manner be fine, I deſire to know why there is nothing like it to be found in any Greek writer, not even in the ſophiſts of later times, who write orations of ſhow and oſtentation, not of buſineſs, ſuch as thoſe of Cicero? And, indeed, I cannot help ſaying, that it is a ſtyle altogether unfit for buſineſs and real life, ſuch as could only have been produced in a ſchool of declamation, and fit only to gain the applauſe of the boys there, or of a people as rude and untaught as the generality of the people of Rome were in the days of Cicero.

or, if examples were neceſſary, theſe two which I have given from Cicero's orations, *pro Milone*, and *pro Archia Poëta*, are ſufficient; for there we have ſtrings of antitheſes; and beſides, we have the figure of like endings, and a perfect ſimilarity of the ſtructure, both as to the grammatical form of the words, and even the number of them in the ſeveral members of the period. Ariſtotle, in his rhetoric, has given examples of ſuch compoſition, from the epidictic or panegyrical orations of Iſocrates[*]; but it is uſed with much more moderation, even by Iſocrates. And, as to Demoſthenes, there is no ſuch playing with words to be found in him; for he wrote the ſtyle of buſineſs, not of pleaſure and oſtentation.

Theſe figures laſt mentioned belong to the ſound of the compoſition, of which I have already treated, as well as to the ſtructure of the words, of which I am now

---

[*] Thus Iſocrates, when ſpeaking of Xerxes' expedition againſt the Greeks, ſays, πλευσαι μεν δια της ηπειρου, πεζευσαι δε δια της θαλασσης τω μεν Ελλησποντον ζευξας, τον δε Αθω διορυξας; *Ariſtot. Rhetor. lib.* 3. *cap.* 10.

speaking. And, indeed, a good composer will, in every ornament he uses, study the pleasure of the ear, as much as is consistent with sense and propriety. But I am now to mention one or two figures which have little or no relation to the sound, but regard only the syntax.

The first I shall mention is called in Greek ἀνακολυθια, that is, *inconsequence* or in-connection, when the words, as they stand, will not at all connect together in construction, nor without supplying some other words, or changing in some way the structure of the sentence. If this produced no obscurity, it was judged by the antients an agreeable variety of composition, and it is used as such by Homer*, the great fountain of eloquence, as well as poetry, and

---

* Of this kind there is a remarkable instance in the second Iliad, in Nestor's speech, v. 350.

'Φημι γαρ, ὀι κατανευσαι ὑπεργυια Κρονιωνα,
'Ηματι τῳ, ὁτι νηυσιν ἐν' ὠκυποροισιν ἐβαινν
Ἀργειοι, Τρωεσσι φονον και κηρα φεροντες,
Ἀστραπτων ἐπι δεξι', ἐναισιμα σηματα φαινων.

where we have ἀστραπτων, instead of ἀστραπτοντα, and we must make out the connection by resolving the paniciple

who has practised, if not invented, every art of speech that has been used since his time, or, I believe, can be devised. The Greek prose-writers likewise use this figure, especially such of them who, like Thucydides, affect the austere character of style; for it is not a pleasant figure. And, as the Roman writers formed themselves up-

---

into the verb, and making it ιστρωστι, or αστιαττατ ω; see the life of Homer above quoted, p. 307. And if we add the adverb τητι, the connection will be evident. Another example is in Iliad 6. v. 510. where, speaking of a horse that had broke out of the stable, he says,

ὁ δ' ἀγλαΐηφι πεποιθως,
Ῥίμφα ἑγονα φερει μετα τ' ήθεα και νομον ἱππων·

where, in order to make out the syntax, we must likewise change the participle into the verb, and then, with the addition of an ιππος, or some such word, both the sense and syntax will be completed.

Again,

Τω δε διακρινθεντε ὁ μεν μετα λαον Ἀχαιων
'Ηϊ' ὁ δ' ἐς Τρωας ὁμαδον κιν.

where the resolution of the participle into the verb will do without more; or it may be construed by making τω διακριθεντε a nominative absolute, such as the Greeks use frequently. And, indeed, every case absolute, or απολυτος, as they say, whether nominative, genitive, dative, or accusative, (for the Greeks use them all) may be considered as a species of ἀνακολουθια.

on the Greek, we are to expect to find it in them. There is a remarkable one in the Hecyra of Terence, act 3. sc. 1. which runs thus: 'Nam nos omnes, quibus est 'alicunde aliquis objectus labos, omne quod 'est interea tempus, prius quam id rescitum 'est, lucro est;' where, according to the rules of construction, it should be *nobis omnibus—lucro est*. To make it, therefore, construe as it stands, we must supply *quoad*, or some such word.

It is no doubt a figure that varies the style, and throws it much out of common speech. But the use of it is dangerous; and, if it makes the style obscure or ambiguous, it ought to be condemned as a solecism, of which it has, no doubt, the appearance; and, accordingly, the Greek critics call it σολοικοφανες. Our English writers do not attempt it, unless we dignify with the name of this figure some such anomalous expressions as *methinks*, and *he would needs do it*. But we must except Milton, who was resolved to be an antient in this respect, as well as every other. There is one instance that I remember, among others that may be found. It is in the third book of Paradise Lost, beginning at verse 344.

> No sooner had the Almighty ceas'd, but all
> The multitude of angels, with a shout,
> Loud, as from numbers without number, sweet,
> As from blest voices uttering joy, heaven rung
> With jubilee, and loud hosannahs fill'd
> The eternal regions.

The lines are so wonderfully fine, that if it were a real solecism, not to be justified by any antient authority, I could excuse it. But it is to be justified in the same way as those passages I have quoted from Homer. And I have no doubt but that Milton, who had all Homer by heart, as Dr. Bentley somewhere says, had those passages in view, particularly the first, which very much resembles this of Milton. I would, therefore, make out the syntax by supplying the verb *shouted*, or *received*; so that the full construction will be, *The angels shouted with a shout*, or *received*, viz. what God Almighty had said *with a shout, loud as from numbers without number*, &c. But, whatever way we solve the difficulty of the syntax, there is nothing obscure in the sense; and therefore I cannot condemn the figure, though it be, no doubt, a very unusual one in English*.

The next figure I am to speak of is, perhaps, more properly a figure of construction than any I have hitherto mentioned. For it is a change of the natural construction of the language into one that is foreign to it,

---

* This passage may be so construed as to need no supplement or alteration of the words to make out the sentence, viz. by connecting the words *uttering joy*, with *all the multitude of angels*, and then it would be no more but an ablative absolute, which indeed is a gaping, unconnected syntax, but so common in English, as well as in Greek and Latin, that it is not reckoned a figure. But this, in the first place, would be making the connection too remote, when the natural connection is with the word immediately preceeding, viz. *voices*, so that the construction is, *voices uttering joy*. And, secondly, the sense is better if we follow the natural connection, as *uttering joy* accounts so well for the sweetness of the voices. I therefore think it is better to suppose, that Milton, in imitation of his great model Homer, intended to vary his style, and make it more poetical, by an anomalous construction, but such as does not at all obscure the sense.

Dr. Bentley understands this passage as I do; for he says, the sentence is imperfect, being without a verb. But, instead of making a figure of it, he proceeds, according to his usual method, to correct the text; and, instead of *with* a shout, reads, *gave* a shout.

being taken from a foreign language. It is well known in Latin, under the name of *Hellenism**; for the Romans took their foreign idioms from the Greek. In the fashionable English of this age, the idioms of that kind are Gallicisms. For one of our fine gentlemen, who, perhaps, knows no more of the French language than is sufficient to corrupt his own, will say, *I have given to eat*, instead of saying, *I have given an entertain-*

---

* In the common Latin Grammars, I observe, that many unusual ways of speaking in that language are referred to a figure they call *antiptosis*, or *enallage casuum*; whereas they are truly Hellenisms. Thus, when Horace says, *uxor invicti Jovis esse nescis*, they tell you that *uxor*, the nominative, is there put for *uxorem*, and that the sentence should be *nescis te esse uxorem invicti Jovis*. But it is a Greek idiom, according to which, if the person of the verb, which governs the other in the infinitive, is not changed, the pronoun is not repeated, and the substantive, or adjective, which follows the verb in the infinitive, is of the same case with the person of the first verb, that is, of the nominative. In the same manner, when Cicero says, *rem quemado se habeat vides*, it is not one case for another, viz. the accusative *rem* for the nominative *res*; but it is a Græcism: And, in general, to say, that one case is put for another, without giving a reason for it, is ungrammatical, and, as Dr. Clarke has observed, overturns all the rules of the art.

ment. And it is to be hoped, that he will come at laſt to improve his ſtyle ſo much, as to tell us, that *it does not make day* with him till twelve o'clock. But Milton drew the ornaments of his ſtyle from a better ſource, namely, the Greek and Latin, and chiefly the Greek. For it is evident, that not only his Engliſh, but his Latin, is cut upon Greek, as much, or perhaps more, than that written by any Roman. Of thoſe Greek or Latin conſtructions his works are full. I ſhall give an inſtance of one or two of them. In the ſecond book of Paradiſe Loſt, he makes Beelzebub ſay,

> Upborne with indefatigable wings,
> Over the vaſt abrupt, ere he arrive
> The happy iſle.

The conſtruction in Engliſh is, *arrive* at *the iſle*. But, inſtead of that, he has choſen the Latin idiom of *acceſſit inſulam*, or *ingreſſus eſt inſulam*, or the Greek εισῆλθε τὴν νῆσον.

There is another inſtance in the beginning of book 9. v. 42. where he ſays,

> ——— Me, of theſe
> Nor ſkill'd nor ſtudious, higher argument
> Awaits.

Book IV. Progress of Language. 99

The usual construction in English is, *skilled in a thing;* but the Latin construction is, *peritus alicujus rei.* Again, In book 9. v. 845. he says,

> Yet oft his heart, divine of something ill,
> Misgave him.

which is just the Latin, *mens divina futuri.* Again, speaking of death, he says, that

> ———he upturned
> His nostrils wide into the murky air,
> Sagacious of his quarry;

which is likewise a Latin idiom.

There is a third passage that I remember, which may be referred to this head. It is in the *Comus*, where he makes that magician address the lady in a very high style of classical gallantry:

> Hail, foreign wonder! whom certain these rough shades
> Did never breed; unless the goddess, that in rural shrine
> Dwell'st here with Pan or Sylvan, by blest song
> Forbidding every bleak unkindly fog
> To touch the prosp'rous growth of this tall wood.

As Cicero says of Plato's language, that, if Jupiter were to speak Greek, he would speak as Plato has written; so we may say of this language of Milton—that, if Jupiter were to speak English, he would express himself in this manner. The passage is exceeding beautiful in every respect; but all readers of taste will acknowledge, that the style of it is much raised by the expression —*unless the goddess*, an elliptical expression, unusual in our language, though common enough in Greek and Latin. But if we were to fill it up and say, *unless thou beest the goddess;* how flat and insipid would it make the composition, compared with what it is.

I will mention another idiom of construction in Milton, and which, as far as I know, is neither Greek nor Latin, but intirely Milton's own, and which, I think, does more violence to the language than any other that he has used. It is where he describes Eve just parting from her husband to go to work by herself in the garden, which exposed her to the temptation of the devil. As this is the last description of her in a state of innocence, Milton has bestowed upon her the richest colours of his poetry, and has compared her to every thing most beautiful of the kind that is to be found in the antient fable, with which he found it necessary to adorn even his Christian poem.

> Thus saying, from her husband's hand her hand
> Soft she withdrew, and like a Wood-nymph light
> Oread or Dryad, or of Delia's train,
> Betook her to the groves; but Delia's self
> In gait surpass'd and goddess-like deport;
> Though not, as she, with bow and quiver arm'd,
> But with such gard'ning tools as art, yet rude,
> Guiltless of fire, had form'd, or angels brought.
> To Pales, or Pomona, thus adorn'd,
> Likest she seem'd (Pomona, when she fled
> Vertumnus), or to Ceres in her prime,
> Yet virgin of Proserpina from Jove. b. 9. v. 385.

This expression, *virgin of Proserpina*, is certainly not common English, and many will deny it to be English at all; but let any man try to express the same thought otherwise, and he will be convinced how much Milton has raised and ennobled his style by an idiom so uncommon, but which is, notwithstanding, sufficiently intelligible.

The last example I shall give from Milton of this kind of figure, is one by which the natural construction of the language is not altered, but interrupted and broken in a very unusual way. It is in the Comus, where the lady sitting inchanted, and endeavouring to rise, Comus says to her,

> Nay, lady, fit: *If I but wave this wand,*
> *Your nerves are all chain'd up in alabafter,*
> *And you a flatue; or, as Daphne was,*
> *Root-bound, that fled Apollo.*

where, inftead of faying *root-bound, as Daphne was, that fled Apollo*, he throws in *root-bound* into the middle, betwixt the antecedent and the relative, a trajection altogether unufual in our language, but which muft be allowed both to vary and raife the ftyle; and as the connection is not fo remote as to make the language obfcure, I think it may not only be tolerated, but praifed.

This way of varying the ftyle is a figure very ufual both in Greek and Latin. For, though thofe languages admitted of very much greater variety of compofition than ours; yet, even among them, there were certain tranfpofitions, not only of fingle words, but of the members of fentences, which were unufual. Thefe were marked by their critics, and denoted by the name of *hyperbaton;* a figure much ufed by the beft authors, by Thucydides more than any, and I think too much; but by Demofthenes more moderately, though Longinus feems to think that even he has exceeded in the use of it *. But a much better critic than he, I mean the Halicarnaffian, does not find fault with him in that respect; and it is certainly one of the principal means by which he has raised a style of common words so much above common speech. It is a figure which raises and diversifies style perhaps more than any other; and though the effects of it be felt by every man of good natural taste, it is only the critic who knows the cause. Thus the difference betwixt the Virgilian verse and the verses of Cicero, or even of Lucretius, in the didactic part of his poem, is acknowledged by every man of the least taste; but it is only the man who has studied the rules of writing who knows that it is owing chiefly to the use of the hyperbaton †.

* De Subl. § 22.

† See what I have further said upon this subject, vol. 2, p. 584.

Some may think, that those transpositions of words, which I dignify with the name of a figure, were no more than the ordinary arrangement of words in those learned languages, however extraordinary it may appear to us. Even in the days of the Halicarnaffian, as he informs us in

Thus much I have thought proper to say of figures of construction—a little out of a great deal that might be said upon the subject—but enough, I hope, to excite my reader's curiosity to look into the antient masters of art who have treated of this part of style, such as Dionysius the Halicarnassian, Cicero, and Quintilian. And, if he would have a complete pattern for this kind of figurative style, let him go to Thucydides, who has diversified his composition by

---

his treatise upon Thucydides, c. 51. p. 261. vol. 2. edit. Hudsoni, there were some who thought that the style of Thucydides, which, as I have said, abounds so much with this figure, was the usual style of his age. But the Halicarnassian shews the contrary, by appealing to the writings of other authors contemporary with him. And if we would be convinced that the style of Demosthenes, though not near so much varied and adorned by this figure, was not the common language of his time, we need only compare his public orations, such as his Philippics, his Olynthiacs, and his oration περι στεφανου, with his orations in private causes, or with the decrees of the senate and people of Athens, which are inserted in some of his harangues; and we shall immediately perceive the difference betwixt his artificial high-raised style, and the common language of business, or of conversation, at that time in Athens; and we shall also perceive, that it is the more or less frequent use of the hyperbaton that chiefly makes the difference.

Book IV. PROGRESS OF LANGUAGE. 105

every figure of words that can be imagined, many more than the grammarians or rhetoricians have given names to *.

* The Halicarnaſſian has written two treatiſes upon Thucydides's character of ſtyle and his idioms; not in the epidictic manner, as he ſays, that is, in the way of a popular oration, but in the didactic manner, which he underſtood as well as any body, being by profeſſion a teacher of rhetoric in Rome. He has therefore explained, by examples taken from Thucydides's hiſtory, whatever he has ſaid of his ſtyle, which makes the work exceedingly inſtructive to thoſe who deſire to know accurately all the different forms of compoſition. He has enlarged particularly upon the figures relating to the ſyntax, or grammatical ſtructure of the words, in which Thucydides abounds more than any other writer in proſe; for he moulds and faſhions the language in every way that can be conceived, in order to remove his ſtyle, as far as poſſible, from common ſpeech, uſing nouns ſometimes for verbs, and, *vice verſa*, verbs for nouns, active verbs for paſſive, and paſſive for active, and ſingular and plural numbers interchangeably, making his caſes and genders refer, ſometimes to the things ſignified, ſometimes to the word ſignifying them, ſometimes making perſons ſtand for things, at other times things for perſons; and in theſe, and other ways which the Halicarnaſſian enumerates, torturing, as it were, the words, in order to form a ſtyle peculiar to himſelf, and exceedingly different from that of any other writer. See vol. 2. of the Halicarnaſſian's works, *p*. 215. *edit. Hudſon*. All this is much enlarged upon in

VOL. III.   I

CHAP. VII.

Recapitulation.—Of the figures by which the sense is varied.—These divided into three kinds.—Of the first is Exclamation—Hyperbole — Epithet—Prosopopœia—And Description.

STYLE, as we have said, consists of two parts, words considered singly, and the composition of these words. We have seen how single words may be varied both as to the sound and the meaning; we have seen also that, in composition, the same words may be varied with respect to the sound, and likewise that the grammatical structure of the speech may be changed, the words still continuing the same. It

---

the first treatise, and, as I have said, illustrated by examples. But, in the second, he not only examines the style, but the matter of this author most accurately. And, upon the whole, it is the finest piece of criticism, and, at the same time, the fairest I ever read; for he praises as fully and freely as he censures.

now remains to show how the style may be varied by a change both of the words and the meaning, the subject matter, however, still continuing the same, and the order of treating it. This is done by what is called *figures of the sense or meaning* *. These make so much the nobler part of ornamented composition, by how much the meaning is more excellent than the words.

Figures of this kind, as they vary the composition more than any other, are in number so many, that Quintilian has said they are innumerable †. We must try, however, whether they cannot be reduced to certain heads or classes, so that we may treat of them in order and method. And it appears to me, that they may be properly divided into three kinds: *First*, such as express some feeling or emotion of the mind; *secondly*, such as express the character or manners of the speaker or writer; and, *thirdly*, such as, without expressing

---

* Σχήματα τῆς διανοίας, in opposition to the σχήματα τῆς λέξεως, of which we have already treated.

† Pag. 758. *edit. Burmanni.*

either of thefe, give a turn and form to the thought and expreffion, different from what is ufual in common fpeech. Under one or other of thefe heads may be ranked, as I imagine, every figure of this kind that can be devifed.

By the firſt kind of thefe, the ſtyle is made *pathetic*; by which I do not mean the exciting of grief only, but of every other paſſion or affection of the human mind, ſuch as joy, hope, fear, and the like. Of this fort is a very ſtrong figure, much more uſed in modern writing than in antient; I mean *exclamation*, by which a fpeaker or writer ſtarts from his ſubject, and breaks out into ſome rapturous expreſſion of admiration, aſtoniſhment, or whatever other paſſion moves them. I do not remember one example of it in Homer or Demoſthenes. Cicero, who is certainly not ſo correct a writer as either of thefe, abounds with it; as in the oration for Milo—' O fruſtra fufcepti mei labores! ' O cogitationes inanes meæ! &c. *.' Again, in the fame oration—' O me miferum! O

* Cap. 34.

'infelicem *!' And a little after—'O ter-
'ram illam beatam, quæ hunc virum exce-
'perit †!'—Our Milton has but few of
them: I remember one, which muſt be
allowed to be upon a very proper occaſion.
It is in the ſong of the angels celebrating the
love of the Son of God, when he under-
took to die for men:

——O! unexampled love!
Love no where to be found leſs than divine!
Par. Loſt, b. 3. v. 410.

But, among our more modern authors, it is
become ſo common, that the printers have
invented a punctuation for it, which they
call *punctum admirationis.*

Another figure of this kind, and which
is likewiſe much more common in modern
than in antient writing, is *hyperbole*, by
which a thing is either magnified or dimi-
niſhed beyond what it really is. From this
definition of it, it muſt be evident, that it is
not much uſed by the chaſte writers of antiquity; by the proſe-writers, who deſerve
that character, not at all; and by their

* Cap. 37. † Ib. 38.

poets but very sparingly. Homer has but few of them; though, if we were to judge of his style by that of his translator, we should imagine that he used a great many, and some of them most violent and outrageous *. Virgil has many more, and some

---

* There are, I believe, many English readers, who think Mr. Pope's translation of the Iliad a finer poem than the original. This is a point that I will not dispute with those gentlemen; but I think I shall be able to convince them by an example or two, that, though the style of the translation may be finer than that of the original, it is of a different kind, particularly with respect to the use of this figure of hyperbole. Achilles says in the first Iliad, that the Greeks shall then find the want of him, when many shall fall under Hector the homicide.

———εὖτ' ἂν πολλοὶ ὑφ' Ἕκτορος ἀνδροφόνοιο
Θνήσκοντες πίπτωσιν. V. 242.

This expression is very simple; but see how it is swelled in the translation:

When flush'd with slaughter, Hector comes to spread
The purpled shore with mountains of the dead. v. 319.

This may be a better style, but it is certainly different. Again, Homer describing a battle, says, that the ground flowed with blood,

Ῥεε δ' αἵματι γαῖα,

which is no hyperbole, but is literally true of every bloody battle, especially of such battles as the antient, in which men, drawn up in close and deep order, were en-

of them very violent, such as where he makes one of his heroes lift a stone,

> ' Haud partem exiguam montis.'

gaged hand to hand. But see what a gargantua image Mr. Pope has made of this simple description:

> With streaming blood the slippery fields are dy'd,
> And slaughter'd heroes swell the dreadful tide.

This is an hyperbole with a witness; and, if it had come from the pen of a less celebrated poet, we should have said, that it was not translating Homer, but parodying, or rather burlesquing him.

But, though some severe critics may think that he has not properly translated Homer, I think it is impossible to deny, that he has parodied Virgil exceedingly well in his Dunciad. As where he says, speaking of Curle, and the figures of that piece of tapestry which was one of the prizes in his *high heroic games*,

> Himself among the storied chiefs he spies,
> As from the blanket, high in air he flies.

And again, speaking of a scribbler of the name of Ward,

> From the strong fate of drams if thou gett'st free,
> Another Durphy, Ward, shall sing in thee:
> Thee shall each ale-house, thee each gill-house mourn,
> And answering gin-shops sow'rer sighs return.

These parodies, I think, are incomparable. But perhaps it is not given by Nature to the same man to excel both in the *heroic* and the *mock-heroic*, nor in tragedy and comedy, according to the opinion of the antients; for, among them, the same poet never attempted both. But,

and where he makes Æneas, defcribing a great fea, which lifted their fhips very high, fay,

— ' Rorantia vidimus aftra.'

In Englifh, and more ftill in French, common converfation is moſt unnaturally fwelled, and raiſed by the intemperate uſe of this figure, and from thence it has crept into our writings; fo that a ſtyle, perfectly chaſte and correct in this refpect, is now very rarely to be found. But our great Milton has in this, as well as in other things, faithfully copied his maſters, the antients. For, though his poetical ftyle is, in many paffages, by far the moſt ſublime we have in Englifh; yet it has lefs froth or bombaſt than any modern compofition of the kind that I know. I have elfewhere inſtanced fome expreffions that ſhew the modeſty of his ſtyle, fuch as,

Battle dangerous to lefs than Gods;

befides the mock-heroic, he excelled alfo in fatire; nor do I think any thing keener of that kind is to be found in any author antient or modern. And it muſt alfo be acknowledged, that he has carried the rhyming verfification, in Englifh, to the higheſt point of perfection. And, in his latter works, after he had acquired fome fcience and philofophy, there is a clofenefs and ftrength of expreffion that is rarely to be found in any poet, antient or modern.

and,

> Nor appeared lefs than arch-angel ruined.

And I will here give only one inftance more: It is where he defcribes the rifing of the council of the devils in Pondæmonium, the noife of which a lefs correct and judicious author would have compared to loud thunder; but he compares it to thunder heard at a diftance:

> Their rifing all at once was as the found
> Of thunder heard remote;   Book 2. v. 476.

which is a found not loud or ftrong, but awful, and very like that produced by the movement of a great multitude.

Among the figures of this kind, I reckon the ufe of epithets, by which we commonly exprefs our admiration, love, hatred, or averfion, to any perfon or thing, and by which we denominate or characterize, in a particular manner, any perfon or thing. They are much ufed by the antients in their poetry, and they are the diftinguifhing characteriftic of the poetic ftyle among them*. But they are sparingly used by their best prose-writers, even by their orators; whereas, among us, the *epithetical* style is become so common, as to infect even our ordinary conversation; and, as for our oratory, it makes the greatest part of it. And,

---

* Homer, in the addresses of his speeches, has often joined several epithets together, as

Διογενες Λαερτιαδη πολυμηχαν' Οδυσσευ.

By such magnificent compellations he has raised the dignity both of his heroes and his style. Milton in this, as in other things, has imitated him; he makes Beelzebub address Satan in this manner:

> O prince! O chief of many throned powers,
> That led th' embattled seraphim to war
> Under thy conduct, and in dreadful deeds
> Fearless, endanger'd heaven's perpetual King,
> And put to proof his high supremacy.
> Book i. v. 128.

Adam accosts Eve thus:
> Daughter of God and man, immortal Eve:
> Book ix. v. 291.

And she him in these words:
> Offspring of heaven and earth, and all earth's lord.
> Ib. 273.

Such a style as this, Milton thought
> ———Justly gives heroic name
> To person, or to poem.——— Ib. v. 40.

as all our writings, of every kind, have something of the poetical or rhetorical cast, this style has become universally predominant.

The *Prosopopœia* is a figure likewise used in the pathetic style: By it we introduce personages that are not present, and sometimes such as are no longer existing, nay, inanimate things, and give them voice and speech for the purpose of exciting passions of different kinds in the hearer. It is a strong figure, and belonging more to poetry than oratory; it is, however, used by the orators, and particularly by Cicero, who sometimes even personifies inanimate things, which is altogether poetical, nor do I remember that it is practised by any Greek orator; but Cicero has used it in sundry passages of his orations, particularly in the oration for Milo, where he addresses the Alban groves and altars in this manner: 'Vos enim jam, Albani Tumuli at-
' que Luci, vos, inquam, imploro atque tes-
' tor, vosque Albanorum dirutæ aræ*.'

* Pro Milone, c. 31.

Our poetry is full of addresses of this kind to inanimate things; and if not too frequent, and if introduced upon proper occasions, they have a very good effect. There is a beautiful prosopopœia of this kind in the *Crito* of Plato, who may be reckoned a poet as well as a philosopher. It is in that part of the dialogue where Socrates makes a personage of the laws and community of Athens, and introduces them arguing against his escape out of prison, which Crito had advised, and the argument is carried on by way of dialogue betwixt Socrates and them for several pages *. In the oration which he has given us, in the *Menexenus*, upon those Athenians, who died fighting for their country, he has likewise used this figure very successfully, by raising from the dead those whom he was praising, and making them give very proper exhortations to the children they had left behind them: See the passage quoted and commended by the Halicarnassian †.

* Plat. opera, Ficini, p. 37.
† Περι της διοτητος το Δημοσθεν;, c. 30.

The laſt figure of this kind I ſhall mention, is, what the Greek maſters of the art call διατυπωσις, by which we particularly deſcribe any thing with all its circumſtances; and it is a figure which, more than any other, if properly uſed, moves the mind, and excites paſſion. For this purpoſe, it is much more proper than exclamation, hyperbole, or ſtrong epithets; becauſe it preſents to us the object itſelf, and, as it were, ſets before our eyes whatever is intended to excite our pity, terror, anger, indignation, or whatever other paſſion. This figure is chiefly poetical; for poetry is a kind of painting, and a particular deſcription of any thing, being ſuch as might be painted, is not improperly called a picture of that thing; and, accordingly, it is very much uſed by the poets, and particularly Homer*. It is alſo uſed properly by the orator, when he has

* Ανδρας μεν κτεινουσι, πολιν δε τι πυρ αμαθυνει·
Τεκνα δε τ᾽ αλλοι αγουσι, βαθυζωνους τε γυναικας.

And again,

Δυσμορε, ηΐα πατηρ Κρονιδης ετι γυμαις εσθν
Λυγρη εν οργαλεη φθισει κακα πολλ᾽ επιεοντα,
Υιας τ᾽ ελλημενες, ιδευθεισασι θυγατρας·
Και θαλαμες, κεραιζομενες, και νηπια τεκνα
Βαλλομενα ποτι γαιη εν αινη δηϊοτητι.

a mind to excite our paſſions. But, as the beſt kind of oratory perſuades more by argument than by paſſion, and therefore reaſons more than it deſcribes, we have little of this figure in Demoſthenes*, but a great deal of it in Cicero, who, in his orations, has given us many pictures, ſuch as that of Verres—' Stetit ſoleatus prætor populi 'Romani cum pallio purpureo, tunicaque

---

* In his oration againſt Æſchines, entitled, περι παραπρεσβειας, deſcribing the deſolation of the country of the Phocians by Philip, which he himſelf ſaw, and of which, he ſays, Æſchines was the cauſe, he ſpeaks of houſes demoliſhed, walls razed, a country diſpeopled of men fit for the purpoſes of life, with only a few women and children in it, and poor old men. In ſhort, ſays he, nobody can, by words, deſcribe the miſery that is now to be ſeen there. The ſcholar, however, will be pleaſed to read Demoſthenes's own words: Θεωμε δικει, ω ανδρες Αθηναιοι και ιλιγγια· ετι γαρ κ', εποριευομεθα εις Δελφους, εξ αναγκης ο βραι ημιν παντα ταυτα· οικιας κατεσκαμμενας, τειχη περιηρημενα, χωραν ερημον των εν ηλικια, γυναια δε και παιδαρια ολιγα, και πρεσβυτας ανθρωπους οικτρους· ουδε αν εις ιξικεσθαι δυναιτο τω λογω των εκει κακων νυν οντων. And the critic, in comparing this paſſage with a like deſcription in Homer, juſt now quoted, will be ſenſible of the difference betwixt poetical painting and oratorial deſcription. Demoſthenes has given us little more than the ſubject of the picture, with ſome of the great outlines; but Homer has filled up the piece with every ſtriking circumſtance that could occur to the imagination of a painter.

' talari, muliercula nixus in littore *.' And another of Lucius Piso, much longer and more remarkable †.

* In Verrem, lib. v. p. 446. edit. in ufum Delphini.

† ' Meminifline, cœnum, cum ad te quinta fere hora
' cum C. Pifone veniffem, nefcio quo e gurguftio te pro-
' dire, involuto capite, foleatum? Et cum ifto ore fœti-
' do teterrimam nobis popinam inhalâffes, excufatione te
' uti valetudinis, quod diceres, vinolentis te quibufdam
' medicaminibus folere curari? Quam nos caufam cùm
' accepiffemus, (quid enim facere poteramus?) paulifper
' fletimus in illo ganearum tuarum nidore atque fumo;
' unde tu nos, cum improbiffimè refpondendo, tum tur-
' piffimè eructando, ejecifti. Idem illo fere biduo pro-
' ductus in concionem ab eo, cui fic æquatum præbebas
' confulatum tuom, cùm effes interrogatus, quid fenti-
' res de confulatu meo; gravis auctor, Calatious credo
' aliquis, aut Africanus, aut Maximus, et non Cæfonius
' Semiplacentinus Calventius, refpondes, altero ad fron-
' tem fublato, altero ad mentum depreffo fupercilio,
' *crudelitatem tibi non placere*;' in *L. Pifonem*, c. 6. This
is painting indeed; but it is Dutch painting: And
though it might have been proper enough in a comic
poet, it was not fuitable to the dignity of an orator, a
confular orator too, and then the firft fenator in Rome.
But, with Cicero's great talents, there was a levity of
wit mixed, which he never could fhake off, and which
made Cato fay, upon hearing his oration for Lucius
Muræna, made when he was actually conful, wherein
he was witty upon the ftoical philofophy—*quàm ridiculum confulem habemus*.

For this, and such like descriptions, I am perswaded Cicero was much praised and clapped by his countrymen; but I doubt whether the people of Athens, assembled, either to deliberate on public affairs, or to judge causes, would have borne to be entertained in that way by their orators. For, though they loved poetry, and particularly that of the theatre, more perhaps than any people ever did; yet their taste was so correct, that I do not believe they could have endured to see it mixed with their serious business.

As to other kinds of style, such as the historic or didactic, this figure does not at all belong to them; and therefore, whenever we see in any such composition a particular description tending to move the passions, we ought to consider it as out of the style of the work, and belonging to poetry or rhetoric: I say, *tending to move the passions;* for, if it be a description of any thing, as a subject of art or science, let it be ever so particular, it may be very properly inserted, even in history; and as to works of the didactic kind, such descriptions properly belong to them. The account, therefore, given by Thucydides of the plague in Athens, about the beginning of the Peloponnesian war, though very accurate, and almost as circumstantial as a physician could have given it, is a very proper part of his history.

CHAP. VIII.

Of the second kind of Composition, figured with respect to the sense, viz. by the imitation of characters.—The difference betwixt this kind of style and the pathetic.—The difference betwixt describing and imitating a character.—The Ethic style belongs both to Poetry and Rhetoric, but in different respects.

I Come now to speak of the second way in which the sense is figured, namely, by expressing the character of the speaker or writer. The effect of this turn given to the composition is felt by every reader of any taste or judgment; but the nature of the thing appears to me to be little understood by our modern critics; at least I do not know any modern work of criticism in which it is treated of as a matter of art or science. Among the antients, it was well known under the name of the τὸ ἠθικον*, and in Latin *morata oratio* †; and is treated of by them in every book which they have written upon the subject of rhetoric or poetry; but, as it is so little understood among us, it will be necessary to explain the nature of it at some length.

And, first, it is to be carefully distinguished from the expression of passion, of

---

* In the Scholia upon the antient Greek authors, where any thing is said of this kind, it is observed by the Scholiast to be ηθικως, or ἐν ἤθει λεγομενον.

† In this sense Horace uses the word *morata* when he says,

——Speciosa locis, morataque recte
Fabula, nullius veneris, sine pondere et usu,
Valdius oblectat populum, meliusque moratur,
Quam versus inopes rerum, nugæque canoræ.
Ar. Poët.

where the reader, not learned, would imagine, that by *Fabula recte morata*, was meant a *fable of good moral*; but it is a fable or dramatic piece, in which character and manners are properly represented. What we would call the morals of the piece, are denoted by the *speciosa locis*, which signifies, that the common topics, the subject of which was almost always something moral and useful in life, were there well handled.

which we have treated in the preceeding chapter. For though a speaker or writer may shew himself to be full of anger, grief, indignation, or any other passion, he does not for that speak or write *ethically*, if I may be allowed the expression, because *character* and *passion* are two things quite different; and, accordingly, Aristotle, in his Poetics, has accurately distinguished them: Character, says he, is that which directs us in our choice of actions, and makes us be denominated such or such a man, that is, good or bad, just or unjust, and the like. By passion, on the other hand, we grieve or rejoice, hope or fear, and, in short, are liable to every emotion or alteration of the mind *.

Secondly, There is a great difference between *describing* a character and *representing* it; and the one may be intirely without the

---

* The words of Aristotle are, τα δι ηθη, καθ' α ποιας τινας ιναι φαμεν τας πραττοντας. And again, ιστι δε ηθος μεν το τοιουτον, ο δηλοι την προαιρεσιν, οποια τις εστιν, εν οις μη εστι δηλον ή προαιρειται, ή φευγει ο λεγων. Po.l. 1, 6.

other. A poet may reprefent characters very well without defcribing any; and my Lord Shaftfbury has very well obferved, that, though Homer has reprefented or imitated characters exceedingly well, he has defcribed none *. And again, an hiftorian may defcribe characters very well, as my Lord Clarendon has done, and yet imitate none. But what is the difference betwixt the two? It is this: When I defcribe a character, I only *tell* what it is; whereas, when I reprefent it, I *fhew* or *exhibit* what it is. This diftinction will be perfectly underftood with refpect to the body and its operations. If I fay, that a man made fuch and fuch motions or geftures, looked fo and fo, and fpoke with fuch a tone of voice; though I defcribe all this ever fo accurately and particularly, ftill I do but *defcribe*; but if I am a mimic, and move, look, and fpeak as he

* There is, however, one paffage in the Iliad, where Homer has defcribed the character of his hero from the mouth of Patroclus:

Οὐδὶ γλυκιθυμ:ς ἀϊκρ ϰϛ, ὑδ᾽ ἀγανόφρων,
Ἀλλὰ μαλ᾽ ἰμμιμαως.——

does, then I *reprefent* or *imitate* him, and become, as it were, that man*.

According to this account of the matter, when an author either exhibits himfelf un-

---

* This is the nature of Imitation, as defcribed by Plato in a paffage of the third book de Republica, too long to be here tranfcribed, but of which I will give the fubftance in Englifh, becaufe it further explains the nature of imitation, and of that kind of ftyle which I call Ethic. Plato, in this paffage, after having fhewn what the fubject fhould be of the poetical fables, and mythological tales, which were to be taught to children in his commonwealth, comes next to explain in what manner the fubject was to be handled in fuch fables or tales; and he begins with laying it down, that whatever was faid by poets or mythologifts, was a narrative of what had been, what was, or what would be; and this narrative was either fimple, or by imitation, or both ways. The Interloquutor Adimantus did not underftand this laft, and defired an explanation of it: 'I am, it would feem, fays Socrates, a ridiculous teacher; and I muft do, I find, as thofe do who have not learned the art of fpeaking ; I muft explain the thing, not in whole, but in parts, and make you conceive what I mean by examples. You remember the beginning of the Iliad, where the poet introduces Chryfes the prieft, defiring the ranfom of his daughter; and, when he could not obtain it, praying to the god Apollo to avenge him of the Greeks for the refufal. In this narrative, down to thefe lines,

———Και λισσοντο παντας Αχαιους,
'Ατρειδα δε μαλιστα, δυω κοσμητορε λαων,

der a certain character, or introduces persons into his piece who so exhibit themselves, then does he write in the style I am describing, and is what I would call an *ethic writer*. But, if there is no character repre-

the poet speaks himself, and there is no change of person in the narrative; but the same person, namely, Homer, continues to narrate. But, after this, he speaks not as Homer, but as Chryses the priest, endeavouring, as much as he can, to make us forget him, and attend only to the priest; and in these two ways the narrative goes on through the whole Iliad and Odyssey.' The first of these ways, when the poet appears, and narrates *in his own person*, I call *simple narrative*; but, *when he becomes another*, and speaks not as Homer, but as that other, I call it *narrative by imitation*; because the poet, in that case, imitates, as much as he can, the person whom he introduces as speaking. And he may be said to be a mimic, with as much propriety as a man is so called, who imitates the figure, gesture, or voice of another. If the poet never disappeared himself, but went on narrating that such or such things were done or said, then would the whole poem be simple narrative; but if, on the other hand, the poet never appeared at all himself, but the whole story was told by other persons, introduced as speakers, then would the whole be imitation: And this is the case, says Plato, of tragic and comic poetry; whereas the former is the nature of Dithyrambic poetry. And, lastly, if the story is told partly by the poet himself, and partly by other speakers, then is the poem mixed of plain narrative, and of imitation; and of this kind are the Iliad and Odyssey.

sented in his piece, neither belonging to himself, nor to any other person, then, whatever other excellence there may be in his work, there is no *character* or manners in it. And it is not enough, that the persons he introduces as acting, may shew their characters by their actions; for, unless they shew them by speaking, it is not such character as I mean, which must be exhibited by speeches, not by actions.

This kind of style belongs both to poetry and oratory, but in different respects. The orator ought to represent himself as a good man, a lover of truth, just, humane, and benevolent, especially to those to whom he addresses himself*. But, if he introduces any other persons as speaking, he

---

* The character of the orator is one of the three methods of persuasion mentioned by Aristotle, in the beginning of his books of rhetoric. We persuade, says he, by arguments, drawn either from the nature of the subject, from the passions of the hearers, or from the character of the speaker; lib. 1. c. 2. This shews the necessity of every orator assuming a proper character, which is often more convincing with the people than either of the other two. For the people sometimes may not understand the best arguments, and the subject may not

need not make them exhibit any character. The poet, on the other hand, needs never appear in his own piece; and Homer, I think, has been very juftly praifed for never fo appearing; but the perfons he introduces muft neceffarily have a character, which they ought to fhew by their fpeaking, otherwife his piece is very imperfect. And from this difference proceeds another, that, though many bad and wicked characters may be *defcribed* in an oration, the character *reprefented* in it, being that of the orator himfelf, is always a good character; whereas, the characters reprefented by the

admit of much paffion: But all men will be difpofed to believe what a good man, and a well-wifher of theirs, tells them. An orator, therefore, though he be not ftrong in argument, and though he have not the faculty of moving the paffions; yet, if he can fpeak thus, is not to be defpifed: And the poffeffing this talent was of the greateft ufe to the antient orator, not only in his deliberative orations, but in his judicial; for, as the pleadings were by the parties themfelves, at leaft in Athens, though the fpeeches were fometimes compofed by others, it was proper that the party fhould affume a character throughout the whole oration, and particularly in the narrative, which is not fo neceffary for our pleaders to do.

poet may be, and often are, very bad characters.

As poetry is an art imitative of characters, as well as of actions, the poets ought, above all others, to excell in this figure of style; and, accordingly, Homer, the father of poetry, is most eminent in it. All the characters he has imitated are of the heroic kind, excepting only one ridiculous personage, that he has but once exhibited, I mean *Therſites*. But he has contrived, notwithstanding, to give them a great variety; for Achilles, Ajax, Hector, Diomede, &c. are all heroes, but very different from one another. Virgil, it has been observed, has not such a variety; and indeed the truth is, that he has only three, Æneas, Turnus, and Dido; whereas we may reckon in Homer a dozen that are distinctly characterized. Milton's subject is particularly unfortunate in this respect; for it is such as affords him only one character fit for poetry. His divine personages are such as cannot have characters, like those of Homer's deities, who are as much characterized as his heroes: And Adam and Eve, while in their ſtate of perfection, can hardly be conſidered as human characters; and, after their fall, the part they act is very ſhort; ſo that there remains only Satan, of whom he indeed has made a very fine poetic perſonage, but not without doing ſome violence to his character as devil. For he has not made him perfectly bad, which would not have been a character ſo fit for poetry; but he has mixed with his deviliſh qualities ſome remorſe and feeling of what goodneſs is; and, by doing ſo, he has brought the character nearer to human.

Milton appears to have been ſenſible of this defect of his ſubject; and, accordingly, he has been at great pains to ſupply it; for, in the council of the devils, in the ſecond book, he has exhibited different characters of them in very fine ſpeeches, the fineſt, in my opinion, that are to be found in Engliſh. But thoſe devils appear only there, and are no more ſeen; ſo that Satan may be truly ſaid to be his only character; for he is carried through the whole poem, and every where appears like himſelf, of which I ſhall give but one example out of many. It is the end of his speech, with which he concludes the debate in the council of Pandæmonium; where, after setting forth the dangers that any one must run who should undertake the discovery of the new created world, he says,

> But I should ill become this throne, O peers!
> And this imperial sov'reignty, adorn'd
> With splendor, arm'd with power, if ought propos'd
> And judg'd of public moment, in the shape
> Of difficulty or danger, could deter
> Me from attempting. Wherefore do I assume
> These royalties, and not refuse to reign,
> Refusing to accept as great a share
> Of hazard as of honour, due alike
> To him who reigns, and so much to him due
> Of hazard more, as he above the rest
> High honour'd sits? Go therefore, mighty pow'rs,
> Terror of Heav'n, though fall'n, intend at home,
> While here shall be our home, what best may ease
> The present misery, and render hell
> More tolerable: If there be cure or charm,
> To respite or deceive, or slack the pain
> Of this ill mansion; intermit no watch
> Against a wakeful foe, while I abroad,
> Thro' all the coasts of dark destruction, seek
> Deliv'rance for us all: This enterprize
> None shall partake with me.——
>
> Book ii. v. 445. & seqq.

The whole paſſage is wonderfully beautiful in every reſpect. But the reaſon why I have quoted it is, to ſhew how he ſupports Satan's

> Monarchal pride, conſcious of higheſt worth,

as he expreſſes it. In the firſt of theſe lines I have no doubt but he had in view the ſpeech of Sarpedon in Homer; but he only took the hint from that poet; and to ſhew the learned reader how far he is from a ſervile imitator, even of Homer, I have tranſcribed the paſſage below *.

---

* Γλαυκε, τιη δη και τετιμημεσθα μαλιστα
Εδρη τι, κρεασιν τι, ιδε πλειοις διπαεσσιν,
Ἐν Λυκιη, παντις δι θεος ὡς ἰσορωσι,
Και τιμενος νεμομεσθα μεγα Ξανθοιο παρ' οχθας,
Καλον, φυταλιης και αρουρης πυροφοροιο;
Τω νυν χρη Λυκιοισι μετα πρωτοισιν ιοντας
Εσταμεν, ἠδε μαχης καυστειρης ἀντιβολησαι.
       Lib. μ. v. 310.

Here we may obſerve, that indeed the thought is Homer's; that a King, being moſt honoured, ſhould likewiſe expoſe himſelf moſt to danger. But Milton has given it ſo much of the rhetorical caſt, and dreſſed it ſo up with ſentences and enthymemas, after the manner of Demoſthenes, who, as I have ſaid elſewhere, was his model for ſpeeches, that Homer is hardly to be found in it.

As to characters of common life, they are finely imitated in Terence's comedies, where we have ordinary and natural characters reprefented, fuch as give both pleafure and profit to an intelligent fpectator, not fuch abfurd and ridiculous characters as thofe of our comedy often are, affording nothing but laughter, and that only to the mere vulgar.

There is lately fprung up among us a fpecies of narrative poem, reprefenting likewife the characters of common life. It has the fame relation to comedy that the epic has to tragedy, and differs from the epic in the fame refpect that comedy differs from tragedy; that is, in the actions and characters, both which are much nobler in the epic than in it. It is therefore, I think, a legitimate kind of poem; and, accordingly, we are told, Homer wrote one of that kind, called *Margites*, of which fome lines are preferved*. The reafon why I mention it

---

* Ariftotle, in his Ethics *ad Nicomachum, lib.* vi. *c.* 7. has given us the following paffage of Homer's Margites:

Τον δ' ατ' αξ σκαπτηρα θεοι θεσαν, ετ' αροτηρα,
Ουτ' αλλως τι σοφον.

ie, that we have, in English, a *poem* of that kind, (for so I will call it) which has more of character in it than any work, antient or modern, that I know. The work I mean is, the *History of Tom Jones*, by Henry Fielding, which, as it has more personages brought into the story than any thing of the poetic kind I have ever seen; so all those personages have characters peculiar to them, in so much, that there is not even an host or an hostess upon the road, hardly a servant, who is not distinguished in that way; in short I never saw any thing that was so much animated, and, as I may say, *all alive* with characters and manners, as the History of Tom Jones.

This configuration of style has not been so much explained, even by the antient authors, nor so accurately divided into its several species, as other figures have been:

a character very common in these days, but, it would seem, rare in those antient times. And Plato, in the *Alcibiades* II. has preserved another line of it:

Πολλα επιστατο εργα, κακως δ' ηπιστατο παντα;

a character likewise not uncommon now-a-days; but, I believe, not so common in those times.

There is only one species of it that has been defined and explained. It is when the speaker assumes a character and sentiments different from his own. This figure is known by the name of *Irony*, which Socrates practised more than any man we have heard of, and it was the distinguishing characteristic of his style and manner. But there may be as many speciefes of this figure, as there are different characters that may be represented by an author or speaker, whether they be assumed characters, or his own natural character. If the subject were to be divided, and treated of in this manner, it would take in the definition and explanation of all the different characters of men—a thing very necessary to be known both by poet and orator. And accordingly, Aristotle, in his books of rhetoric, has spent several chapters upon that subject, which are a most valuable part of that valuable work. And Horace also, in his art of poetry, has some very fine lines upon the same subject. As, therefore, this work is so much better done to my hand, I will say no more of it, but will here conclude what I have to say upon this part of style.

CHAP. IX.

The great variety of Composition illustrated by an example.—Of the third kind of figures of the sense.—Some of these named, such as Interrogation—Antithesis—Simile—Allegory—Many more of such figures have no name.—The use of them in composition.—Examples of them from Virgil's Georgics, and Dr. Armstrong's Poem on Health.—Praise of that Poem.—Conclusion of what relates to the Figures of Speech.—Apology for the Author's being so minute in explaining them.

THE reader, who is not learned in the critical art, if he has had the patience to accompany me so far in what I have said concerning all those niceties of composition, will be surprised to find that there is so much variety in this matter; and he will be still more surprised to be told, that the variety is not yet exhausted; and that, besides all the several forms and figures of composition which I have explained, relating both to the sense and the sound, there remain others without name or number, which serve to vary and adorn the composition, as well as those that have been already mentioned.

In order to help him to conceive this variety, I will take a period of some length, and show him the different ways in which it may be composed. The example I shall use is a period that I have mentioned more than once before, viz. that of Milton in Satan's first speech in the council of devils, in the second book of Paradise Lost; and I will take in the whole passage, containing an argument which shews, as much as any thing in the whole work, Milton's rhetorical faculty; for by it he endeavours to prove, that hell is, at least in some respects, better than heaven:

> Me tho' just right, and the fix'd laws of Heaven
> Did first create your leader; next, free choice;
> With what besides, in council or in fight,
> Hath been atchiev'd of merit; yet this loss,
> Thus far at least recover'd, hath much more

Book IV. Progress of Language. 139

Eſtabliſh'd in a ſafe unenvied throne,
Yielded with full conſent. The happier ſtate
In heaven, which follows dignity, might draw
Envy from each inferior; but who here
Will envy whom the higheſt place expoſes
Foremoſt to ſtand againſt the Thund'rer's aim
Your bulwark, and condemns to greateſt ſhare
Of endleſs pain? Where there is then no good
For which to ſtrive, no ſtrife can grow up there
From faction; for none ſure will claim in hell
Precedence; none, whoſe portion is ſo ſmall
Of preſent pain, that with ambitious mind
Will covet more. With this advantage then
To union, and firm faith, and firm accord,
More than can be in heav'n, we now return
To claim our juſt inheritance of old,
Surer to proſper than proſperity
Could have aſſur'd us; and by what beſt way,
Whether of open war or covert guile,
We now debate: Who can adviſe, may ſpeak.

As every compoſition is made up of certain materials, let us conſider, *firſt*, of what materials the compoſition here is made. And theſe are the following propoſitions (for there is no need to analyſe it further): 1*ſt*, I was created your leader, by the fixed laws of Heaven: 2*dly*, I was likewiſe by you choſen for leader: 3*dly*, This choice was confirmed by my atchievements: 4*thly*, But, I was liable to envy while in heaven: For,

5*ibly*, there is envy in heaven, becaufe there is in it good for which to contend: But, 6*ibly*, There is no envy here in hell, becaufe there is no good to contend for. From thefe premifes, the conclufion is drawn, that he was more eftablifhed in his throne, and they in a better condition, and furer to profper than before their fall. Thefe materials may be put together in the following plain manner, without any figure or other ornament of language.

'Being created your leader, by juft right,
' and Heaven's fixt laws, then by your free
' choice, and next by my own atchieve-
' ments in battle and in council; I am fur-
' ther eftablifhed in this right by the lofs
' we have fuftained, a lofs, at leaft, fo far re-
' covered; for, by this lofs, I am delivered
' from the danger of envy, which attends
' dignity in heaven, but which cannot be
' here, where there is no good to contend
' for, and where the higheft dignity only
' expofes to the greateft mifery. With the
' advantage, then, of greater union and
' firmer concord than can be in heaven, we

'are in a better condition, and furer to
'profper than we were before our fall.'

This is the plain fenfe of the paffage; but it will be fomewhat ornamented, if it be turned in this way;

'What could have eftablifhed me more
'in my throne than this very lofs that we
'have fuftained, thus far, at leaft, repair-
'ed? Before, indeed, I was created your
'leader, by the fixt laws of Heaven. This
'creation was confirmed, firft by your free
'election, next by my own atchievements
'in council and in battle; but ftill I was
'in danger, from that envy which attends
'all fuperior dignities in heaven. Now
'that is at an end; for who will envy him
'who is here condemned to fuffer the
'greateft fhare of pain? And how can there
'be contention, when there is no good for
'which to contend? With the advantage,
'then, of fo much greater unanimity and
'concord than we could enjoy in hea-
'ven, let us return to claim our juft inheri-
'tance, being now affured to profper more
'than profperity could have affured us.'

Or thus, with a little more ornament, and more of the rhetorical caſt.

' As uſurpation, the want of the people's concurrence in the election of a monarch, and the defect of perſonal merit in the monarch himſelf, make a throne inſecure; ſo, on the other hand, nothing eſtabliſhes a throne more than juſt right and fixt laws, the free election of the people, and the atchievements of the monarch in council and in battle. All theſe advantages I enjoy. But there is one thing which makes my throne ſtill more ſecure: What is that? It is this very loſs that we have ſuſtained; by which that envy which attends ſuperior dignities in heaven is at an end. For who will here envy him who is condemned to ſuffer the greateſt miſery? With more unanimity, therefore, and firm concord than can be in heaven, let us deliberate how we are to repair our loſſes, thus far already recovered.'

Other turns might be given to this ſentence; but theſe will ſuffice to ſhew, *firſt*, how much more copious the language of

Milton is, and how much more rounded, compact, and nervous his compofition is, than any that I, at leaſt, can give to this paſſage. 2*do*, If there be ſo much variety in turning one ſingle argument, how much more muſt there be in the compoſition of a whole difcourſe or oration, though the ſubſtance of the matter, and the order of treating it, ſtill continue the ſame? *Laſtly*, And, what is more to our preſent purpoſe, it may be obſerved, that all the variety is here produced, without uſing any of the figures, of which I have treated in the two preceeding chapters; for there is here neither the pathetic nor the ethic, nor any thing but the argument variouſly turned and figured. This then ſhews, that there are ways of figuring the ſenſe of a compoſition otherwiſe than either by paſſion or by manners; and it is of ſuch figures that I am now to treat.

Some of them have got names; and with theſe I ſhall begin. And, *firſt*, there is *Interrogation*, a figure uſed by Milton in this period, and likewiſe by me in the two laſt ways I have turned it. It is a figure that serves to excite the attention, and gives life and spirit to the composition. It is, therefore, much used both by poets and orators, and particularly by Demosthenes, who frequently throws pungent interrogations into the middle of his arguments and periods, by which he not only varies the meaning, but the sound of his composition, and often much inforces the sense and argument. It is a figure that is likewise commonly used in ordinary conversation especially when we argue; for it belongs more to argument than to narrative; and therefore it is little used by historians.

Another figure, likewise belonging more to argument than to narrative, is *Antithesis*; a figure I have already mentioned among the figures of construction. It is also a lively figure, which, by opposing things to one another, throws greater light upon both. It is a figure also of pleasant sound; for, at the same time that it makes an opposition in the sense, it produces a similarity in the structure of the words; and, when joined with some other figures above-mentioned, such as the Paronomasia, and like endings, as it sometimes happens*, it makes the style altogether panegyrical, and even theatrical. It is much used by modern authors, particularly by those who are thought to write smartly and wittily; for it is the figure of wit, as I shall shew, when I come to treat of that kind of style.

There is another figure of the kind we are now speaking of, and which likewise has a name, and that is the *Simile*, of great

---

* Of this kind a great deal is to be found in Isocrates; and in Plato too, when he affects to write rhetorically; as in his funeral oration in the Menexenus, where we have such sentences as the following: τας μεν παιδευοντες κοσμιως, τας δε γηροτροφουντες αξιως.—Again, νεκρωντες μεν τας παλαμας, λυταμενοι δε τας φιλιας.—Again, τας μεν τετελευτηκοτας ικανως επαινεσαι, τας δε ζωσι ευμενως παραινεσαι —Further, πολιτεια ανθρωπων τροφος εστι, η μεν αγαθη αγαθων, μη καλη δε κακων; where we have altogether the Paronomasia, like endings, the Antithesis, and every other species of the Parisosis. But the frequent use of such figures is blamed by the Halicarnassian—περι της των Δημοσθενος δεινοτητος; c. 26. as making the style unfit for business and action, and such as I have described it above, fit only for theatres and panegyrical assemblies, when men meet for the purpose only of being entertained, by having their ears and fancies amused.

use in poetry, and particularly in heroic poetry; for it both raises and varies the style. Homer has used it much, and so has our Milton; who, though he has not copied from Homer any one simile servilely, as far as I remember, has imitated his manner more than any other poet I know, without excepting even Virgil, who has copied more from Homer, but has not, in my judgment, imitated him so well. For Milton's similes are, like Homer's, descriptions of the thing, without being confined to the point of similitude; and he often animates them, as Homer likewise does, by introducing human sentiments and passions into them *. This also is a figure of wit

---

* Of this kind is Milton's simile of the fallen angels, contracting their forms, and crouding into Pandæmonium:

——They but now who seem'd
In bigness to surpass earth's giant sons,
Now less than smallest dwarfs, in narrow room
Throng numberless, like that Pygmæan race,
Beyond the Indian mount; or fairy elves,
Whose mid-night revels, by a forest's side,
Or fountain, some belated peasant sees,
Or dreams he sees, while over-head the moon
Sits arbitress, and nearer to the earth

among our modern authors, and particularly is very much used by our writers of comedy.

What simile is to a metaphor, an allegory is to a simile. For, as a simile is a

> Wheels her pale course; they on their mirth and dance
> Intent, with jocund music charm his ear;
> At once, with joy and fear, his heart rebounds.
> *Book* 1. v. 777.

He has another beautiful simile of the same kind in the 4th book of Paradise Lost, beginning v. 980. where he compares the angels surrounding Satan with a grove of spears, bending towards him, to a field of corn waved with the wind:

> While thus he spake, the angelic squadron bright
> Turn'd fiery red, sharp'ning in mooned horns
> Their phalanx, and began to hem him round
> With ported spears, as thick as when a field
> Of Ceres, ripe for harvest, waving bends
> Her bearded grove of ears, which way the wind
> Sways them: 'The careful plowman doubting stands,
> 'Lest on the threshing-floor his hopeful sheaves
> 'Prove chaff.'

This is exactly after the manner of Homer in many of his similes, particularly in the following, where he compares the fires of the Trojan camp to the heavens, in a clear, starry, and moon-shine night:

lengthened metaphor, so an allegory is a lengthened simile. It is drawn out to so great a length, by some modern authors, as to run through a whole piece, and make

> Ὡς δ' ὅτ' ἐν οὐρανῷ ἄστρα ἀμφὶ σελήνην
> Φαίνετ' ἀριπρεπέα, ὅτε τ' ἔπλετο νήνεμος αἰθήρ,
> Ἐκ τ' ἔφανεν πᾶσαι σκοπιαὶ, καὶ πρώονες ἄκροι,
> Καὶ νάπαι· οὐρανόθεν δ' ἄρ' ὑπερράγη ἄσπετος αἰθήρ,
> Πάντα δὲ τ' εἴδεται ἄστρα· γέγηθε δέ τε φρένα ποιμήν.
>
> Il. θ. v. 555.

Again, in the fine simile of the two torrents meeting, to which he compares the shock of two armies engaging, he places a shepherd at a distance, hearing the noise, just as a painter who had been to draw the scene he describes would have enlivened his landskip, by setting down such a figure in it;

> Ὡς δ' ὅτε χείμαρροι ποταμοὶ, κατ' ὄρεσφι ῥέοντες,
> Ἐς μισγάγκειαν συμβάλλετον ὄμβριμον ὕδωρ,
> Κρουνῶν ἐκ μεγάλων, κοίλης ἔντοσθι χαράδρης·
> Τῶν δέ τε τηλόσε δοῦπον ἐν οὔρεσιν ἔκλυε ποιμήν.
>
> Lib. δ. v. 452.

It is by such descriptions that Homer has furnished so many good subjects for painters, more, I believe, than any other poet; for, as he paints in words, it is easy to copy him in colours; whereas, a poet that does not paint, but gives only a general description, as most of our modern poets do, cannot be copied by the painter. Some modern critics find fault with such similes, as containing many particulars that have nothing to do in the comparison; and particularly Mr. Perault, the

what we call an *allegorical poem*. I do not know that whole works of that kind were known in antient times; but it was used by them as an ornament and figure of style, and but very sparingly, even in that way. Homer has but very few; though certain critics, antient as well as modern, have found a great many in him. Some indeed have allegorized every thing in him, the human as well as the divine personages. Virgil has been blamed, and I think very justly, for drawing out to so many lines the allegorical desciption of Fame, which Homer has dispatched in two*.

French critic, condemns them, and calls them similes *a longus qurn*, or *long-tailed similes*. But such critics do not consider, that the Epic is a poem of great extent, and which does not hasten to its conclusion so much as tragedy. Therefore it admits of episodes, and such descriptions and digressive similes, as they may be called, and, in short, of every thing that can raise or embellish the style, provided it be not altogether foreign to the purpose.

* Besides this allegorical description of Fame, I do not recollect any allegory, either in the Iliad or Odyssey, except the story which Phœnix tells to Achilles of *prayers*, which, he says, are the daughters of Jupiter, and follow *Ate*, repairing the mischiefs that she does; Il. i. v. 498. And the story of the two casks, that Achilles

And Milton, with greater reason, has been blamed for making such allegorical personages, as *Sin* and *Death*, act so considerable a part in his poem.

These are all, or, at least, the principal figures of this kind that have got names; but every way by which the meaning may be any ways affected, and the composition varied from plain grammatical speech, is properly called a *figure*. And that there may

tells to Priam, out of which Jupiter mixes the cup of mortals; Il. 24. v. 527. Aristarchus, therefore, the great antient critic, was mistaken, when he said there was no allegory at all in Homer; but he was very much nearer the truth than those critics who allegorized every thing, even the human personages; such as Hector and Achilles: See Eustathius on Iliad First. The truth is, that even what is called the mythology of Homer, is not allegory; but, like all the rest of the mythology of Greece, historical facts much disguised, indeed, by fable, with this difference, however, betwixt Homer's mythology and the later Greek mythology, that the former is made up of stories of the antient Egyptian kings, or gods, as they call them, with little or no addition from the invention of the Greeks; except changing the scene of their adventures from Egypt to Greece; the latter is the history of the Egyptian gods, much enlarged by Greek fables. For the Egyptian religion, when it was transplanted to Greece, flourished exceedingly there, and produced a large growth of new divinities.

be many such, as many as there are different ways of turning the same sentence, is evident, both from the reason of the thing, and from the examples I have given.

But it will be said, what is the use of turning the same thing so many different ways? And are not the methods I have already pointed out sufficient, and more than sufficient, for the purpose of men communicating their thoughts to one another? And, indeed, if nothing more were required than plain speech, a great deal more than enough has been said upon the subject. But we are speaking of ornamented language; and for this is required, *first*, that things should be expressed in a way somewhat different from the common and ordinary. Now, it may be improper to vary the composition of common speech by any of the figures hitherto mentioned, and yet, some way or other, it must be varied, otherwise it would not be ornamented language. 2*dly*, There must be a change even of ornament; for variety, as I have before observed, is absolutely necessary in all the works of art, in order to make them please; and the finest composition in the world, if it were to continue always the same, would, in the end, very much disgust [*]. One of the greatest faults, therefore, of composition is, that noted by Quintilian [†], under the name of *Homoiologia*; and It is one of the greatest praises of the style of Demosthenes, and is mentioned by the Halicarnassian as a well known mark by which his composition is distinguished from that of every other orator, the varying his periods, and members of periods, and, in short, every part of his composition, by different figures and forms

---

[*] See what the Halicarnassian has said upon this subject, in his most valuable treatise περὶ συντάξεως τῶν Δημοσθένους. c. 48. where he compares ornate composition to what it resembles more or less in all languages, but most of all in Greek; I mean music; and he supposes that a musician was perfect as to melody, but had no regard to rhythm, could we endure, says he, such a musical composition? Again, let us suppose, that both the melody and rhythm are compleat, but that he continues always the same melody, and the same rhythms, without any change or variety, would not this spoil all?

[†] P. 698. Edit. Burmanni.

of expression*. And all this variety may be so ordered, by a judicious speaker or writer, that the sense and matter, which ought to be the principal in all compositions, may not only not be hurt, but even aided and inforced by it.

* After having mentioned the melody and rhythm of his composition, of which we have so little idea, and made these two the first distinguishing marks of his style, he adds, τρίτον ἔτι καὶ τέταρτον ἰδώμα τῆς συνθέσεως τὰ ῥήτορος ὦ, τοῖς τε ἐξαλλάττων ποικιλώτατον, καὶ τὸ σχηματίζω ποικίλως, τὰ καλὰ καὶ τὰς τερψιας. ἐδὲν γάρ ἐστω ἐδὲς ἀπλῶς τοτος, ὡς οὐχι διαστεσκιλται ταῖς τι ἐξαλλαγαις και ταῖς σχηματισμοῖς, ᾗς ἅπαντις ἴσμεν· καὶ μοι δαλει ταῦτα μη λογον διδώαι, γνωριμα και τοῖς φαυλτατοῖς ὄντα· Περὶ τῆς διντετος τε Δημοσθένης, p. 315. And again, in his second treatise upon Thucydides, c. 53. p. 263. speaking of Demosthenes, he says, ταις μεταβολαις και τη ποικιλια, και τω μηδν ἀπλως ἀσχηματιστον ἰνφερν νομα, καθαρω τω φρασιν. And, according to Cicero, Demosthenes was reckoned the first of orators, on account of the variety of the figures, and *conformations*, as he calls them, of his sentences. It is where he is speaking of Antonius, a Roman orator, contemporary with Lucius Crassus. Of him he says, that he excelled ' in sententiarum orna-
' mentis et conformationibus, quo genere, quia præstat
' omnibus Demosthenes, idcirco a doctis oratorum est
' princeps judicatus. Σχηματα enim, quæ vocant Græci,
' ea maximè ornant oratorem; eaque non tam in verbis
' pingendis habent pondus, quàm in illuminandis sen-

This variety of compofition is not only moſt beautiful and pleaſing, but, more than any thing elſe, ſecures an author or ſpeaker againſt parodies, or ridiculous imitations. For it is a fameneſs in the ſtyle, and certain forms of expreſſion often recurring, that makes a ſtyle liable to be *taken off*, according to the common expreſſion. For proof of this, we ſee how the ſtyle of Salluſt or Tacitus has been imitated by ſome writers of later times; not indeed in the way of parody, but as ſomething fine and excellent of the kind: Whereas, the variety of Demoſthenes's compofition it is impoſſible to ridicule, and exceedingly difficult to imitate. And, in general, it may be ſaid of a good ſtyle, as of a good face, that it has no ſtrong or diſtinguiſhing features, but it is the ſymmetry and juſt proportion of the whole that pleaſes. Such a face, however, is much more difficult to imitate in painting or ſculpture, than a face with any thing prominent, or out of due proportion.

' tentiis.' De Cl. Oratoribus, c. 37. And it is the compoſition which Æſchines, who ſhould have beſt known to what he owed his ruin, praiſes moſt in his antagoniſt, as the Halicarnaſſian informs us.

There is no author, as far as I know, that has attempted to divide and clafs, under different heads, all this variety of figures. It would not be an eafy tafk; and I doubt whether it would be worth the while. I fhall therefore do, as Plato fays the unlearned do, when they would explain any thing: Inftead of taking the whole together, dividing and fubdividing, and unfolding it by definition, they go to particulars, and explain it by examples*. And as fome, even of my learned readers, may not be familiarly acquainted with Demofthenes, who, as I have faid, excelled fo much in the variety of his figures, I will take my examples from an author better known, viz. Virgil. This author lived to finifh only two pieces, his *Eclogues*, and his *Georgics*, both mafter-pieces of ftyle and compofition, but different, in that refpect, one from the other. The ftyle of the Eclogues is elegant and ornamented; at the fame time, it has much of rural fimplicity (not the Dorick rufticity of

* See Plato in the paffage quoted above, p. 126. from the third book de Republica.

Theocritus); so that it is rather sweet and pleasant, than highly and richly ornamented*. I except, however, the fourth Eclogue, of which, as the subject is not rural,

---

* It is of that kind of style which Horace characterizes by the epithets of *molle et facetum*,

———— *Molle atque facetum*
Virgilio annuerint gaudentes rure Camœnæ ;

where the English reader would be much mistaken if he should translate *facetum* by the word *facetious*, derived from it, of which there is nothing in the style of Virgil's eclogues; but it answers to what the Greek critics call the τὸ γλαφυρὸν in composition, which may be translated *sweet and elegant*. This shews us, that it is impossible thoroughly to understand the Latin, and what the Latin authors have written upon the subject of any art, without knowing the language of their masters, the Greeks: And, *secondly*, it confirms the observation made above, that a great part of the Latin words we have adopted into our language are taken from a false and barbarous Latinity.

For a specimen of the *molle et facetum* of the style of the Eclogues, I refer the reader to the beginning of the eighth Eclogue, which runs thus:

Pastorum musam Damon.is et Alphesibœi,
Immemor herbarum quos est mirata juvenca,
Certantes, quorum stupefactæ carmine lynces,
Et mutata suos requierunt flumina cursus;
Damonis musam dicemus et Alphesibœi.

the style is much more raised and embellished than that of any other of them; and, accordingly, the poet, in the beginning of this Eclogue, tells us, that he is to raise his style above the country*. The Georgics, on the other hand, are embellished with every ornament of style that can be imagined; even the didactic part of them is ornamented; in which, as I shall take occasion to observe afterwards, he differs from Lucretius. But, as to the digressions, they are the richest pieces of composition that are extant; and, it would seem, that, as in the Eclogue, which sings of the return of the golden age, and the renovation of all things, he wanted to make his *woods* worthy of a consul; so, in his Georgics, he studied to make his *fields* worthy of his great patron, Augustus Cæsar. It is from the digressions, therefore, that I shall take my examples—a few out of many that might be given, but sufficient, I hope, to shew how much and how agreeably the style

---

* Sicelides Musæ, paulo majora canamus;
Non omnes arbusta juvant, humilesque myricæ.
Si canimus sylvas, sylvæ sint Consule dignæ.

may be varied otherwise than by any of the figures hitherto mentioned.

In describing the different prognostics of the weather, towards the end of the *first* Georgic, after mentioning the actions of different animals, by which they presage a storm, and particularly that of the *cornix*, or *raven*, he says of her, that

> ———Plena pluviam vocat improba voce,
> Et sola in sicca secum spatiatur arena.

He then changes the form of the style, as well as the prognostic, in the following lines:

> Nec nocturna quidem carpentes pensa puellæ
> Nescivere Hiemem; testa cum ardente viderent
> Scintillare oleum, et putres concrescere fungos.
>
> v. 390.

Then he goes on still changing:

> Nec minus ex imbri soles et aperta serena
> Prospicere, et certis poteris cognoscere signis.
>
> v. 393.

After describing some appearances of the morning, he tells us what the consequences of those appearances will be, in the following manner:

> Heu, male tum mites defendet pampinos uvas;
> Tum multa in tectis crepitans falit horrida grando.
>
> v. 448.

Immediately after this, in paffing to the omens that are to be taken from the evening, and the fetting-fun, he gives this turn to the compofition:

> Hoc etiam, emenfo cum jam decedet Olympo,
> Profuerit meminiffe magis.—— v. 450.

And he tells us the effect of certain appearances at that time, in the following beautiful manner:

> ——Non illa quifquam me nocte per altum
> Ire, neque a terra moneat convellere funem.
>
> v. 456.

Where, inftead of telling us fimply that it would be a tempeftuous night, 'Let no-'body,' fays he, 'advife me to unmoor my 'bark, or put to fea in that night.'

With the omens of the weather, and particularly thofe which are drawn from the appearances of the fun, he connects the prodigies that appeared about the time of Julius Cæfar's death in the following lines;

> Denique, quid vesper serus vehat, unde serenas
> Ventus agat nubes, quid cogitet humidus Auster,
> Sol tibi signa dabit: Solem quis dicere falsum
> Audent? Ille etiam cæcos instare tumultus
> Sæpe monet, fraudemque et operta tumescere bella.
> Ille etiam extincto miseratus Cæsare Romam,
> Cum caput obscura nitidum ferrugine texit,
> Impiaque æternam timuerunt sæcula noctem.
> v. 461.

Then he changes the form thus:

> Tempore quanquam illo tellus quoque, et æquora ponti,
> Obscænique canes, Importunæque volucres,
> Signa dabant.   v. 469.

Then he changes again:

> —— Quoties Cyclopum effervere in agros
> Vidimus undantem ruptis fornacibus Ætnam,
> Flammarumque globos, liquefactaque volvere saxa!

After this he proceeds to mix, with this artificial, some plain composition, telling us simply what happened:

> Armorum sonitum toto Germania cœlo
> Audiit; insolitis tremuerunt motibus Alpes.
> Vox quoque per lucos vulgo exaudita silentes
> Ingens, et simulacra modis pallentia miris
> Visa sub obscurum noctis, &c.   v. 474.

And so he goes on for several lines, till he again figures the style in this manner:

Book IV. PROGRESS OF LANGUAGE. 161

> ——— Nec tempore eodem
> Triſtibus aut extis fibræ apparere minaces,
> Aut puteis manare cruor ceſſavit.   v. 485.

Then, after going on a little farther in this form, he changes to another of this kind:

> Non alias cœlo ceciderunt plura ſereno
> Fulgura, nec diræ toties arſere cometæ.   v. 487.

Then he proceeds to tell what happened in conſequence of theſe omens; and, with the ſubject, he changes the phraſeology:

> Ergo inter ſeſe paribus concurrere telis
> Romanas acies iterùm videre Philippi.   v. 489.

Then he takes another figure:

> Nec fuit indignum ſuperis, bis ſanguine noſtro
> Emathiam, et latos Hæmi pingueſcere campos.

Then he changes again:

> Scilicet et tempus veniet, cum finibus illis
> Agricola, incurvo terram molitus aratro,
> Exeſa inveniet ſcabra rubigine pila,
> Aut gravibus raſtris galeas pulſabit inanes,
> Grandiaque effoſſis mirabitur oſſa ſepulchris.

And ſo he goes on (for it would be tedious to mention more particulars) to the end of the book, diverſifying and adorning his composition, by figures which have no name, but of which every reader of taste must feel the effect, though he do not, perhaps, know the cause.

In the second Georgic, there is a most beautiful digression in praise of Italy, his native country, which he has adorned with the richest colours of his poetry. He had before described a remarkable tree that grows in Media. With this description he connects the praises of Italy in the following manner:

> Sed neque Medorum sylvæ, ditissima terra,
> Nec pulcher Ganges, atque auro turbidus Hermus,
> Laudibus Italiæ certent; non Bactra, neque Indi, &c.
> Georg. 2. v. 136.

He goes on in this negative form for a few lines, till he comes to

> Sed gravidæ fruges, et Bacchi Massicus humor,
> Implevere; tenent oleæ armentaque læta.

Then he changes again:

> Hinc bellator equus campo sese arduus infert, &c.

And so he goes on for some lines, and then he gives us a new form:

Book IV. PROGRESS OF LANGUAGE. 163

> At rabidæ tigres abfunt, et fæva leonum
> Semina.——

Then he leaves this form, and gives us another;

> ——Nec miferos fallunt aconita legentes.

And, after dwelling upon this for two lines more, then he changes again;

> Adde tot egregias urbes, operumque laborem.

And, after continuing this ftyle a little longer, he changes to this form:

> An mare, quod fupra, memorem, quodque alluit infra,
> Anne lacus tantos?——

Then he ufes a ftronger figure, and which has got a name, being called *Apoftrophe:*

> ——Te, Lari maxime, teque
> Fluctibus et fremitu affurgens, Benace, marino?

And fo he goes on, ftill varying, till he concludes the digreffion with a form altogether different from any he has hitherto ufed, viz. a falutation of his native country, in thefe beautiful lines:

> Salve, magna parens frugum, Saturnia tellus,
> Magna virum: Tibi res antiquæ laudis et artis

> Ingredior, sanctos ausus recludere fontes;
> Ascræumque cano Romana per oppida carmen.
>
> v. 173.

If I had not said enough, and perhaps more than enough, to explain what I mean by those nameless figures of composition, so many, and so various, I would refer the reader to several other passages in this highly finished work, and particularly to what he has written in praise of a country-life, in the end of the second Georgic. There, besides the figures of variety we are now speaking of, he has described the city-life, with a pomp of language that nothing can exceed:

> Si non ingentem foribus domus alta superbis
> Mane salutantum totis vomit ædibus undam,
> Nec varios inhiant pulchra testudine postes,
> Illusasque auro vestes, Ephyreïaque æra;
> Alba neque Assyrio fucatur lana veneno,
> Nec Casia liquidi corrumpitur usus olivi.

Then he changes his style at once; and, in contrast to the pomp of the city-life, describes the simple country-life, in a language as simple, only sweetened and enlivened a little by the figure *Repetition*:

> At secura quies, et nescia fallere vita,
> Dives opum variarum, at latis otia fundis,

Speluncæ, vivique lacus; at frigida Tempe,
Mugitusque boum, mollesque sub arbore somni,
Non absunt.——

I shall have done with Virgil, when I have observed, that it is not the variety of the structure only which I commend in the verses I have quoted; but they have, besides, almost every other ornament, either of single words, or of composition, and are in every respect most beautiful, and well worthy of the labour which, we are told, he bestowed on making them.

Milton, in this variety, has not been deficient, any more than in other ornaments of style. But, as I have already quoted a great deal from him, I will not trouble the reader with any more of his, but will go to a living author, that I may shew, that even these *coster-monger* days, to use a phrase of Shakespeare's, have produced, at least, one poet, that deserves to be quoted as a model of good composition; and, that I may not incur the suspicion of envy and malignity, which Horace throws upon some critics of his time:

*Ingeniis non ille plaudit favetque sepultis;
Nostra sed invidet, nos nostraque lividus odit.*

The person I mean is Dr. Armstrong, author of the Poem upon Health; the best didactic poem, without dispute, in our language, and such as will bear comparison even with the Georgics of Virgil, whose elegance of style he has chosen to imitate, rather than the dry philosophic manner of Lucretius. Besides elegance, the Doctor has nerves in his style, more, I think, than any writer of this age; and there is in it the closeness and density of Thucydides, without the obscurity. Much more might be said in praise of this poem; but what I quote it for at present, is chiefly to observe the variety of its composition.

Though Virgil be his pattern of style, in the didactic part of the work, he has imitated Lucretius in his exordium, and in the beginnings of his books. He opens his poem, therefore, with an invocation of the goddess *Health*, in a very high strain of poetry, finely varied and ornamented. He begins,

Book IV. Progress of Language. 167

> Daughter of Pæon, queen of every joy,
> Hygeia; whose indulgent smile sustains
> The various race luxuriant nature pours,
> And on the immortal essences bestows
> Immortal youth; auspicious, O descend!
> Thou cheerful guardian of the rolling year.

Then he varies the form of the composition in these two beautiful lines, finely contrasted with one another:

> Whether thou wanton'st on the western gale,
> Or shak'st the rigid pinions of the north.

He goes on in this way for two lines more, and then he changes again:

> When thro' the blue serenity of heaven
> Thy power approaches, all the wasteful host
> Of pain and sickness, squalid and deform'd,
> Confounded, sink into the loathsome gloom,
> Where, in deep Erebus involv'd, the fiends
> Grow more profane.——

Then he has another change of the phrase:

> ——Whatever shapes of death
> Shook from the hideous chambers of the globe,
> Swarm thro' the shuddering air.——

This figure he carries on through several very beautiful lines, in which he enumerates the different causes of diseases, but not without this beautiful variety towards the end:

5

> —— Or if aught
> The comet's glare amid the burning sky,
> Mournful eclipse, or planets ill combin'd,
> Portend difaftrous to the vital world.

The period is very long, confifting of no lefs than twenty lines and a half; but it is only the more beautiful on that account, having the greater variety, and being, at the fame time, fo well compofed, as not to be in the leaft obfcure; and we may obferve in it a very fine imitation of Horace, though at fo great a diftance as hardly to be perceptible. It is where he fpeaks of

> —— The pale tribes halting in the train
> Of vice and headlefs pleafure. ——

where, I believe, the Doctor has had in view the *pœna pede claudo* of Horace.

In the next paragraph he renews his invocation in lines alfo very beautiful, and, at the fame time, propofes his fubject in a ftyle as fimple as that with which Virgil propofes his in the beginning of his Georgics, thus imitating both the pomp of the exordium of the one poet and the plainnefs of that of the other.

His compliment to Dr. Mead is finely turned.

> Nor should I wander doubtful of my way,
> Had I the lights of that sagacious mind,
> Which taught to check the pestilential fire,
> And quell the dreaded Python of the Nile.

Having thus invoked the goddess that presides over health, proposed the subject, and complimented his patron, he enters upon the subject, and begins with warning those who have a regard to their health, to beware of the air of the city, the bad qualities of which he has described in the strongest words that the English language, or, I think, any other affords, put together in numerous verse, and most beautiful and various composition, in which the nervous and austere is very judiciously mixed with the sweet and flowing. This last is particularly remarkable, where he recommends the country air, and the situation of some country places about London. It would be too much to quote the whole; and to quote any part of it divided from the rest, would be doing injustice to the author. I shall, therefore, only further add, that the matter in this passage, and indeed through the whole work, is, as far as I am a judge, as excellent as the style and composition.

Nor is it in the exordium, or firſt book only, that he has ſtudied this variety of compoſition; but, throughout the whole work, he has varied and changed the form of expreſſion more than any author that I know in Engliſh, whether of proſe or of verſe; and yet his changes are ſo natural, and ſo much adapted to the ſubject, that they ſeem to be not at all ſtudied, though any perſon, who has experience in writing, muſt know, that they have coſt him a great deal of pains and ſtudy. I will give but a few inſtances more, out of hundreds that might be quoted. In the ſecond book, ſpeaking of the difference of food, he apoſtrophiſes certain of his readers in this way,

——But ye, of ſofter clay,
Infirm and delicate, and ye who waſte,
With pale and bloated ſloth, the tedious day,
Avoid the ſtubborn aliment, avoid
The full repaſt.——   Book 2, v. 51. & ſeqq.

This is a very lively figure; for it very much animates the ſtyle, and raiſes the attention of the reader. The Doctor, therefore, uſes it much, but not too much, nor ever to ſatiety.

Book IV. Progress of Language.

Again, speaking of the sweet sleep of the labouring man, he says,

—— He not in vain
Invokes the gentle deity of dreams;
His powers the most voluptuously dissolve
In soft repose, &c.   Book 3. v. 382.

Where he appears to have had in view what Virgil says, speaking of a farmer who practises certain things:

—— Neque illum
Flava Ceres alto necquicquam spectat Olympo.
                Geor. lib. 1. v. 96.

And again, speaking still of sleep, he varies his style by a classical idiom, much used by Virgil:

—— Nor does it ought avail
What season you to drowsy Morpheus give,
Of the ever-varying circle of the day.
                    Book 3. v. 425.

Again, speaking of hot weather,

—— Me, near the cool cascade
Reclin'd, or saunt'ring in the lofty grove,
No needless flight occasion should engage
To pant and sweat beneath the fiery noon.
                    Ib. v. 370.

Here the Doctor appears likewise to have

N 2

had Virgil in view, in the paſſage above quoted, where he ſays,

> Non illa quiſquam me noċte per altum
> Ire, nec a terrà moment convellere ſuhem.

In theſe, and many more paſſages, the Doctor has imitated Virgil; and I do not heſitate to ſay, that, in ſome of them, he has even exceeded his original, particularly, in one where he deſcribes the celeſtial bodies in this manner:

> —— Ye eternal fires,
> That lead through heaven the wand'ring year;

Which, I think, is better than Virgil's

> ——Vos, O clariſſima mundi
> Lumina, labentem cœlo qui ducitis annum:

Becauſe *wandering* is a more ſignificant epithet, denoting, in poetical language, the obliquity of the ecliptic, than *labentem*, which expreſſes no more than the gliding motion of the year.

The Doctor, among other varieties, has that of digreſſions, ſome of them extremely beautiful: One particularly pleaſes me. It is that in which he describes the simplicity of the first ages of the world, contrasted with our modern refinements. The passage is so fine, that, though it be long, I cannot help transcribing it. It is in the second book, where he recommends the drinking of water:

> No warmer cups the rural ages knew,
> None warmer sought the fires of human kind;
> Happy in temperate peace, their equal days
> Felt not th' alternate fits of fev'rish mirth,
> And sick dejection; still serene and pleas'd,
> They knew no pains, but what the tender soul
> With pleasure yields to, and would ne'er forget:
> Blest with divine immunity from ails,
> Long centuries they liv'd; their only fate
> Was ripe old age, and rather sleep than death.
> Oh! could those worthies, from the world of Gods,
> Return to visit their degen'rate sons,
> How would they scorn the joys of modern times,
> With all our art and toil improv'd to pain?
> Too happy they! But wealth brought luxury,
> And luxury on floth begot disease!

There is another which pleases me still more. It is in the same second book, where he recommends a right use of wealth. The passage is too long to be all transcribed, and I shall only give the reader those lines of it in which he describes the various miseries of life that may be relieved by money, properly applied:

> ——Form'd of such clay as yours,
> The sick, the needy, shiver at your gate;
> Even modest want may bless your hand unseen,
> Tho' hush'd in patient wretchedness at home.
> Is there no virgin, grac'd with ev'ry charm,
> But that which binds the mercenary vow?
> No youth of genius, whose neglected bloom,
> Unfoster'd, sickens in the barren shade?
> No worthy man, by Fortune's random blows,
> Or by a heart too gen'rous and humane,
> Constrain'd to leave his happy natal seat,
> And sigh for wants more bitter than his own?
> There are, while human miseries abound,
> A thousand ways to waste superfluous wealth,
> Without one fool or flatt'rer at your board,
> Without one hour of sickness or disgust.

The passage is, in every respect, exceedingly beautiful; but what I chiefly quote it for is, to shew that the author, among other talents of a great writer, possesses the tender and pathetic.

Besides the various turns and figures which the Doctor gives to his thoughts, there is a variety in his versification which I much admire. And I praise his style for another thing, which, though it be but a negative commendation, may be reckoned a great praise in this age. What I mean is, that there is nothing in it like point, or affectation of wit. In thefe two refpects his compofition is very different from that of Mr. Pope. For, though Mr. Pope's verfification be very fweet and flowing, and I think, upon the whole, the beft rhyming verfification in Englifh, there is in it an uniformity which is not pleafing to my ear; and in his ftyle there is too much of the witty figure called *Antithefis*; and he gives a quaint turn to the thought and expreffion, which is far removed from the noble fimplicity of antient compofition. Thefe peculiarities in his ftyle and verfification are fo well marked, that it is not difficult *to take them off*; and, accordingly, he has been exceedingly well imitated in both by the author of verfes upon tobacco, which were publifhed in a Magazine about forty years ago, and which, I have been told, affected Mr. Pope more fenfibly than any thing that ever was written againft him; and, I think, with good reafon, as they fhewed the two greateft defects in his poetry. Now, let any man try to imitate, in that manner, Dr. Armstrong's style and versification, and he will find, that the Doctor deserves the praise which I have bestowed upon Demosthenes, of not having a style and manner liable to be parodied, or caricatured.

I should go much too far from my present purpose, if I were to praise all the beauties of this admirable poem. But, I hope, I have quoted enough to shew that it particularly excells in that beauty of style of which I am now treating, namely, the variety of figures, and turns of expression, concerning which I shall only further observe, that, though poetry admit and require many more of them than prose does *,

---

* In this matter of variety, as in every thing else, there may be an excess: And I recollect a story which Seneca the rhetorician relates of one Oseus, a famous declaimer of his time, who was so great a lover of the figured style, that he insisted every thing should be expressed in that round-about way, and nothing in a plain and simple manner. Another declaimer, who was of a different opinion, meeting him one day, instead of saluting him according to the ordinary way of *ave, Ofee*, accosted him with a figured salutation—*peteram, inquit, dicere—ave, Ofee*; Lib. 5. Controvers. in præfat.

yet, even in prose, and particularly in rhetorical composition, if this variety be not studied, I will venture to affirm, that the performance will not please a judicious critic, nor even a man of good natural taste, who will desiderate something in it, though perhaps he cannot tell what it is: And, however trifling these observations may appear to some, it was chiefly by a particular attention to this part of style that Demosthenes, as we have seen, obtained the reputation of the greatest orator that ever lived.

I have insisted the more upon this ornament of style, because I think the greatest part of our later English authors are very deficient in it. The style of my Lord Bolingbroke is both nervous and elegant, full of matter and argument; but it is not sufficiently varied. At first he appears to have formed his taste upon the style of Seneca; for his letters on exile, which, I believe, was the first thing he wrote, are professedly in imitation of that author. This style, from its nature, cannot have sufficient variety: And it was, perhaps, for this reason that my Lord grew disgusted with Seneca's *fond without lime*, and began to compose in a better taste. But, though he made his sentences longer, sometimes, I think, too long, there was not variety enough in the composition; for he still retained a tincture of Seneca's manner, and therefore the members of his long sentences are either altogether unconnected, or inartificially connected, and not aptly inserted into one another, so as to give a roundness and compactness to the whole. And, in general, though my Lord Bolingbroke excells in the choice of words, he is, I think, defective in the art of composition, and, for that reason, is sometimes obscure. Dr. Atterbury, Bishop of Rochester, a contemporary of his, composes much better; his words too are correct and elegant: And, upon the whole, I think him the best composer of sermons in English; but neither has he sufficient variety of turns and figures of composition. To be convinced of this, we need only compare his style with that of my Lord Shaftsbury, who, like his master Plato, is as various in his composition as he is rich and copious in words.—There is great force, as well as propriety, in the words of Dr. Swift's ftyle: But he likewife does not diverfify fufficiently the ftructure of his language; and therefore the ftyle, in which he chiefly excells, as I fhall afterwards obferve, is the fimple ftyle, where very little variety of compofition is required.

And here I finifh what I had to fay upon the ornament of words, whether confidered as fingle, or joined together, and which I call the materials of compofition. There are, I know, who will defpife the labour I have beftowed, in thus minutely diffecting the feveral parts of ftyle. Thefe are critics, who think their genius ftands not in need of the affiftance of learning, and who like the perfons of quality, of whom Moliere fpeaks, *underftand every thing, without having learned any thing*. But men of learning and modefty know, that the greateft things, both in nature and art, arife from fmall beginnings, and that there are elements of every art, and of the critical, among others, without the ftudy of which we can never be able performers, nor even accurate judges. Such men will rather think, that, inftead of being too minute and particular, I have not explained many things so much as I might and ought to have done. But, I hope, I have done all that I professed to do in the beginning of this part of my work, which was to direct the attention of the reader to what is most material in style and composition, and to point out to him the authors that could instruct him better than I am able; at the same time, laying down a method, which will take in every thing belonging to the art, ranged in its proper order.

CHAP. X.

An apology for the style of the Author.—The three general characters of style: The simple, the highly ornamented, and the middle between those two.—Nature and use of the simple style.—Lysias, the first who brought this style to perfection.—Menander, and his Translator, Terence, are perfect models of it.—Among the moderns, Dean Swift, in his Gulliver's Travels, has excelled in it.

THERE is an objection which will naturally occur to every reader, that, if the study of the minute things belonging to composition be so useful as I would make it, and so conducive to the forming a style of elegance and ornament, how comes it that my own style is so plain and unadorned, without that variety of composition which I admire and praise so much in other authors?

To this I answer, that, as I said in the beginning of this volume, genius, as well as knowledge of the rules, is necessary for excelling in every art. Though, therefore, I may be defective in genius (for pains and labour should not be wanting in any thing that a man presents to the public,) it ought not to discredit my rules, which may be very useful to others, though I cannot give an example of them myself. For I may, as Horace says, serve the purpose of a whetstone, and sharpen the wits of other men, *exsors ipse secandi*. 2dly, I say, that, in a work like this, not of the rhetorical or poetical kind, which is not intended to move or excite passion, or even to persuade without instructing, a style much figured or ornamented would be improper. Order and method in the matter, and plainness and perspicuity in the diction, are the chief beauties of such a work. Variety, however, in the style, to a certain degree, it will admit; and this I have so far studied, as to endeavour to avoid a tiresome sameness in the composition. I hope likewise, that I have so far profited by studying those chaste and correct models of antiquity, upon which

I have formed my taste, as to have avoided a fault in writing, which, at the same time that it gives much trouble to the author, is perhaps, of all others, the most offensive to a judicious reader; I mean labouring much to write ill. For it often happens, that writing in bad taste costs much more trouble than writing well. This odious affectation, I trust, I have avoided, by not aiming at too much ornament. At the same time, I am far from denying, that there might have been more of variety and ornament, even in such a didactic work as this, and without any impropriety. For there is another advantage, at least I reckon it so, of proposing to yourself the best patterns of imitation, that you cannot be over fond of your own productions: Whereas, if your standard of perfection be an inferior one, you may, with genius and application, get beyond it, and so imagine that you have attained to a height of perfection, that no man before you ever reached. But, if the great antient models are your standard, your vanity will be constantly mortified, by observing how much you fall short of them; and you will discover that, what the modeſt Virgil ſaid of his imitations of Homer, is true of the imitation of all the great authors of antiquity, 'That it is more eaſy to 'take the club from Hercules, than a line 'from Homer.' If, therefore, the reader would ſee a ſtyle of criticiſm more ornamented, I muſt refer him to the Halicarnaſſian's critical works, where he will find as much variety and ornament as, I think, are compatible with that accurate ſcience, which, at the ſame time, is to be found in thoſe works. Cicero's books upon the rhetorical art may alſo be recommended for the ornaments of ſtyle; and indeed, in my judgment, they are ornamented in a better taſte than his orations. But, as he was more an orator than a philoſopher, or man of ſcience of any kind, and had never practiſed teaching, as the Halicarnaſſian did, we cannot expect in him the ſame accuracy of ſcience; though neither is that wanting. But he was no more than a ſcholar of the Greek maſters; and, I am ſorry to ſay it, not a grateful one [*]. But, to return to our ſubject.

---

[*] I am really provoked at the contempt with which Cicero ſometimes ſpeaks of the Greeks, from whom, as he confeſſes himſelf, he learned all his philoſophy; to which,

In the preceeding chapters, I have treated of the various forms and figures that words assume, whether single or in composition. These may be said to be the mate-

as he says, he owed his reputation in oratory; for he boasts, that he proceeded an orator, not out of the shops of rhetoricians, but from the walks of the academy, ' Se non ex ' rhetorum officinis, sed ex academiæ spatiis, oratorem ' extitisse;' *Orator. ad M. Brut.* c. 12. And in the rhetorical art itself, it is a well known fact, that he owed his chief improvement to Molo, a Greek rhetorician, under whom he practised, both at Rome, where he had an opportunity of hearing him twice, and also at Rhodes, to which place it appears he went on purpose, in order to be instructed by Molo, who was of that island. By his lessons he was corrected of a bad manner, which he had acquired in the Latin schools of declamation, and returned from his travels to Rome, changed, as it were, into a new man, as he tells us himself in his book *De clar. Orator.* which he has inscribed to Brutus. But, notwithstanding all these obligations he had to the Greeks, he calls them by the diminutive name of *Græculi*; speaks of them as an idle prating people, *otiosi et loquaces*; Lib. i. de Oratore, c. 22. He says, that, though they are *inepti* more than any other people, yet they have not a name for the thing; for he even prefers the Latin language to the Greek, as more rich and copious; Lib. i. de Fin. c. 3. And the genius of his countrymen, he says, excelled that of all other nations; Lib. i. de Oratore, c. 4. *in fine*. And, in another place, he says, that they had either invented every thing better than the Greeks, or improved what they had received from the Greeks; Tusc. Quæst. Lib. i.

VOL. III. O

rials of which style is made; and, according as these materials are used, style takes different *colours*, as I call them, by which it is denominated such or such a kind of style; simple, for example, or ornamented—historical, rhetorical, or didactic; and it is of these colours of style that I am now to treat.

What we call *style*, being, as I have said, something different from plain grammatical speech, and more or less ornamented, the first and most natural division of it is taken from the greater or less degree of ornament bestowed upon it. And, as every thing in which quantity is considered is least, or greatest, or middle and betwixt the two, so it is with style; that which is least ornamented we call the *Simple style*;

n. 1. But Cicero was very vain; and the vanity of the individual, as I have elsewhere observed, naturally goes to the nation; for every thing belonging to a vain man must needs be excellent of the kind. And, what is worst of all, vanity very often acquits itself of every obligation of gratitude, receiving all good offices, not as *favours*, but as *debts* paid to extraordinary merit.

that which is moſt, we call the *High ſtyle*; and that which is betwixt the two, is the *Middle ſtyle*; and theſe make the three general colours, or characters, as they are commonly called, of ſtyle *.

The firſt kind is ſo little ornamented, that it appears not to be ornamented at all, and to be no better than common ſpeech; for it has no *ambitious* ornaments, as they may be called, nothing prominent, or, as it were, ſticking out; and what Petronius Arbiter ſays of a good ſtyle, will, in a particular manner, apply to this, when it is brought to perfection—' naturali pulchritudine exſur-' git †.' This is ſo true, that a man, not learned in the critical art, or who has not formed a taſte by much reading and obſervation, will be apt to think, that all is nature in this ſtyle, and no art at all. But, when he comes to try to imitate

---

* This is the way that the Halicarnaſſian has proceeded in conſidering ſtyle—διαιρῶντος τὴν λέξιν εἰς τρεῖς χαρακτῆρας τῆς γινομένης, τόν τε ἰσχνὰ, καὶ τὸν ὑψηλὸν, καὶ τὸν μεταξὺ τούτων—περὶ τῆς διαιρέσεως τῶν Δημοσθενος; cap. 33.

† *Satyric. in initio.*

it, he will find that what Horace says is true,

>———— Sudat multum, fruſtraque laborat
> Auſus idem. ————

The Halicarnaſſian tells us *, that all the hiſtorians of Greece, before Herodotus who firſt ornamented hiſtory, wrote in this ſtyle †; all the antient philoſophers too of Greece, who wrote upon ſubjects of natural philoſophy; and the whole Socratic ſchool, Plato only excepted, who firſt ornamented philoſophy, as Herodotus had done hiſtory; the antient orators too, as the Halicarnaſſian ſays, ſpoke and wrote in this character of ſtyle ‡; and the ſame, no doubt, was the

---

* Περι της διυνατος τα Δημοσθενις, cap. 7. et de Thucyd. cap. 23.

† Such were Hecatæus, Hellanicus, and others, who wrote what the Halicarnaſſian calls *Genealogical and Topical Hiſtories*. Joſephus, in his firſt book againſt Apion, c. 22. has preſerved to us ſome paſſages from Hecataeus, by which the learned reader will judge of the ſimplicity of his ſtyle. And there is a fragment of Hellanicus preſerved, but I cannot recollect in what author, which is ſtill more ſimple.

‡ See Cicero, de clar. Orator. c. 7. where he gives us a hiſtory of the progreſs of eloquence in Greece.

style of the first orators of Rome, after speaking became an art in that city, which, as Cicero informs us, did not happen till about the time of Ennius the poet, who praises one M. Cornelius Cethegus as a good speaker*. In the more antient times, both of Greece and Rome,

> Cum neque mufarum fcopulos quifquam fuperârat,
> Nec dicti ftudiofus erat——

as old Ennius says, there was no doubt a great deal of speaking, as it was in that way that all public affairs were conducted in both nations; but it was only in later times that it became an art; fo that, till then, the orators could not properly be said to speak in any *style*, but only to deliver their sentiments in a rude artless manner.

This simple style was brought to perfection, as the Halicarnaffian says †, by Lyfias the Athenian orator; and, indeed, what remains of him well juftifies the praise which this critic has bestowed upon him. In the narrative particularly he is admi-

* Cicero, de clar. Orator. c. 15.   † *Ubi fupra.*

rable; and it is to that part of an oration that this style is most suitable. For if a narrative is much ornamented, it has not the appearance of truth, but of a tale, designed either to impose upon the hearer, or to make an ostentatious shew of the author's genius. Hence it comes, that the narrative of Homer is more credible than that of Virgil, not only because it is more circumstantial, which also gives a great air of truth to a story, but because it is less ornamented.

Demosthenes, as he had all the great talents of an orator, so he possessed this faculty, among others, of writing most simply, and without the least appearance of art, though he was master of every art belonging to the profession. Indeed, I was never thoroughly convinced of his being so perfect in the art, till I came to read the narratives of some of his orations in private causes, particularly one quoted by the Halicarnassian, from his oration against Conon, which is so much in the style of Lysias, that, as this critic says, if it were not for the title and inscription, it would be impossible to say, whether it belonged to Lysias or Demosthenes; for the words, as well as the composition, are all plain and simple, without trope or figure, or adscititious ornament of any kind. And it is full of the τὸ ἠθικον, or *ethic*, which is the chief ornament of this kind of style, and is more persuasive, at least among the people, both in narrative and argument, than any thing else belonging to style, because it touches the heart more*.

Among the most perfect models of this kind of style were the authors of the new comedy in Athens, particularly Menander. His comedies are now unfortunately lost; but in Terence we have excellent imitations of them, or rather translations; for the Romans, when they first began to write, stuck so close to the Greek originals, that they translated them. And Donatus, the commentator upon Terence, tells us, that Terence would have valued himself less upon

---

* Dionys. the Halicarnassian περὶ τῆς Δημοθους ἰσοτητος c. 12. and 13.

writing a comedy of his own, than upon tranflating from the Greek. The ftyle of Terence is, in good Latinity, called *purus fermo*. Thus Julius Cæfar, in his verfes upon Terence*, calls him *puri fermonis amator*; and Terence himfelf, in the prologue to the *Heautontimorumenos*, calls the ftyle of that comedy *pura oratio*. It is called, I think, with propriety enough, *pure*, as not being difcoloured, or, as it were, *troubled* with tropes and figures, but altogether fimple and of one colour. For though, in every good ftyle, there fhould be one colour predominant, there is in other ftyles a mixture to a certain degree. For example, though the general colour of the ftyle of Homer be the high heroic, yet, in many paffages, where the fubject requires it, the ftyle is perfectly fimple, as fimple as that of Terence's comedies. And it is a fault in Virgil's Eneid, that there is little or no variety of ftyle, all of it having more or lefs of the heroic fwell. In fuch works, a poet muft know how to vary properly the colour of his ftyle:

* See Suetonius's Life of Terence.

Book IV. PROGRESS OF LANGUAGE. 193

> Defcriptas fervare vices, operumque colores
> Cur ego, fi nequeo ignoroque, poëta falutor?

Whereas, in the comedy of Terence, the ſtyle is all of the ſame colour, that is, perfectly ſimple, without any tumor or ſwell; or, if there be any thing of that kind upon any particular occaſion, it is noted as ſomething extraordinary. As when Chremes, in the *Heautontimorumenos*, being extremely provoked againſt his ſon for his diſorderly life, accoſts him in this way:

> ——Non fi ex capite fis meo
> Natus, item ut aiunt Minervam eſſe ex Jove, ea cauſa magis,
> Patiar, Clitipho, flagitiis tuis me infamem fieri;
>
> Act. v. fc. 4.

Which makes Horace ſay,

> Interdum tamen et vocem comœdia tollit,
> Iratuſque Chremes tumido delitigat ore *.

---

* The diction of Terence was, I believe, as *pure* as that of Menander; and, indeed, it appears to me, that there can be nothing purer. But his fable, and the texture to his pieces, was not near ſo pure. For he tells us, in more than one place, *Prol. Andr. et Prol. Heautontim.* that his adverſaries accuſed him of *contaminating* his fables, that is, of joining two Greek fables together, and in that way, as they ſaid, making one bad Latin piece out of two Greek ones. And Donatus has obſerved, in his Com. on the

To distinguish this style from the low and the vulgar, is a matter of pretty nice judgment; for that is the extreme which it borders upon; and we see from Terence's prologue to the Phormio, that his pieces were said, by his adversaries, to be written

Andrian, that, besides one young man, Pamphilus, and his slave *Davus*, there is another young man, viz. *Charinus*, introduced, and another slave, *Byrrhia*, who are not to be found in the Andrian of Menander; *in Andr. act. 2. sc. 1.* And, in general, we may observe, that, in all Terence's comedies, there is something of a double plot; for there are commonly two young men, two fathers, two mistresses, and two cunning slaves. Terence, in those prologues I have quoted, does not deny the charge, and only justifies himself by the example of the comic poets before him, such as Plautus and Cæcilius. And the truth appears to have been, that so perfect a simplicity as that of Menander's pieces, would not have pleased the taste of the Romans of that time, which was little better than barbarous; for the taste of all barbarous nations delights much more in variety than in simplicity and uniformity. Thus we see what a variety there is in the Gothic architecture; not a gate, not a window, hardly a capital of a pillar, ornamented like another; and it was the same in the writing art. Before Shakespeare's time, there was a tragedy called *Cambyses*, which bore in its title to be *a most lamentable tragedy, full of excellent mirth*; and in Shakespeare's own tragedies, there is not wanting mirth sufficient, but not always *excellent*, whether it were his own taste, or only compliance with the barbarous taste of his time.

tenui oratione et scriptura levi, that is, in a style too simple, and too little raised. But not only the learned critic, but even a man of good natural taste, will perceive the difference. And, however easy it may seem to imitate such a style, any one who tries it will find, that it is true what Horace says,

——— Sudet multum, frustraque laboret
Aufus idem.———

And, indeed, take the style of Terence altogether, the expression of characters and manners in it, as well as the elegance and wonderful simplicity, I do not know but it is more difficult to imitate than even the style of Homer.

The author, in English, that has excelled the most in this style is Dr. Swift, in his *Gulliver's Travels;* of which the narrative is wonderfully plain and simple, minute likewise, and circumstantial, so much, as to be disgusting to a reader without taste or judgment, and the character of an English sailor is finely kept up in it. In short, it has every virtue belonging to this style; and I will venture to say, that those monstrous lies so narrated, have more the air of probability than many a true story unskilfully told. And, accordingly, I have been informed, that they imposed upon many when they were first published. The voyage to Lilliput, in my judgment, is the finest of them all, especially in what relates to the politics of that kingdom, and the state of parties there. The debate in the King's council, concerning Gulliver, is a master-piece; and the original papers it contains, of which he says he was so lucky as to get copies, give it an air of probability that is really wonderful. When we add to all this, the hidden satire which it contains, and the grave ridicule that runs through the whole of it, the most exquisite of all ridicule, I think I do not go too far when I pronounce it the most perfect work of the kind, antient or modern, that is to be found. For, as to Lucian's true history, which is the only antient work of the kind that has come down to us, it has nothing to recommend it, except the imitation of the grave style of the antient historians, such as Herodotus; but it wants the satire and exquisite ridicule that is to be found in the Dean's work.

This plain style is not, as I have observed elsewhere, much used in our prose compositions, and is altogether out of fashion in our verse. But it was not so in the days of Milton, as I have already shewn, by examples from him, and shall shew, by examples from others of our antient poets, when I come to speak of the style of poetry.

CHAP. XL.

Of the ornamented style—This divided into two kinds, the austere and the florid.— Of the first kind is the style of Thucydides. —Character of that style.—Of the style of Sallust.

THE opposite style to the simple is that which is highly ornamented, and I divide it into two kinds; for the ornaments are either of the grave and severe kind, or of the gay and florid. Of the first sort is the style of Thucydides, the most extraordinary, perhaps, that is to be found; and, as the Halicarnassian says, the first and last of the kind; for at the time the Halicarnassian wrote, no other historian had attempted to imitate him, nor any orator, except in part[*]. And, since the days of the Halicarnassian,

[*] De Thucydide judicium, c. 52. et 53.

few, I believe, have underftood him, but none fet him up as a model of imitation. The fingularity of his ftyle is not fo much in the choice of words, which, however, were many of them obfolete and unufual, even at the time he wrote, as in the compofition, which is fo varied by every figure of conftruction and arrangement, many more than the grammarians have found names for, that he may be faid to have rung all the changes poffible upon words. His fenfe in the narrative part of his hiftory is, I think, plain enough; but, in his fpeeches, the fentences and arguments are often fo crouded and complicated together, as to be a perfect riddle. His numbers are auftere, and often harfh and uncouth, cheating the ear by abrupt claufules. But, though his ftyle be thus fingular, and more a *made* ftyle, as I may call it, than any that I know in profe, yet it is ftill profe, and not poetry; nor can we deny that it is the ftyle of hiftory, though of an extraordinary kind; for the narrative is altogether hiftorical, without being loaded with epithets, or adorned with poetical defcriptions, which is generally the cafe of our modern hiftories; nor

does it attempt, in any way, to excite the
paffions of the reader, or to inftruct him
by reflections on events or the characters
of men. And as to the fpeeches, all we can
fay of them is, that the rhetoric of them is
of an extraordinary kind, and that we could
have wifhed the fame fenfe to have been delivered in plain words.

Salluft, the Roman hiftorian, is commonly reckoned an imitator of Thucydides; and
no doubt he had read and ftudied him,
for fome of the beft fentences in his book
are taken from him. And his ftyle, fo far
as concerns the choice of words, refembles
that of Thucydides; for he ufes antiquated
words, and common words in an unufual
fenfe. But his compofition is very different; for Thucydides compofes in long periods, very often too long, and fometimes
much involved and implicated, fo as to be
exceedingly obfcure; then his compofition
is all connected, both the periods, and the
feveral members of periods. On the
other hand, Salluft writes in fhort fentences,
abundantly clear and perfpicuous, but unconnected with one another, and the differ-

rent parts of the same sentence likewise without connection; so that his composition is gaping and disjointed, and, in some places, hardly deserves the name of composition. Nor is there any author, that I know, that abounds so much in a figure, well known among the grammarians under the name of *Asyndeton*. He is the first, as far as I know, Greek or Roman, who affected this character of style. We see the authors before him using the figure above-mentioned upon occasions; but a whole history, or any other work, written all in that style, was a thing unknown before his time. For it is not in his speeches only that he uses this figure so much, but in his narrative, his reflections, and characters, with which he abounds; so that there is wanting in Sallust that diversity of composition which we observe in Thucydides, whose style in his narrative is exceedingly different from what it is in his speeches. As to characters and reflections, Thucydides does not deal in them; for that was something new with respect to the matter, which Sallust appears first to have introduced into history. Before his time, this species of writing confined itself to the narrating of facts, leaving the reader to form his own reflections upon them, as well as to judge from them of the characters of men.

This censure of Sallust's style will, I know, be thought by many too severe: It may not, therefore, be improper to support my judgment by examples, which will shew, that, in all the four parts of his work above-mentioned, and which comprehend the whole of it, viz. the narrative, the reflections, characters, and speeches, the same incoherent and disjointed style, the same *sand without lime*, is to be found.

In the introduction to his history of Catiline's conspiracy, speaking of the Romans in the earliest times of the commonwealth, he says, ' Romani, domi militiæque intenti, ' festinare, parare, alius alium hortari, ho- ' stibus obviam ire, libertatem, patriam, ' parentesque armis tegere.' In the same introduction, speaking of his countrymen in later times, he says, ' Igitur ex divitiis ' juventutem luxuriâ atque avaritiâ cum

'superbia invasere; rapere, consumere; sua
' parvi pendere, aliena cupere; pudorem,
' pudicitiam, divina atque humana promis-
' cua, nihil penfi atque moderati habere.'
In the defcription of a battle, which Jugur-
tha fought with Metellůs, he writes thus:
' Numidæ alii poftremos cædere; pars a
' finiftra ac dextera tentare; infenfi adeffe
' atque inftare; omnibus locis Romanorum
' ordines conturbare;' c. 50. de bello Jug.
And again, in his account of the fame action, ' Cæterum facies totius negotii varia,
' incerta, fœda atque miferabilis; difperfi
' a fuis pars cedere, alii infequi; neque fig-
' na, neque ordines obfervare; ubi quem-
' que periculum ceperat, ibi refiftere ac
' propulfare; arma, tela, equi, viri, hoftes,
' cives permixti; nihil confilio, neque im-
' perio agi; fors omnia regere;' c. 51.
Thefe may fuffice for fpecimens of his narrative ftyle. In his reflections, or what may
be called the philofophy of his hiftory, the
ftyle is of the fame kind. ' Avaritia fidem,
' probitatem, cæterafque artis bonas fubver-
' tit; pro his fuperbiam, crudelitatem, deos
' negligere, omnia venalia habere edocuit.
' Ambitio multos mortales falfos fieri fube-

'git; aliud claufum in pectore, aliud in
' lingua promptum habere; amicitias ini-
' micitiafque non ex re, fed ex commodo
' æftumare; magifque vultum, quàm inge-
' nium bonum habere;' Bell. Cat. c. 10.
His characters are as deficient in copula-
tives as either his narrative or his reflections.
For proof of this I need go no farther than
the character of Catiline, in the beginning
of his hiftory of that confpiracy: ' Corpus pa-
' tiens inediæ, vigiliæ, algoris, fupra quam
' cuique credibile eft. Animus audax, fubdo-
' lus, varius, cujus rei libet fimulator ac diffi-
' mulator; alieni appetens, fui profufus;
' ardens in cupiditatibus; fatis loquentiæ,
' fapientiæ parum. Vaftus animus, immo-
' derata, incredibilia, nimis alta femper cu-
' piebat;' c. 5. In his characters of Cæfar and
Cato, he has joined to this fhort and disjointed compofition a ftring of *antitbefes:* ' Cæfar
' beneficiis ac munificentia magnus habeba-
' tur; integritate vitæ Cato. Ille manfue-
' tudine et mifericordia clarus factus; huic
' feveritas dignitatem addiderat. Cæfar
' dando, fublevando, ignofcendo; Cato ni-
' hil largiundo gloriam adeptus; in altero
' miferis perfugium, in altero malis perni-

' cies; illius facilitas, hujus conſtantia lau-
' dabatur;' c. 54.

The rhetorical ſtyle leaſt of all admits of this gaping compoſition, becauſe it demands a flow, and a roundneſs, proper to fill the ears of the people. Yet Salluſt is the ſame in his ſpeeches, or very little different from what he is in the other parts of his work. What orator of Greece or Rome, that had any reputation, ever began an oration to the people in the manner that Salluſt makes Memmius the tribune begin his: 'Multa
' dehortantur a vobis, Quirites, ni ſtudium
' reipublicæ omnia ſuperet; opes factionis,
' veſtra patientia, jus nullum; ac maxume
' quod innocentiæ plus periculi, quam ho-
' noris eſt;' de Bell. Jug. c. 31. If he had not put this ſtyle into the mouth of Memmius, who, he tells us, at that time was a great and powerful orator, I ſhould have thought that what he makes Marius ſay to the people, was an attempt to imitate his rude and incompoſed manner of ſpeaking; for he was intirely unlearned, and a profeſſed deſpiſer of the Greek arts. He makes him ſpeak thus: ' Non ſunt compoſita ver-

'ba mea; parum id facio; ipsa se virtus
'satis oftendit; illis artificio opus eft, uti
'turpia facta oratione tegant: Neque litteras
'Græcas didici; parum placebat eas difcere,
'quippe quæ ad virtutem doctoribus nihil
'profuerunt. At illa multo optuma reipubli-
'cæ doctus sum; hoftem ferire, præfidia
'agitare; nihil metuere, nifi turpem fa-
'mam; hyemem et æftatem juxta pati; hu-
'mi requiefcere; eodem tempore inopiam et
'laborem tolerare;' c. 85. But it is evident that the ftyle of this fpeech, no lefs than of every other fpeech in the book, is intirely his own.

Not only in the fpeeches, but in every part of an hiftorical work, fuch a bounding hopping compofition is unfuitable: *Firſt*, becaufe it has no fweetnefs or flow; and, *fecondly*, becaufe it has no gravity or dignity, fuch as the hiftorical ftyle requires; Nor do I know any kind of writing that it is fit for, except the epiftolary, which ought to have the air of being unpremeditated, without ftudy of compofition or ornament of any kind. Salluft has preferved to us an original letter of Lentulus, one of Catiline's affociates, written in that manner.

It was addressed to Catiline, and is in these words: 'Quis sim, ex eo quem ad te misi cognosces; fac cogites in quanta calamitate sis, et memineris te virum; consideres quid tuæ rationes postulent: Auxilium petas ab omnibus, etiam ab infimis;' de Bell. Cat. 43. This is a very proper style for a letter; but, I think, very improper for a history; nor is it justifiable by any good authority. For, except Sallust and Tacitus, no antient historian has used it; nor orator or poet, except upon particular occasions. But, though I be thus severe upon the style of Sallust, it must not be imagined that I think meanly of him as an historian; for I esteem his matter as much as I blame his style. His narrative, though, I think, ill composed, is clear and distinct; his reflections are sensible and judicious, particularly those upon the state of the Roman commonwealth, and the manners of that people. For, as to his philosophy, I think it is no better than common place; and, though it had been better, I think it might have been spared. His speeches are, in my judgment, by far the best part of the work; and there are more splendid sentences to be picked from them than from those of any historian or orator that I know. Julius Cæsar's speech in the senate, upon the subject of the punishment to be inflicted on the conspirators, is a master-piece; nor do I know any thing of the kind, antient or modern, in which there are arguments more plausible, or sentences of greater weight and gravity. And, though the composition be clearly his own, and not that of Cæsar, I am persuaded the matter is from Cæsar. Thus much, at least, we are sure of, from Cicero's speech on the same occasion, that what he makes Julius say of a future state, was actually said by him.

This opinion of Sallust, and the difference I make betwixt his speeches and the rest of his history, appears to have been the judgment of the critics of his own time, at least, of the next age; for so I understand a passage in Seneca the rhetorician's declamations, Lib. 3. in præfatione, where, speaking of the different talents of men, he says, ' Virgil's happy genius forsook him in prose,

'Cicero's eloquence deserted him in verse;' then he adds, 'Orationes Sallustii in hono-'rem historiarum leguntur:' The sense of which words I take to be, that it was chiefly his orations which did honour to his history.

CHAP. XII.

Of the style of Tacitus—That style considered by many as a model—Not an original style, but an imitation of Sallust.—General observations upon it—Particular examples—Of his unconnected composition—Of abrupt and harsh—Of obscure brevity—Of affectation in the expression, and obscurity thence arising—Compared in this respect with Julius Cæsar.—Poetical diction of Tacitus—Poetical description—Quaintness and affectation of smartness.—Praise of Tacitus as to his matter—Some things also in his style commendable.—Effect that the imitation of him has had upon the style of modern writers.—The best imitation of him is in Mr. Mallet's Life of Chancellor Bacon.

THE next author I shall mention, remarkable for the kind of style of which I am now speaking, is Tacitus, an author of so high reputation at present, that

I have thought proper to bestow an intire chapter upon him. No body ever thought of setting him up for a model of style, till Justus Lipsius brought him into fashion, and, by imitating him, wrote a style very different from that of the other scholars of the age, and different even from what he himself wrote in his younger days. From that time Tacitus has been the model of the French writers, as many of them as had learning enough to understand him, and of a great many British, who have imitated him either directly from the original, or at second-hand from the French. What I shall say, therefore, of his style will not, I know, please the many; but for them, as I have more than once said, I do not write.

Tacitus himself was no original, though the contrary is generally believed; for he plainly imitates the author last mentioned, Sallust. This is evident, not only from particular obsolete words and phrases, which he has borrowed from Sallust, as has been observed by the commentators, but from the general colour and complexion of his style *. And, indeed, there was at that time no other historian, either Greek or Latin, who had written in that style; for, as I observed before, the composition of Thucydides, though affecting the same character of style, is very different from that of Sallust, or his imitator Tacitus.

Besides this imitation of Sallust, there is in Tacitus a great tincture of the style of the schools of declamation, the fashionable

---

* I will give two or three examples of this.—Every body who has studied Sallust knows, that the style in which he describes characters is remarkable: Here is one from Tacitus, which is plainly an imitation of that manner. It is the character of Sejanus: 'Corpus illi laborum tolerans; animus audax, sui obtegens, in alios criminator; juxta adulatio et superbia; palam compositus pudor; intus summa apiscendi libido;' Ann. Lib. iv. c. 1. The character of Galba is given in the same manner by antithesis: 'Pecuniæ alienæ non appetens, suæ parcus, publicæ avarus;' Hist. Lib. i. c. 49. His descriptions too are often in the style of Sallust, that is, in single unconnected words, as in the description of the rout of an army: 'Non arma, non ordo, non consilium; sed pecorum modo, trahi, occidi, capi;' Ann. Lib. i. c. 25. In the same manner Sallust describes the same thing: 'Sequi, fugere, occidi, capi, equi, viri, adflicti;' B. Jug. c. 101.

style, as I shall afterwards observe, of that age; and it is from thence chiefly that the differences to be observed betwixt his style and that of Sallust, in whose time the declamatory style was not so much in fashion, arise.

There is one fault in the style of Tacitus which is obvious, and will strike every man of sense, though he have not studied the rules of writing. It is this, that he draws our attention too much to his style. This is so true, that I will venture to affirm, that a man who had only studied the great antient masters of composition, such as Demosthenes, Cicero, Julius Cæsar, or any other who has written in a plain natural manner, would at first, when he came to the reading of Tacitus, be employed almost intirely about the words, wondering at the strangeness of the composition, so different from what he had been accustomed to, or, perhaps, admiring and falling in love with it, as Lipsius did.

Now, the greatest praise, in my opinion, that can be bestowed upon any style is, that we are carried away by the sense and argument, without attending to the words. This is the peculiar praise of Demosthenes, whose words are all of common use, and seem only put together in such a way as to convey the meaning clearly and distinctly. Nor, unless we know something of the critical art, do we perceive any art at all in a composition, the most artificial which is to be found in prose. The beauties, therefore, of Demosthenes's style are, of all others, the most genuine, being such as are not *prominent*, and do not stick out, as it were, from the body of the work—' Quæ non ' extra corpus orationis eminent,' to use the expression of a very elegant writer*, but are so incorporated with it, that, though the effects of them be felt by every one, the art is only perceived by the critic—' Grandis, ' et, ut ita dicam, pudica oratio non est ' maculosa, nec turgida, sed naturali pul- ' chritudine exsurgit †.' Now, this natural beauty of style is certainly not predominant in Tacitus; but, on the contrary, it is evident, that he studies, like Mr. Bayes in the

---

* Petron. Arbit. Satyric.　　† Id. Ibid.

Rehearsal, to *elevate and surprise* by a kind of composition, which is any thing but plain and natural. And, if the art of Tacitus's style were good, which, I think, it is not, it is too conspicuous; so that he wants the greatest art of all in speaking and writing, which is to conceal art.

Another general observation I would make upon Tacitus's style is, that though the chief thing to be studied in composition is not the pleasure of the ear, nor what is called a flow of words, yet that is not to be neglected; and much less ought a writer to affect to distinguish himself by a composition abrupt and gaping, and altogether harsh and offensive to the ear; and yet this is the most distinguishing characteristic of Tacitus's style, and in this he has far surpassed his original, it being generally the fate of imitators, that, if there be any fault in the model, they aggravate and make it worse.

I will now proceed to give examples of the peculiarities of Tacitus's style, as I did of those of Sallust, beginning with his un-

connected composition, so unconnected, abrupt, and broken, that it hardly deserves the name of *composition*. My first example shall be the very beginning of his work, I mean his introduction to his *Annals*, where one should have expected some kind of flow and smoothness of composition, such as we find in other authors, even in those who, in other parts of their work, study composition very little*. He begins thus: ' Urbem Romam a principio reges
' habuêre. Libertatem et consulatum L.
' Brutus instituit. Dictaturæ ad tempus
' sumebantur; neque Decemviralis potestas
' ultra biennium, neque tribunorum militum consulare jus diu valuit. Non Cinnæ, non Sullæ longa dominatio; et Pompeii Crassique potentia cito in Cæsarem;
' Lepidi atque Antonii arma, in Augustum

---

* Aristotle, in his abstruse philosophical works, which he intended only for the use of his scholars, has nothing that can be called *composition*, though it deserves that name as well as a great part of Tacitus's history. But, in his popular works, and particularly in the exordiums of them, there is very good composition, as in the beginning of his book of poetry.

Book IV. Progress of Language. 217

cessere.' In what he calls his history,
where it is commonly thought, but, in
my judgment, without reason, that the
composition is more copious and flowing,
he enters upon his subject in this manner:
' Opus aggredior opimum casibus, atrox
' præliis, discors seditionibus, ipsa etiam
' pace sævum. Quatuor principes ferro in-
' terempti. Tria bella civilia, plura exter-
' na, ac plerumque permixta. Prosperæ in
' oriente, adversæ in occidente res. Tur-
' batum Illyricum; Galliæ nutantes; per-
' domita Britannia, et statim missa; coortæ
' in nos Sarmatarum ac Suevorum gentes,
' nobilitatus cladibus mutuis Dacus. Mota
' etiam prope Parthorum arma falsi Nero-
' nis ludibrio. Jam vero Italia novis cladi-
' bus, vel post longam sæculorum seriem
' repetitis, afflicta. Haustæ aut obrutæ ur-
' bes fœcundissima Campaniæ ora. Et urbs
' incendiis vastata, consumptis antiquissimis
' delubris, ipso capitolio civium manibus
' incenso. Pollutæ cærimoniæ; magna
' adulteria; plenum exiliis mare; infecti
' cædibus scopuli; atrocius in urbe sævitum.'
A little after speaking of prodigies that happened about that time,—' Cœlo terraque

' prodigia, et fulminum monitus, et futu-
' rorum præsagia, læta, triftia, ambigua,
' manifefta.' Upon this paffage, I cannot
help fetting down the remark of his tranflator and great admirer, Mr. Gordon. ' In
' this,' fays he, ' there is an infinite pathos.
' What can be more folemn, founding, and
' fublime, even in Lucretius?'

Let any man compare thefe exordiums of Tacitus with the exordium of Livy, or even of Thucydides, whofe ftyle Tacitus is thought by fome to have imitated, and the difference will appear ftriking; and let him compare them, at the fame time, with the exordiums of Salluft, and he will perceive a great refemblance, and that it is Salluft whom he has imitated in this disjointed ftyle, and not Thucydides.

The narrative of hiftory fhould certainly be put together with fome kind of art; and there fhould be a certain dignity in the compofition, as well as the words. But Tacitus narrates in this manner in his hiftory, for from thence I chufe to take my examples, for the reafon above given: ' In-

' terim civilis vetera circumſedit. Vocula
' Geldubam, atque inde Noveſium conceſſit.
' Civilis capit Geldubam. Mox haud pro-
' cul Noveſio, equeſtri prælio proſperè
' certabit *.' Again—' Nec Sequani detrec-
' tavère certamen. Fortuna melioribus af-
' fuit. Fuſi Lingones, Sabinus feſtinatum
' temerè prælium, pari formidine deſe-
' ruit †,' &c. To quote more would be to
tranſcribe a great part of the work.

Such ſhort ſentences, or rather mutilated
ſentences, *amputatæ ſententiæ*, as Seneca
calls them ‡, can be ſaid with propriety to be
only the materials of compoſition: And, had
there been nothing preſerved of Tacitus but
a few fragments of this kind, and if I had
not known his taſte of ſtyle, and manner of
writing, I ſhould have thought that theſe
were only heads, or memorandums of what
he was afterwards to put together in regular compoſition.

* Hiſtor. Lib. iv. c. 36.

† Ibid. c. 67.

‡ Senec. Philoſ. Epiſt. 114.

In the speeches there is something more of composition; but these likewise are, for the greater part, cut into short sentences, commonly in the form of interrogation, after the manner of the schools of declamation. Thus the Pannonian legions, when they mutinied, were addressed by their officers: 'Quousque filium imperatoris obside-
'bimus? Quis certaminum finis? Percen-
'nione et Vibuleno sacramentum dicturi
'sumus? Percennius et Vibulenus stipendia
'militibus, agros emeritis largientur? De-
'nique, pro Neronibus et Drusis imperium
'populi Romani capessent? Quin potius ut
'novissimi in culpam, ita primi ad pœni-
'tentiam sumus? Tarda sunt quæ in com-
'mune expostulantur: Privatam gratiam
'statim mereare, statim recipias *.'

In some of the passages I have quoted, the sentences are not only short, but abrupt, and ending harshly and unexpectedly; so that we may apply to him what Seneca the rhetorician says of the style of Fabianus, a declaimer of his time: 'Quædam tam su-

---

* Annal. Lib. i. c. 28.

Book IV. PROGRESS OF LANGUAGE. 221

'bito definunt, ut non brevia fint fed abrup-
'ta *.' And what Seneca the philofopher
fays, fpeaking of the compofition of certain
writers of his time,—' Quidam præfractam
' et afperam probant, difturbant de induftria,
' fi quid placidius effluxit. Nolunt fine
' falebra effe juncturam ; virilem putant et
' fortem quæ aurem inæqualitate percu-
' tiat †.' Of this I will only give two more
inftances, out of innumerable that might
be given: For it is evident that he affected
thofe harfh claufules, having a pleafure, as
it would feem, to furprife the reader, by dif-
appointing his expectation, and cheating his
ear. In giving the character of one Vi-
nius, he fays, that he was—' Audax, calli-
' dus, promptus, et prout animum intendiffet
' pravus aut induftrius eâdem vi ‡.' Again,
in giving an account of what Antonius the
general of Vitellius faid to his troops, when
they were in poffeffion of Verona, which
they had a mind to fack and pillage, and

* Lib. ii. Controverf. in initio.

† Epiftol. 114.

‡ Hiftor. Lib. i. c. 48.

Q 3

accordingly afterwards did so, he says, 'Vocatos ad concionem Antonius alloquitur magnificè victores, victos clementer, de Cremona in neutrum*.' Where, in order to make the last member of the sentence as short and abrupt as possible, he has made it obscure; for you must be well acquainted with Tacitus's idioms, to know that, by the expression *de Cremona neutrum*, he means that Antonius said nothing at all of Cremona, neither in the way of praise or censure, intending, as the event shewed, to leave the soldiers to follow their own inclination with respect to that town.

And this leads me to observe another fault in Tacitus's style, namely, an *obscure brevity*. This, with the other peculiarities above-mentioned, is imputed to Sallust by Seneca the philosopher, in the epistle above quoted, in these words: 'Sallustio vigente amputatæ sententiæ, et verba ante expectatam cadentiam, et obscura brevitas fuere pro cultu.' And, as imitators commonly aggravate the faults of their

* Histor. Lib. iii. c. 32.

original, so, compared with Tacitus, Sallust may be said to be a clear and perspicuous writer. For Tacitus has so many short and elliptical expressions, that he may be said to write a kind of short-hand style. Thus, speaking of the dissimulation and feigned behaviour of the Roman nobility, upon the decease of Augustus, and the accession of Tiberius, he says,—' Quanto quis illustrior,
' tanto magis falsi ac festinantes, vultuque
' composito, ne læti excessu Principis; neu
' tristior primordio, lacrymas, gaudium, quæ-
' stus, adulatione miscebant*:' Where the word *primordio* has no meaning at all, unless we supply *principatus Tiberii*. Again, speaking of Primus Antonius, the general of Vitellius, his behaviour after the taking of Cremona, he says,—' Primus Antonius
' nequaquam pari innocentia post Cremo-
' nam agebat †:' Where, unless you supply the word *captam*, there is no sense in the passage.

* Annal. Lib. i. c. 7.

† Histor. Lib. iii. c. 49.

Another caufe of obfcurity in this author is, the affectation of expreffing common things in an uncommon manner; as where, fpeaking of the wonders of Egypt, and particularly of the lake Mœris, he calls it ' Lacus effoffa humo, fuper-fluentis Nili re-ceptaculum, atque alibi anguſtiæ, et pro-funda altitudo, nullis inquirentium fpatiis penetrabilis*:' Where all that is meant by this fhort and obfcure fentence is, that the lake Mœris was in fome places wider, in fome narrower, and, where it was narrow, it was of an unfathomable depth. Again, fpeaking of one Celfus, who was accufed before Otho the Emperor for his adherence to Galba, the preceeding Emperor, againft whom Otho had rifen in rebellion and killed, he fays,—' Celfus conftanter fervatæ erga Galbam fidei crimen confeffus, exemplum ultro imputavit †:' Where the only difficulty that can be is in the manner of the expreffion, not in the thing expreffed. And the moſt probable meaning

* Annal. Lib. ii. c. 61.

† Hiftor. Lib. i. c. 71.

that, I think, can be put upon the words
(for, when an author so expresses himself,
we can but guess at his meaning) is, that
Celsus not only confessed his adherence to
Galba, but reproached Otho for not shewing the same example of fidelity. Again,
In describing the bloody battle betwixt the
troops of Vitellius and Otho, where the soldiers on the different sides knew one another, he has these words: ' Noscentes
' inter se, cæteris conspicui, in eventum to-
' tius belli certabant *:' Where the meaning plainly is, though Tacitus seems to
have intended to conceal it from the reader, that the soldiers on the different sides,
knowing one another, and wanting to distinguish themselves, fought each of them
as if the whole fortune of the war had
depended upon his single valour. Again,
in his treatise *de moribus Germanorum*, speaking of the condition of freedmen among
them, he says, ' Liberti non multum supra
' servos sunt, raro aliquid momentum in
' domo, nunquam in civitate, exceptis dun-

---

* Histor. Lib. ii. c. 42.

'taxat iis gentibus quæ regnantur ; ibi
enim et super ingenuos, et super nobiles
ascendunt, apud cæteros impares libertini
libertatis argumentum sunt *:' Where,
from the context, and whole sense of the
passage, not from the words, the meaning
appears to be, that in all those German
states, except those which were under regal
government, the unequal condition of freedmen was a proof of the value of liberty.
In the same place, a little after, speaking of
the German way of possessing their lands,
he says, ' Agri pro numero cultorum ab
universis per vices occupantur, quos mox
inter se secundùm dignationem partiun-
tur.' This I never should have understood, if I could not have explained it from
the passage of an author who writes plainly
and naturally; I mean Cæsar, who, in the
account he has given us of the manners of
the Germans, Lib. vi. de B. Gallico, tells us,
that the magistrates among them made a
distribution every year of a certain quantity
of land to each tribe or family, and they
no doubt would, as Tacitus says, subdivide

* Cap. 25.

it among themselves, giving to each man according to his dignity. I will subjoin Cæsar's words, from which we may see the difference between a plain natural account of a thing, and the same account given with an affected and obscure brevity: 'Agricul-
'turæ non student; neque quisquam agri
'modum certum ac fines proprios habet;
'sed magistratus in annos singulos gentibus
'nationibusque hominum, qui una coierunt,
'quantum eis et quo loco visum est, attri-
'buunt agri, atque anno post alio transire
'cogunt.' Again, in the same book, speaking of the situation of the Catti in Germany, he has these words: 'Catti initium se-
'dis ab Hercynio saltu inchoant, non ita
'effusis ac palustribus locis, ut cæteræ ci-
'vitates, in quas Germania patescit; durant
'si quidem colles, paulatimque rarescunt;
'et Cattos suos saltus Hercynius prosequi-
'tur simul atque deponit*.' The conclusion of this sentence favours more of the operose diligence of the sophist than of the gravity of the historian; for it expresses, in a quaint and artificial manner, a very plain

* Cap. 30.

and simple thing, namely, that the territory of the Catti extended along the Hercynian forest, and went no farther than that forest. And, lastly, that I may not tire the reader with more examples of what, indeed, is to be seen in almost every page of Tacitus, in describing the form of our island, ' Formam ' totius Britanniæ Livius veterum, Fabius ' Rusticus recentium, eloquentissimi aucto- ' res, oblongæ scutulæ vel bipenni assimi- ' lavère ; et est ea facies citra Caledoniam, ' unde et in universum fama est trangref- ' sa [*] : Where the sense is plain enough, namely, that the form of the southern part of the island, terminated by the Frith of Forth, or the Scottish sea, was ascribed to the whole. But the expression is not plain or natural, but has much of what the Greek critics call περιεργια σοφιστικη.

I have insisted the more upon this obscurity in Tacitus, arising from an affectation to raise his style by an uncommon phraseology, that I think it is one of the most distinguishing characteristics of his

---

[*] Agricolæ vita, c. 10.

style. And the great difference in this respect between him and Thucydides is, that, though Thucydides be likewise obscure, more obscure, I think, than Tacitus, his obscurity is all in his orations, arising from his perplexed and involved enthymemas. For his narrative is abundantly clear and perspicuous; whereas the obscurity of Tacitus is chiefly in his narrative, for he wants to adorn the plainest facts. Now an ornamented narrative can hardly be very accurate and distinct. And, as narrative is the most essential part of history, it is this which makes the commentaries of Julius Cæsar, or even the history of Livy, though his narrative be not near so plain as that of Julius, so much more valuable than the history of Tacitus.

Tacitus so far resembles a modern author, that his prose, in many places, is very poetical. Speaking of Germanicus's voyage, along the coast of Germany, he says, 'Ac 'primo placidum æquor mille navium re- 'mis strepere, aut velis impelli *.' This is

* Annal. Lib. ii. c. 23.

poetical painting, not hiſtorical narrative. Again, ſpeaking of the ſoil of Germany, he ſays, 'Terra ſatis ferax, frugiferarum arborum impatiens, pecorum fœcunda, ſed plerumque improcera, ne armentis quidem ſuus honor, aut gloria frontis *.' And, a little after, ſpeaking of the culture of the lands in Germany, he tells us, that they do not cultivate the fruits of the garden; and he adds, ' Sola terræ ſeges imperatur †.' Again, ſpeaking of the rebuilding of the capitol under Veſpaſian, which had been burnt in the civil war betwixt him and Vitellius, he tells us, that, among other things that were thrown into the foundation of it, there were ores of different kinds, which he expreſſes in this manner: ' Metallorum primitiæ nullis fornacibus victæ, ſed ut gignuntur ‡.' In theſe examples the diction is altogether poetical, ſuch as is not to be found even among orators, who write

---

* De Mor. Germ. c. 5.

† Ibid. c. 26.

‡ Hiſt. Lib. iv. c. 53.

Book IV. PROGRESS OF LANGUAGE. 231

chastely and correctly, but it is not to be tolerated in an historian. He abounds also with poetical descriptions, some of them drawn out to a great length: Such is that describing the field of battle, where Varus and his legions fell: ' Prima Vari castra lato ambitu, et dimensis principiis, trium legionum manus ostentabant; dein semiruto valla, humili fossa, accisæ jam reliquiæ consedisse intelligebantur: Medio campi albentia ossa, ut fugerant, ut restiterant, disjecta vel aggerata; adjacebant fragmina telorum, equorumque artus, simul truncis arborum antefixa ora, lucis propinquis barbaræ aræ, apud quas tribunos, ac primorum ordinum centuriones mactaverant. Et cladis ejus superstites, pugnam aut vincula elapsi, referebant, *hic cecidisse legatos; illic raptas aquilas; primum ubi vulnus Varo adactum; ubi infelici dextra, et suo ictu mortem invenerit; quo tribunali concionatus Arminius; quot patibula captivis, quæ scrobes; utque signis et aquilis per superbiam inluserit**.' It is in

* Annal. Lib. i. c. 61.

this way that Virgil paints the field of battle before Troy:

Hic Dolopum manus, hic sævus tendebat Achilles;
Classibus hic locus; hic acies certare solebant.

Æn. ii. v. 29.

Tacitus's poetry is here the less excuseable, that the defeat of Varus and his legions was an event that did not fall within the period of his history, having happened several years before. But he has another description which belongs to his subject; and, as it is less poetical, is for that reason more beautiful, and such as, I think, may be tolerated, if not praised, by the severest critic. It is where he describes a most dangerous sedition and mutiny of the German legions, upon the death of Augustus, which rose to such a height, that Germanicus, who commanded them, was obliged to send away his wife and infant son, who happened to be at that time in the winter-quarters of the legions. Their leaving the camp, and the effect that had upon the minds of the soldiers, is thus finely described: ' Incede-
' bat muliebre et miserabile agmen, profu-
' ga ducis uxor parvulum sinu filium ge-

Book IV. PROGRESS OF LANGUAGE. 233

'rens; lamentantes circum amicorum con-
'juges, quæ fimul trahebantur; nec minus
'triftes qui manebant. Non florentis Cæ-
'faris, neque fuis in caftris, fed velut in ur-
'be victa facies, gemitufque ac planctus,
'etiam militum aures oraque advertere.
'Progrediuntur contuberniis: *Quis ille fle-*
'*bilis fonus? Quod tam trifte? Fæminas il-*
'*luftres, non centurionem ad tutelam, non*
'*militem, nihil imperatoriæ uxoris, aut co-*
'*mitatûs foliti, pergere at Treveros, et ex-*
'*ternæ fidei*.*' This is a picture well de-
figned, and exceedingly well coloured; and,
indeed, it appears to me, that in fuch defcriptions Tacitus indulged his genius,
which, I think, was as much adapted to
poetry as to hiftory. But it is one of thofe
dulcia vitia, againft which I would warn
all writers of hiftory; for, if the writer
happens to be a dull man, and of a genius
not favoured by the Mufes, he will make a
forry piece of it; and, if he have a poetical
genius, and fucceed, though he may gain
popular applaufe, he will probably not pleafe

* Annal. Lib. i. c. 40, 41.

a good judge of writing, who will think the defcriptions mifplaced, and unfuitable to the nature of the work, giving to hiftory the air of romance. And, in fact, it always happens, that there are many circumftances in fuch defcriptions either altogether feigned, or much exaggerated, which makes the faith of the author fufpected in other things.

The laft fault I fhall obferve in Tacitus's ftyle is alfo one which is much imitated by modern writers, and greatly admired by moft readers; and that is a fmart and unexpected turn which he gives to the thought, as well as the expreffion: As where, fpeaking of the mathematici or aftrologers in Rome, he fays, that they were ' genus ho-
' minum potentibus infidum, fperantibus
' fallax, quod in civitate noftra et vetabitur
' femper, et retinebitur *:' Where every reader is furprifed to find *vetabitur* and *retinebitur* joined together. Again, in giving a character of Galba the Emperor, he fays,
' Major privato vifus, dum privatus fuit, et
' omnium confenfu capax imperii, nifi im-

* Hiftor. Lib. i. c. 22.

'peràffet *.' Again, speaking of a horrid thing that was done in the civil war between Otho and Vitellius, which every body detested and execrated, he says, ' Factum
' esse scelus loquuntur, faciuntque †.' Again, describing Burrus, the Prefect of the Prætorian Cohorts under Nero, attending the Emperor while he was performing upon the stage, he says, that, among his other attendants, were ' cohors militum centurio-
' nes tribunique et mœrens Burrus ac lau-
' dans ‡.'

These, and such like turns, are, I know, commonly reckoned very fine and witty, and some of them, as I remember, are much praised by his translator Mr. Gordon; but the noble simplicity of the true classical writing rejects all such points and turns, which serve only to surprise the reader, and catch his admiration, not to instruct him. Nor do I know any mark by which the

* Histor. Lib. i. c. 49.

† Ibid. Lib. iii. c. 25.

‡ Annal. xiv. c. 15.

genuine claffics are more readily diftinguifhed from the writers of later times and ages of lefs correct tafte.

But, though I thus cenfure very freely the faults of Tacitus's ftyle, I am very far from thinking contemptibly of his matter, or that he is not, upon the whole, a very valuable author. His fubject, I think, is grand and noble. It is the hiftory of the fall of a great people, greater than any that ever exifted in arms and government, and in the extent and duration of their empire. Other nations may have been more glorious in their rife, or in their profperity, but none was ever fo great in its fall; and the period of Tacitus's hiftory affords more extraordinary examples of virtues and vices, fometimes mixed in the fame man, than are to be found any where elfe in the hiftory of mankind. For the Romans were great in their vices, as well as their virtues, and in both almoft exceeded humanity.

In treating this fubject, Tacitus never falls below the dignity of it, at leaft, as to the matter; nor is it, I think, without reason that he speaks himself of the gravity of his work *. He shews himself every where a lover of virtue, and of virtuous men, and expresses, in the strongest terms, his detestation of cruelty, and every kind of vice. He speaks with admiration of philosophy and its teachers, as often as he has occasion to mention them, knowing that it was philosophy that had produced those extraordinary characters which he celebrates, such as that of Thrasea Pætus, and Helvidius Priscus †. Nor do I think the charge of malignity, commonly made against him, and of exaggerating too much the vices of men, is well founded: He has not made a Tiberius or a

* ' Ut conquirere fabulosa, et fictis oblectare legen-
' tium animos, procul *gravitate* cœpti operis crediderim,
' ita vulgatis traditisque demere fidem non ausim ;' Hist.
Lib. ii. c. 50.

† Speaking of this last, he says, ' Ingenium illustre
' altioribus studiis juvenis admodum dedit; non, ut plerique, ut nomine magnifico segne otium velaret, sed
' quo firmior adversus fortuita rempublicam capesseret;
' doctores sapientiæ secutus est, qui sola bona quæ honesta, mala tantum quæ turpia ; potentiam, nobilitatem, cæteraque extra animum, neque malis, neque bonis annumerant ;' Hist. Lib. iv. c. 5.

Nero so bad as Suetonius has made them; and he sometimes rejects imputations of bad motives to actions that were commonly made at the time, even to the actions of Tiberius, the most cunning, as well as the most wicked of men: As, where he mentions the motives of Tiberius for not being present at the shews of the gladiators, but allowing his son Drusus to attend them: 'Edendis gladiatoribus, quos Germanici 'fratris ac suo nomine obtulerat, Drusus 'præsedit, quamquam vili sanguine nimis 'gaudens: Quod vulgus formidolosum, et 'pater arguisse dicebatur; cur abstinuerit 'spectaculo ipse variè trahebant; alii tædio 'cœtus, quidam tristitia ingenii, et metu 'comparationis, quia Augustus comiter in-'terfuisset. Non crediderim ad ostenden-'dam sævitiam, movendasque populi offen-'siones, concessam filio materiem; quam-'quam id quoque dictum est*.'

But, though he be not malignant, he is very sagacious in divining the motives of men's actions, and the sentiments of their heart; and, if the men are bad, it is natural

* Annal. Lib. i. c. 76.

to suppose that the motives and sentiments of their heart are likewise bad. In speaking of the disadvantage he was under in writing the history of times so near his own, he says, ' Multorum qui Tiberio regente pœnam vel ' infamias subiere posteri manent. Utque fa- ' miliæ ipsæ jam extinctæ sint, reperies, ' qui, ob similitudinem morum, aliena male- ' facta sibi objectari putent. Etiam gloria ac ' virtus infensos habet, ut nimis ex propin- ' quo diversa arguens *.' Again, he assigns various motives for Tiberius continuing the same men so long in the same governments: ' Id quoque morum Tiberii fuit, continuare ' imperia, ac plerosque ad finem vitæ in ' iisdem exercitibus, aut jurisdictionibus ha- ' bere; causæ variæ traduntur: Alii *tædio no-* ' *væ curæ semel placita pro æternis serva-* ' *visse:* Quidam *invidia ne plures fruerentur;* ' sunt qui existiment, *ut callidum ejus inge-* ' *nium, ita anxium judicium; neque enim* ' *eminentes virtutes sectabatur, et rursum* ' *vitia oderat: Ex optimis periculum sibi* ' *a pessimis dedecus publicum metuebat* †.'

* Annal. lib. iv. c. 33.

† Ibid. lib. i. c. 80.

Again, speaking of the same Tiberius refusing the title of *parens patriæ*, and of *dominus*, he says, 'Neque tamen ob ea *parentis patriæ* delatum et antea vocabulum assumpsit, acerbèque increpuit eos, qui *divinas occupationes*, ipsumque *dominum* dixerant; unde angusta et lubrica oratio, sub principe *qui libertatem metuebat, adulationem oderat* *.'

His political wisdom has been much celebrated; and, no doubt, he was a prudent man, and had the experience of business. But I deny that he had gone far into the philosophy, or even the history of government; otherwise, he never would have said that a form of regimen mixt of the power of a king, or chief magistrate, nobles, and people, might be praised in theory, but could hardly ever exist in fact; or, if it did exist, could not be of long continuance †. An obser-

---

* Annal. lib. ii. c. 87.

† Nam cunctas nationes et urbes, populus, aut primores, aut singuli, regunt: Delecta ex his et constituta reipublicæ forma laudari facilius quam evenire, vel, si evenit, haud diuturna esse potest. *Annal.* lib. iv. c. 33.

vation that has been applied by some English writers to the British constitution, with much exultation and triumph over the rudeness and simplicity of antient times, that could not devise a form of government so perfect as has been invented in this island, and which even so great an author as Tacitus speaks of, as only a fine speculation. But the fact truly is, that all the free states of antiquity were governed in this way. Such was the government of Sparta, and likewise of Athens in antient times, and such was even the original form of government in Rome, not only under their Kings, but under their consuls; with this difference only, that, under their consuls, they had two chief magistrates, in place of one that they had before. And Tacitus, if he had been deep in this part of philosophy, would have known from theory, that there can be no government truly free which is not so mixed. But it is evident, that Tacitus himself had studied philosophy with that moderation which he commends in his father-in-law, Julius Agricola *; a clear proof of which, among

---

* ‘ Memoria teneo folitum ipfum [Agricolam] narra-
‘ re, ſe in prima juventa ſtudium philoſophiæ ac juris, ultra

others, that might be quoted, is his doubting whether the gods, propitious or angry, had denied gold and silver to the Germans*. His model Sallust was, in this respect, a better philosopher; for he, speaking of avarice and money, says, ' Avaritia pecu-
' niæ studium habet, quàm nemo sapiens
' concupivit; ea, quasi venenis malis im-
' buta, corpus animumque virilem effemi-
' nat: Semper infinita, insatiabilis, neque
' copia, neque inopia minuitur †.' And he might have known from history, that Lycurgus, the law-giver of Sparta, whose wisdom, according to the judgment of the oracle, exceeded human, laboured nothing more, in the form of polity that he gave to the Spartans, than to exclude wealth from

---

* *quàm concessum Romano ac senatori hausisse: Ni prudentia*
' *matris incensum ac flagrantem animum coërcuisset;* scilicet
' sublime et erectum ingenium, pulchritudinem ac speciem
' excelsæ magæque gloriæ vehementius quàm cauta
' appetebat; mox mitigavit ratio et ætas; retinuitque,
' quod est difficillimum, ex sapientia modum;' Agricolæ vita, c. 4.

* ' Argentum et aurum propitii an irati dii negave-
' rint, dubito;' De Morib. Germ. c. 5.

† Conj. Catilin. c. 11.

among them: And the fame oracle, while yet their ftate was flourifhing, foretold, that nothing elfe but the love of money could ruin them*.

I think, however, as I have already faid, that Tacitus's hiftory is, upon the whole, a valuable work; even the ftyle, which is moft exceptionable in it, is not the ftyle of a little fophift, fuch as there were many in later times, who, unacquainted with human life and bufinefs, applied themfelves only to adorn words, and to tickle the ears, and pleafe the fancy of their hearers and readers. Some of thefe orators, in the very age in which Tacitus lived, boafted that their performances might be *fung* or *danced* to †. The ftyle which Tacitus has ftudied is of a kind quite oppofite; for it is of the auftere kind, uncouth and harfh to excefs. This I afcribe chiefly to his being fo unlucky in his choice of a model and pattern for compofition; I mean Salluft, whom he

---

* Ἀ φιλοχρηματια Σπαρται ἑλει, ἄλλο δε ὐδι.

† Dialog. de caufis corruptæ eloquentiæ, cap. 26. Neque enim oratorius ille.

commends, as 'Rerum Romanarum floren-
' tiſſimus auctor *.' For that, if he had choſen a better model, he had genius enough
to make better compoſition, I have no doubt;
of which, I think, it is but fair, as I have
quoted ſo much againſt him, to give one or
two inſtances. Speaking of one Lepidus, a
wiſe man of thoſe times, who kept well
with Tiberius, and yet moderated and re-
ſtrained his cruelty, which others flattered,
he ſays, ' Hunc ego Lepidum, temporibus
' illis, gravem et ſapientem virum fuiſſe
' comperio. Nam pleraque ab ſævis adu-
' lationibus aliorum in melius flexit; neque
' tamen temperamenti egebat, cum æqua-
' bili auctoritate et gratia apud Tiberium
' viguerit. Unde dubitare cogor, fato et
' forte naſcendi, ut cætera, ita principum
' inclinatio in hos, offenſio in illos; an ſit
' aliquid in noſtris conſiliis, liceatque inter
' abruptam contumaciam, et deforme obſe-
' quium, pergere iter ambitione ac periculis
' vacuum †.' Not only the words here are
very elegant, and well choſen, but the com-

* Annal. Lib. ii. c. 30.

† Ibid. Lib. iv. c. 20.

Book IV. PROGRESS OF LANGUAGE. 245

position is numerous and fine, especially in the latter part of the sentence. In his harangues he has, as I have already observed, more of composition than in his narrative; and there is the beginning of the Emperor Galba's speech to Piso, when he adopted him, which is as well composed as almost any thing that is to be found in any Latin author. It runs thus: 'Si te privatus, lege curiatâ apud Pontifices, ut moris est, adoptarem, et mihi egregium erat tunc, Pompeii et M. Crassi sobolem in penates meos adsciscere; et tibi insigne, Sulpiciæ ac Lutatiæ decora, nobilitati tuæ adjecisse. Nunc me deorum hominumque consensu ad imperium vocatum, præclara indoles tua, et amor patriæ impulit, ut principatum, de quo majores nostri armis certabant, bello adeptus, quiescenti offeram; exemplo Divi Augusti, qui sororis filium Marcellum, dein generum Agrippam, mox nepotes suos, postremo Tiberium Neronem privignum, in proximo sibi fastigio collocavit *.'

* Histor. Lib. i. c. 14.

These, and other instances that might be quoted, shew that Tacitus was capable of writing much better than he has done. But his taste was corrupted by the imitation of Sallust, and the fashion of the times, which, as he tells us, approved much of the style of Seneca: 'Fuit illi viro ingenium amœ-'num, et temporis ejus auribus accommo-'datum *.' It is not, however, the style of Seneca that Tacitus has imitated; for, though Seneca's sentences be as short, with generally more of point and turn in them, they are better smoothed and rounded, and are just what Petronius Arbiter, speaking of the style of the declaimers of his time, calls 'melliti verborum globuli.'

And here I conclude my criticism upon Tacitus, which has drawn out to the greater length, that I have illustrated what I have said of him by examples from him; because I find that, in matters of criticism, general observations instruct little, unless they be explained by examples. I have been the fuller upon this author, so much celebrated

* Annal. Lib. xiii. c. 2.

in modern times, that, I believe, the imitation of his style has contributed very much to corrupt the present taste of writing in Europe. To be convinced of this, we need only compare the English writers of the last century with those of this, and particularly the English writers before, or about the time of the restoration, such as Hooker, Milton, Lord Clarendon, Bishop Wilkins, and Dr. Spratt, with the generality of the British writers of this century. At that time there were no other models for the writing art known, except the great and genuine classics, such as Demosthenes, Thucydides, Herodotus, Xenophon, Plato, among the Greeks, and Julius Cæsar, Cicero, and Livy, among the Latins; and, accordingly, we find in those English authors I have named, a colour of style quite different from what is presently the fashion. In place of the short, smart, unconnected sentences, the *vibrantes sententiolæ*, as Petronius calls them, of these later writers, we have periods in them, well composed, consisting of members connected, and aptly inserted into one another, and full of sense and argument, instead of point and turn, and what is commonly called wit. The opinion of those writers seems to have been, that their words ought to be connected as well as their sense and meaning. And I have generally observed, that where a connection is wanting in the style, there is the same want in the sense and argument. I must however acknowledge, that, as it is difficult to hit the exact middle in any thing, some of those English authors above-mentioned have run out into so great a length of period, that all their skill in composition cannot sometimes make the sense sufficiently clear, without looking farther back, and carrying on the attention longer than most readers are capable of doing.

But, whatever hurt the imitation of Tacitus may have done to a good taste in writing, I think it is a piece of justice that I owe to the British authors to acknowledge, that the best imitation of him, far exceeding any thing that I have seen in French, is to be found in Mr. Mallet's life of Chancellor Bacon: Nor is it possible to refuse a great deal of merit, in point of style, to that work, if it be true that Tacitus is a model for style and composition. But I hope I have said enough to shew, that he is not a proper model; and that, though his works be highly finished, and have no doubt cost him a great deal of pains and study, they are not finished in a good taste; and therefore the negligence, and even vulgarity, of such a writer as Polybius, with all his *Megalopolitan* idioms, is preferable to the studied obscurity and affected sententiousness of Tacitus.

CHAP. XIII.

The style of Tacitus has the general character of the style of the age.—The schools of declamation the cause of so general a corruption of taste among the Romans coming on so fast.—The beginning of those schools at Rome, and the progress of them.—The bad effects of them upon the taste of writing of all kinds.—Some specimens of their style.—Seneca the philosopher's style of the same kind.

THE style of Tacitus, though it have its peculiarities, has the general character of the style of the age in which he lived, as is evident from the writings of Seneca, who lived before Tacitus, and of Pliny the younger, who lived at the same time. This makes it a matter of some curiosity to inquire how the Romans, who at first copied only the best Greek masters, and had formed, about the time of Cicero, a good national taste of speaking and writing, should, in so short a time, have declined so much from that taste. Many things, no doubt, in the degenerate times of any state, contribute to the depravation of taste in all the arts. Several of those causes are enumerated in that elegant dialogue *de causis corruptæ eloquentiæ* *; but there is one which, I think, not only accounts for the Romans falling off from the true taste of eloquence, but for their adopting that particular bad taste which prevailed in the age of Tacitus; and it is the education of the youth in the schools of declamation, where they practised speaking upon fictitious subjects, some of them altogether out of real life †; or, if not fictitious, rare and

---

* This dialogue is by some ascribed to Tacitus, by others to Quinctilian; but, though it appear to have been written about the time in which they lived, it is of a character of style much superior to that of either of them, and is by far the best written piece which remains of that age.

† Of this kind Petronius, in the beginning of his Satyricon, mentions some cases. His words are, ' Et ideo ' ego adolescentulos existimo in scholis stultissimos fieri, ' quia nihil ex iis, quæ in usu habemus, aut audiunt aut

unusual, and such as were of no use in the common business of life *.

The practice began among the Greeks, not the Athenians, but the Asiatic Greeks, from whom it came to Athens, and from Athens, it is likely, to Rome †. At what

' ydent; sed piratas cum catenis in litore stantes, sed
' tyrannos edicta scribentes, quibus imperent filiis, ut pa-
' trum suorum capita præcidant; sed responsa in pesti-
' lentia data, ut virgines tres aut plures immolentur.'
Such subjects are what the author of the dialogue above-mentioned, *de Causis corruptæ Eloquentiæ*, calls ' fic-
' tæ, nec ullo modo ad veritatem accedentes controver-
' siæ, quæ linguam modo et vocem exercebant;' c. 31.
And, if the reader desires to see examples of such questions, and their manner of treating them in those schools, he will find them in Seneca the rhetorician's collection, which he calls *Controversiæ*, of which I shall speak more a little after.

* Of this last kind Suetonius, in the beginning of his book *de Claris Oratoribus*, has given us two examples.

† ' Nuper ventosa illhæc et enormis loquacitas A-
' thenas ex Asia commigravit, animosque juvenum ad
' magna surgentes, velut pestilente quodam sidere adfla-
' vit. Simulque corrupta eloquentiæ regula stetit et
' obmutuit;' Petron. Satyric. initio. This is that unphilosophic eloquence of which the Halicarnassian complains very much; but observes, that it was beginning in

time it began among the Greeks is not certain: Quinctilian says, that it was about the time of Demetrius Phalereus; but one thing is certain, that it was not known in Athens in the days of Demosthenes, Hyperides, and those other great orators, ten of whom were produced in that single city; and, in general, every kind of fine writing had come to perfection in Greece before any school of declamation was opened *.

his time to yield to a better taste and manner, under the patronage and protection of some of the great men of Rome; *Dionysius de Antiquis Oratoribus, Commentarii, in initio.*

This Asiatic eloquence, as Cicero informs us in his book *de Claris Oratoribus*, was of two kinds: ' Genera autem Asiaticæ dictionis duo sunt, unum sententiosum, et
' argutum, sententiis non tam gravibus et severis, quàm
' concinnis et venustis. Aliud autem genus est non tam
' sententiis frequentatum, quàm verbis volucrè atque in-
' citatum.' Of the first kind was the eloquence of the schools of declamation, as is evident from the specimens of it, which Seneca the rhetorician has preserved to us, and of which I shall say more hereafter.

* ' Nondum juvenes declamationibus continebantur,
' cùm Sophocles aut Euripides invenerunt verba, quibus
' deberent loqui. Nondum umbraticus doctor ingenia
' deleverat, cum Pindarus novemque Lyrici Homericis
' versibus canere timuerunt. Et, ne poëtas quidem ad

In Rome, it did not begin till a little before the days of Cicero, who, when he was a boy, heard the first Latin declaimer, one L. Plotius Gallus *. At first, this kind of exercise was not at all approved of by the wiser men of Rome; and it was prohibited by a decree of the senate, mentioned by Suetonius in his book *de Claris Rhetoribus*, and afterwards by an edict of the censors Cn. Domitius Ahenobarbus, and D. Licinius Crassus the orator, who mentions this decree in Cicero's third book *de Oratore*, and calls the schools of those declaimers *ludi impudentiæ*, the schools of impudence †.

---

* 'testimonium citem, certè neque Platona, neque Demosthenem ad hoc genus orationis accessisse video;' Petronii Satyric.

* Sueton. de Clar. Rhetor. c. 2.

† From the words of this edict of the censors, which Suetonius has preserved to us in the beginning of the book above quoted, it appears, that the word *rhetor* was not at that time naturalized in Rome; and, before Cicero's time, the word *declamatio* was not known, as Seneca the rhetorician informs us, in the preface to his first book of Controversies.

Before this declamatory exercise was introduced into Rome, the author of the dialogue above-mentioned has informed us, how the young gentlemen of Rome were taught the art of speaking: They applied themselves, says he, to some famous orator of the time; him they followed—him they attended, as often as he had occasion to speak in any public or private cause, or in the assembly of the people. By this means, they heard not only him, but every other famous speaker, and grew acquainted with business and the courts of justice *. In this way they became very soon fit themselves for pleading causes; and, accordingly, our author tells us, that L. Crassus accused C. Carbo, when he was only nineteen years, Cæsar Dolabella, when he was one and twenty, and Asinius Pollio C. Cato, when he was two and twenty; and he adds, that their orations in those causes were, in his time, read with admiration †. And, in the same manner, the orators of Greece were bred by attending the courts of justice, and the assemblies of the people, hearing other orators, and then practising themselves, first

* Cap. 34. † Ibid.

in private caufes, as Demofthenes began by calling his tutors to account for their bad management, and, afterwards, when they came to the proper age, in the affemblies of the people.

Cicero was bred in the old way; and, from his earlieſt youth, attended the bufineſs of the forum, and ſtudied the manner of the different orators of his time, of whom he has given a very particular account in his book *de Claris Oratoribus*. But he likewife practifed declamation very much, which was now become exceedingly fafhionable*: And it is to this practice that I afcribe thofe faults of his ſtyle, which I have fo freely obferved; for it was certainly from the fchool of declamation that he got that tincture of the Afiatic oratory, which was obferved in him by his contemporaries †.

---

* He declaimed in Greek, fays Suetonius, down to his prætorfhip, and in Latin after he was conful, and an old man;—' Cicero ad præturam ufque Græcè de-
' clamabat; Latinè vero fenior quoque, et quidem cum
' confulibus Hirtio et Panfa, quos difcipulos et grandes
' prætextatos vocabat;' *de Claris Rhetoribus, Cap.* 1.

† See the dialogue above quoted, c. 18. and Quinctilian, who fays that ' Ciceronem fuorum temporum bo-

Yet it was chiefly with the Greek rhetoricians that he practised; for he tells us, that, when he inclined to put himself to school to *L. Plotius*, the first Latin rhetorician, as I have said, in Rome, he was restrained by the authority of the most learned men then in Rome—' Qui existimabant
' Græcis exercitationibus ali melius ingenia
' posse*.' And, in his book *de Claris Oratoribus*, he tells us, that he declaimed much in Latin, but in Greek more, both because

---

' mines incessere audebant, ut tumidiorem et Asianum
' et redundantem.' That it was the school of declamation which had given him this taint appears, I think, from this, that it is only to be found in his orations; for, in his critical and philosophical works, his style appears to me quite faultless, and abounding with great beauties. But, as to his string of antitheses, upon the subject of parricide, in the oration ' pro Roscio Amerino,' and his pretty little rounded sentences, upon the subject of self-defence, in the oration pro Milone, where not only single words, but the members of the period, answer to one another, like so many tallies, I think it is impossible they could be the work of a man who had only practised in business and real life, but must have been produced by the mimic pleadings of the school of declamation, where men spoke not to convince, but to be applauded and admired, like players.

* Dial. de Cauf. Cor. Eloq. c. 2.

he improved his Latin ſtyle by the imitation of the Greek, which ſupplied ſo many more ornaments of ſpeech, and becauſe he could not be corrected and taught by the Greek maſters, unleſs he declaimed in Greek.

After his time, it appears that the practice of declamation in Greek was given over by the Roman youth; ſo that eloquence became intirely Latin, both in ſtudy and practice; and not only the Greek maſters were forgot, but even Cicero was not ſtudied; and Seneca the rhetorician mentions a declaimer whoſe ſcholars preferred him to Cicero *.

The bad effects of this upon the taſte of ſpeaking and writing were ſoon perceived

* Lib. 3. Declamat. in præfatione, ‘ Hi non tantum diſertiſſimis viris, quos paulo ante retuli, ſed etiam Ciceroni Ceſtium ſuum præferrent, niſi lapides timerent. Quo tamen uno modo poſſunt, præferant; hujus enim declamationes ediſcunt; illius orationes non legunt niſi eis quibus Ceſtius reſcripſit.’ What a ſtrange depravation of taſte this muſt have been, to get by heart the declamations of a ſchoolmaſter, and not read Cicero!

by the men of sense among the Romans, and are expressed in very strong terms by some of them. Petronius Arbiter ascribes the destruction of the Roman eloquence to those masters of this declamatory art; for, addressing himself to them, he says, 'Pace 'vestrâ liceat dixisse, primi omnium elo-'quentiam perdidistis. Levibus enim at-'que inanibus sonis ludibria quædam exci-'tando effecistis ut corpus orationis ener-'varetur et caderet *.' And, a little before that, after ridiculing the ridiculous pathos which they affected upon those feigned sub-jects, calling out, 'Hæc vulnera pro liber-'tate publica excepi; hunc oculum pro vo-'bis impendi; date mihi ducem, qui me 'ducat ad liberos meos, nam succisi poplites 'membra non sustinent.' He adds, 'Hæc 'ipsa tolerabilia essent, si ad eloquentiam 'ituris viam facerent; nunc, et rerum tu-'more, et sententiarum vanissimo strepitu, 'hoc tantum proficiunt, ut, cùm in forum 'venerint, putent se in alium terrarum or-'bem delatos.' After that, he proceeds to tell us, that the ill taste acquired in the

* Initio Satyrici.

schools of declamation had affected every kind of composition: 'Ne carmen quidem 'sani coloris enituit; sed omnia quasi eodem 'cibo pasta non potuerunt usque ad senec- 'tutem canescere.' This is undoubtedly true of the age of Tacitus, and of Seneca the philosopher; and I say further, that it is true, in some degree, even of the preceeding, I mean the age of Augustus; for there is not any writer of that age that has intirely escaped this taint, or, as Petronius has expressed it, *the malign influence of this inauspicious star to good taste*, Horace only excepted; for I do not except even the divine Virgil; and I appeal to his speeches in the Æneid, which let any man of good taste compare with those of Homer, and he will perceive a difference of style, which, I think, cannot be otherwise accounted for, but from the general prevalence of the taste of declamation, even in that age so general, that, as Petronius, who, I think, it is probable, either lived in the age of Augustus, or much nearer it than is commonly supposed, has told us, it infected not only the prose, but the poetry. But Horace had studied at Athens, Virgil at Naples; after writing his Æneid, he did indeed intend to have passed the remainder of his life in Greece, and to have bestowed three years there upon correcting that poem; but he was prevented by death. And, therefore, though I think he passed much too severe a sentence upon it, when he ordered it, by his will, to be burnt; yet I have always considered it as an unfinished poem, very far from being so perfect in its kind as either the Georgics or Pastorals. It is, therefore, not to be wondered that Horace, so educated, following himself the advice he gave to the Pisones, and studying, night and day, the great Greek masters *, has kept free of the general infection, while Virgil has not escaped it. To be convinced of this, I desire any man to read a speech which he has put into the mouth of Juno, in one of his odes, and compare it with a speech of Juno likewise, in the tenth book of the Æneid †. In the one we find a good deal of the *vibrantes senten-*

---

* ———— Vos exemplaria Græca
Nocturna versate manu, versate diurna.

† Horat. Ode iii. Lib. 3.—Æneid, Lib. x. v. 62. et seqq. The subjects of the two speeches have a resemblance, being both against the Trojans.

tiolæ, and smart pungent interrogations, such as were much used in the schools of declamation; in the other, we have nothing but plain narrative and argument, in the finest poetical language. Even Petronius himself is not altogether free from the taint; for, as he says himself, ' Qui inter hæc nutri-
' untur, non magis sapere possunt, quàm
' bene olere qui in culina habitant.'

The author above quoted, of the dialogue upon the causes of the corruption of eloquence among the Romans, mentions the schools of declamation as one of the principal; and indeed he proves it clearly to have been so, by comparing that method of institution with the antient way of studying eloquence. The passage is much too long to be here transcribed, but it well deserves to be read and studied *.

But no body was better acquainted with the schools of declamation than Seneca the rhetorician; he had been himself a scholar in one of them, and had heard all the famous professors of the art, from the begin-

* Cap. 28.—37.

ning of Auguſtus Cæſar's government, down, as we may ſuppoſe, (for he lived very long) to the end of Tiberius's, or the beginning of Caligula's reign; and he has preſerved to us a large collection of thoſe ſcholaſtic diſputations upon various ſubjects, which is valuable, if it were for no other reaſon than that it is the only monument extant of the eloquence of men famous in their time, ſuch as Portius Latro, Aurelius Tuſcus, Ceſtius Pius, and Gallio, great names in thoſe days, but which, if it had not been for the great induſtry, and ſingular memory of Seneca, would have been utterly loſt to poſterity.

The judgment of this author concerning the practice of declamation, with which he was ſo well acquainted, is the ſame with that of Petronius, and of the author of the dialogue I have ſo often quoted. He gives it firſt under the name of Montanus Votienus, a famous pleader of thoſe times, who, being aſked by Seneca why he did not practiſe declamation, gives ſeveral good reaſons for it: Among others, he ſays, ' That the declaimers ſpeak not to gain a

' caufe, as pleaders do, but to pleafe their
' hearers; therefore they let alone what is
' neceffary or ufeful in the caufe, and only
' ftudy what is capable of flowers and or-
' nament. Then they are not accuftomed
' to anfwer arguments and objections made
' by adverfaries, but only fuch as they make
' themfelves, and which are made to be an-
' fwered; moreover they are fupported in
' this exercife by frequent applaufe, during
' the intervals of which they have time to
' paufe, and affift their memory by recol-
' lection. The faces likewife of all their
' hearers, at fuch exhibitions, are familiar to
' them, and they are never difagreeably in-
' terrupted by laughing, or otherwife. For
' thefe reafons, when they come into the
' forum to plead real caufes, they feem
' tranfported into another world, where they
' are unable to bear the eyes of men they
' do not know, or the noife and tumult of a
' multitude; even the fky above their heads
' frightens them.' And upon this occafion he tells a ftory of Portius Latro, one
of the moft famous profeffors of this art,
who, being employed to plead the caufe of
a friend of his, was fo confounded with ap-

pearances so new to him, that he began his pleading with a solecism, and could not go on, till he persuaded the judge to change the place of the trial to the Basilica, or court of justice, where he had walls and a roof, to which he had always been accustomed. Montanus concludes with saying, that no exercise is useful that is not as like as possible to the business for which it is intended. And he mentions the case of gladiators, who are accustomed to exercise with heavier arms than those with which they fight [*]. He gives much the same opinion concerning the inutility of declamation in another place, under the name of Severus Cassius, a very famous orator of those times, who is not only highly praised by Seneca, but likewise by Quinctilian. Among other things, he says, that we can form no judgment of an orator by so childish an exercise: You might as well estimate the abi-

[*] 'Non est autem utilis exercitatio, nisi quæ operi simillima est illi, ad quod exercet. Itaque durior solet esse vero certamine. Gladiatores gravioribus armis discunt, quàm pugnant;' *Controvers.* Lib. iv. initio.

sities of a sailor by his performance in a fish-pond*.

That the reader may be the better able to judge of this kind of eloquence, which was once so much in fashion in Rome, and which was the chief cause of the corruption of their taste of writing, I will give some specimens of it from Seneca's collection, beginning with his *Suasoriæ*, which is the name they gave to their declamations of the deliberative kind. The subject of the first *Suasoria* is, Whether Alexander, after having over-run India, should attempt to navigate the ocean in search of other countries? To persuade him not to do it, the declaimer accosts him in this way: ' Magni pectoris
' est inter secunda moderatio. Eundem for-
' tuna victoriæ tuæ, quem natura finem fa-
' cit. Imperium tuum cludit oceanus. O
' quantum magnitudo tua, rerum quoque
' naturam supergressa est! Alexander orbi

---

* ' Non est quod oratorem in hac puerili exercitatione
' species. Quid si velis gubernatorem in piscina æsti-
' mare !' *Epitom. Declam. Lib.* iii. *in præfatione.*

'magnus eſt. Alexandro orbis anguſtus eſt.
'Aliquis etiam magnitudini modus eſt. Non
'procedit ultra ſpatia ſua cœlum. Maria
'intra terminos ſuos agitantur. Quicquid
'ad ſummum venit, incremento non reli-
'quit locum. Non magis quicquam ultra
'Alexandrum novimus, quàm ultra ocea-
'num.' Here we have the topic of moderation, and ſetting bounds to extravagant
wiſhes, handled in pretty little acute ſentences, well ſmoothed and rounded.

The ſubject of the ſecond *Suaſoria* is
a deliberation, whether the three hundred
Spartans, who, with other Greeks, were
poſted to guard the paſs of Thermopylæ
againſt Xerxes, ſhould fly, after they were
deſerted by the reſt of the Greeks. Here
the declaimer, ſpeaking of the difference
between the Spartans and other Greeks,
ſays, 'Aliud cæteros, aliud Laconas decet.
'Nos ſine deliciis educamur, ſine Muſis vi-
'vimus, ſine vita vincimus:' Where, beſides
the repetition and ſimilarity of the compoſition, we have the contraſt betwixt *vivimus*
and *ſine vita*, and the paradox of *over-
coming without life*, which no doubt would

be highly applauded by the hearers. Of a'
like kind are the antitheses of another declaimer upon the same subject, with a fine conceit at the end of them, which, from what
Seneca says, appears to have been much
commended. Speaking of Xerxes, he says,
' Terras armis obsidet, cœlum sagittis, maria
' vinculis. Lacones, nisi succurritis, mun-
' dus captus est.'

The subject of the fifth *Suaforia* is, whether the Athenians should not throw down
the trophies which they had erected over the
Persians, Xerxes threatening that he would
return, if they did not. Here one Silo
Pompeius used an argument to persuade the
Athenians not to do it, which Seneca ap-
proves much of: ' Nisi tollitis, inquit, tro-
' phæa, ego veniam. Hoc ait Xerxes, nisi
' hæc trophæa tollitis, alia ponetis.' And,
I think, it must be allowed, that not only
the argument is good in itself, but that the
turn given to it is smart and surprising.
But Seneca mentions an argument used upon the other side by another declaimer,
viz. Gallio, which he commends still more.
Speaking of the Persians, he says, ' Divi-

' illi perire possunt, quàm nos vincere.'
Upon which Seneca's observation is, ' Hoc
' loco disertissimam sententiam dixit, quæ
' vel in oratione, vel in historia ponitur.'
And no doubt the argument was very conclusive, and the turn given to it not so far
fetched, or sophistical, but that it might be
tolerated, even in history, or a serious oration.

The subject of the sixth *Suasoria* is, whether Cicero should beg his life of Antony.
Cestius Pius, one of those famous declaimers above-mentioned, advises him not to do
it, in a style not unlike Cicero's own;
' Si ad desiderium populi respices, Cicero,
' quandoque perieris, parum vixisti ; si ad
' res gestas, satis vixisti; si ad injurias for-
' tunæ et præsentem reipublicæ statum,
' nimium diu vixisti ; si ad memoriam ope-
' rum tuorum, semper victurus es.' Varius
Geminus, another declaimer, took the
other side in this deliberation, and advised
Cicero not to die, but to fly to M. Brutus,
C. Cassius, or Sextus Pompeius : ' Et adje-
' cit,' says Seneca, ' illam sententiam, quàm
' Cassius Severus unicè mirabatur. Quid

'deficiemus? Et refpublica fuos triumviros
' habet. Deinde etiam quas petere poffet
' regiones, percurrit: Siciliam dixit vindi-
' catam effe ab illo, Ciliciam a proconfule
' egregiè adminiftratam, familiares ftudiis
' ejus et Achaiam et Afiam, Deiotari regnum
' obligatum beneficiis, Ægyptum et habere
' beneficii memoriam, et agere perfidiæ
' pœnitentiam, fed maxime illum in Afiam
' et Macedoniam hortatus eft in Caffii et
' Bruti caftra.' Caffius Severus's reflection
(the fame whom I mentioned before, as
not approving of the practice of declamation) is, I think, very fenfible: 'Alios
' declamâffe aiebat, Varium Geminum vi-
' vum confilium dediffe:' By which he
means, that this declaimer had given a
counfel which he might have given to Cicero, if he had been alive; and that his
arguments were fuch as might have been
ufed in real life and bufinefs.

The next *Suaforia* concerns Cicero likewife; for it deliberates, whether Cicero
fhould burn his writings at the defire of
Antony, upon promife of having his life
fpared. Celtius Pius advifes him not to do

it: 'Assere te potius libertati, et unum
'crimen inimico adjice, fac Antonium mo-
'riendo nocentiorem.' The argument, to
be sure, is not obvious, and yet not unnatural, if we could suppose Cicero a man of
determined resolution, and who loved life
less than he hated Antonius. There were
other good things said upon this side, such
as, 'Si scripta combusseris, Antonius pau-
'cos annos tibi promittit; at si non com-
'busseris, populus Romanus omnes.' A-
gain, 'Quamdiu reipublicæ nostræ aut
'fortuna steterit, aut memoria duraverit,
'admirabile posteris vigebit ingenium, et,
'uno proscriptus sæculo, proscribes Anto-
'nium omnibus:' Where there is more of
a flowing composition than is usual in those
declamations.

The declamations of the judicial kind, or *controversiæ*, as they are called, are pretty much in the same style. I will, however, give some specimens likewise from them. The subject of these controversies is generally the application of some law to a case not provided for by that law. The first case I shall mention is singular enough. The law was, that if a man ravished an unmarried woman, she should have the option whether she would marry him, or he be put to death. A man ravished two women in the same night—the one desired his death, the other that he should marry her. Many ingenious arguments are used upon both sides: I shall only take notice of one that was used against the ravisher: 'Perieras, 'raptor, ni bis perire meruisses*.'

Another of these declaimers of controversy, having occasion to mention the sudden deaths that were the effects of luxury and intemperance, gave this turn to the thought and composition: 'Quicquid avium volitat, 'quicquid piscium natat, quicquid ferarum 'discurrit, nostris sepelitur ventribus. Quæ- 're nunc cur subito moriamur? Mortibus 'vivimus.' Seneca is, with good reason, much displeased with this extravagant conceit—'Non sum,' says he, 'ex judicibus se- 'verissimis, qui omnia ad exactam regu- 'lam redigam; multa donanda ingeniis pu-

* Lib. i. Controvers. 5.

' to; sed donanda vitia, non portenta,
' sunt *.'

The last case I shall mention is very singular. A man was shipwrecked, lost his wife and three children, and had his house burnt down: Upon this he hangs himself up. One, passing by accidentally, cuts him down; he is sued for damages by the person whose life he had saved. This was an excellent subject for such mock-trials; and, accordingly, it is very ingeniously argued upon both sides. On the side of the defendant, the topic of the mutability of men's fortunes affords many pretty little sentences: ' Mutantur vices felicitatis humanæ,
' proscriptus aliquando proscripsit; victi fu-
' giunt, proscripti latent, natant naufragi.
' Amisi, inquit, uxorem, liberos, patrimo-
' nium. Tu putabas ea te conditione ac-
' cepisse, ne perderes? Ludit de suis fortu-
' na muneribus, et, quæ dedit, aufert; et,
' quæ abstulit, reddit; nec unquam tutius
' est illam experiri, quàm cum locum inju-

* Præfat. ad Lib. v. Controvers.

'rix non habet.' On the other side, the plaintiff says, ' Injuria eſt, ut, qui meo ar‑
' bitrio debui, tuo moriar. Amiſi uxorem,
' liberos, patrimonium. Fortuna mihi ni‑
' hil præter laqueum reliquit; iſte nec la‑
' queum. Sumpſi inſtrumenta mortis, ſoli‑
' tudinem et laqueum; alterum aptum mo‑
' rituro, alterum miſero. Quiſquis inter‑
' veneris, ſi amicus es, deſle; ſi inimicus
' ſpecta. Cùm a me iſte accuſetur, gravio‑
' rem de me quàm de reo ferte ſententiam.
' Ego, ut moriar, iſte, ut ne prohibeat. Ne
' hæc narrarem, mori volui; præcidit re‑
' medium meum; ſi qua ſides eſt, non ena‑
' tavi, ſed ejectus ſum. Nihil jam timebam,
' niſi vivere. Domus meæ fata claudo,
' nullo miſerior, quàm quod ultimus mo‑
' rior.' The laſt thought I think very good; and it is finely paraphraſed by Mr. Thomſon, in his verſes upon the death of Mr. Aikman:

> Unhappy he! who lateſt feels the blow,
> Whoſe eyes have wept o'er every friend laid low.

From theſe examples, it is eaſy to ſee the nature of this kind of eloquence. The matter of it is arguments from general to‑

pics, very artificially, and sometimes very ingeniously, handled. The style of it is cut into short sentences, very acute, and of wonderful brevity, adorned with those ostentatious figures, which both please the fancy and sooth the ear, of antithesis and similarity of composition, like answering to like, and opposite to opposite. Tacitus's style resembles it, in as far as it is short and disjointed, but differs from it, in as far as it has not so many of those ambitious ornaments; and the sentences are not so well rounded and pared, but more harsh and abrupt. But the style of Seneca the philosopher is, in every respect, so like that of the school of declamation, in which no doubt he had practised much, that, I think, it is impossible to distinguish the one from the other. To be convinced of this, we need only compare what is said in the last controversy I mentioned, upon the mutability of fortune, with what Seneca has said upon the same topic, in more than one place, and we shall find, not only the same thoughts, but almost the same words, with the same composition.

Quinctilian's judgment of the style of this philosopher is so just, and so candid, that the reader will not be displeased to have it here in his own words:—' Ex industria
' Senecam in omnia genere eloquentiæ ver-
' satum distuli propter vulgatam falso de me
' opinionem, quia damnare eum, et invi-
' sum quoque habere, sum creditus; quod
' accidit mihi dum corruptum et omnibus
' vitiis fractum dicendi genus revocare ad
' severiora judicia contendo; tum autem
' solus ferè hic in manibus adolescentum
' fuit, quem non equidem omnino conabar
' excutere, sed potioribus præferri non sine-
' bam, quos ille non destiterat incessere,
' cum diversi sibi conscius generis, placere
' se in dicendo posse iis, quibus illi place-
' rent, diffideret. Amabant autem eum ma-
' gis quàm imitabantur, tantumque ab eo
' defluebant, quantum ille ab antiquis de-
' scenderat; foret enim optandum, pares ac
' saltem proximos illi viro fieri. Sed placebat
' propter sola vitia, et ad ea se quisque diri-
' gebat effingenda, quæ poterat. Deinde
' cùm se jactaret eodem modo dicere, Sene-
' cam infamat, cujus et multæ alioquin et
' magnæ virtutes fuerunt; ingenium facile et

' copiosum, plurimum studii, multa rerum
' cognitio, in qua tamen aliquando ab iis,
' quibus inquirenda quædam mandabat, de-
' ceptus est. Tractavit etiam omnem fere
' studiorum materiam. Nam et orationes
' ejus, et poëmata, et epistolæ, et dialogi
' feruntur. In philosophia parum diligens,
' egregius tamen vitiorum insectator fuit;
' multæ in eo claræque sententiæ, multa
' etiam morum gratia legenda: Sed in elo-
' quendo corrupta pleraque, atque eo perni-
' ciosissima, quod abundant dulcibus vitiis.
' Velles eum suo ingenio dixisse alieno ju-
' dicio. Nam, si aliqua contempsisset, si pa-
' rum concupisset, si non omnia sua amâsset,
' si rerum pondera minutissimis sententiis
' non fregisset, consensu potius eruditorum,
' quàm puerorum amore comprobaretur.
' Verùm sic quoque jam robustis, et seve-
' riore genere satis firmatis, legendus, vel
' ideo, quod exercere potest utrumque judi-
' cium. Multa enim, ut dixi, probanda in
' eo, multa etiam admiranda sunt, eligere
' modo curæ sit: Quod utinam ipse fecis-
' set. Digna enim fuit illa natura quæ me-
' liora vellet; quod voluit effecit *.'

* Lib. x. c. 1.

What Quinctilian here says of the danger there is in those reading him, whose judgment is not confined by severe study, and the imitation of better authors, is certainly true; for they will imitate those *dulcia vitia*, and, as is always the case, multiply them, or make them worse; so that they will write a style of wit altogether, which is, perhaps, the worst of all styles, being the farthest removed from a style of sense and gravity.

I observe, that the witty writers among us, if they study at the same time to give a roundness and smoothness to their sentences (for I cannot call them periods), imitate Seneca more than Tacitus; whereas those who affect sentences of great gravity and wisdom, make Tacitus their model; but I would advise them both to study diligently those remains of the schools of declamation, where, I will venture to say, that they will find as many *fine things*, as they are commonly called, as are to be found in any one book. But, on the other hand, if a man would form a grave, manly style, of that noble simplicity, in which the perfection of all the arts confifts, a ftyle of bufinefs fit to convince and inftruct, or to move and inflame, if that be required; not a ftyle of pomp and oftentation, proper only to be admired by the untaught multitude; let him ftudy the great mafters of more antient times; and when he has, by fuch ftudy, confirmed his tafte and judgment, then he may come without danger to the reading of Tacitus, Seneca, Portius Latro, and the other declaimers, from whom he may gather not only many flowers of fpeech, but many ufeful things.

Thus I have endeavoured to explain the nature of the eloquence of thofe fchools; and it appears, that it anfwers exactly to the defcription of one kind of the Afiatic eloquence given us by Cicero, in the paffage above quoted. Accordingly, I have fhewn that it came from Afia; and it was very natural that fuch an eloquence fhould be produced in a country where it was of little ufe, except for fhow and oftentation. There, inftead of found fenfe and argument, and diftinct narrative of facts, fpeaking would become wit-

ty and clever; and as wit cannot bear to be
diffused into long periods, the composition
would naturally be broken into short smart
sentences, turned and rounded in a manner
agreeable to the ear; and this, as we shall
shew afterwards, is the nature of *wit*.

There have not been, in modern times,
any schools of declamation that I have heard
of, whatever practice there may have been
of it in private clubs or societies. But there
is what the French call the *declamation of
the theatre*, that has been much practised
among people of fashion, both in France
and England. This may be a very good
amusement; but, if it is used as an exercise
preparatory to public speaking, I take upon
me absolutely to condemn it, as a practice
still more useless for that purpose than the
practice of the schools I have been censuring.
For there the genius was exercised in the
invention of arguments, and the expression,
as well as the thought, was the declaimer's
own. But here the practitioner submits to
the mean task of repeating another man's
thoughts and words, in doing which he
commonly mimics some player that is in

fashion, and very often tries to express, by voice and gesture, a passion that he does not feel. This manner, transferred to business and real life, will displease a man of sense and good taste, more than the rudest simplicity, and greatest want of art in speaking. And such an orator loses one of the chief means of persuasion, namely, the character of the speaker: For, if he will assume the manner of a player, he must be contented to pass for a player, not a man of worth and gravity, not the patriot or lover of his country, that he holds out to us.

CHAP. XIV.

Of the other kind of ornamented style, the gay and florid.—Antient authors, who have written in that style.—Modern, such as my Lord Shaftsbury.—Character of this style.

THE other kind of highly ornamented style I call the gay or florid, of which the ornaments are quite different from those of Thucydides's style; for they are of the harsh and austere kind: Whereas the ornaments of this style are all of the sweet and pleasurable sort, amusing the imagination with fine images, and tickling the ear with the most agreeable sounds. Of this kind may be reckoned the poetry of Sappho and Anacreon; the epidictic orations too among the Greeks, such as Gorgias and Hippias, and other antient sophists, used to speak at the games, and other panegyrical assemblies in Greece, were in this style; and likewise the orations of the later sophists, such as Libanius and Themistius, contemporaries of Julian the Emperor. Of this kind also is a great part of the works of Lucian, particularly one of his dialogues, entitled *Amores*, where we have two orations, one in praise of the love of women, another an invective upon women, and extolling the love of boys, in the most florid style of rhetoric that is, I think, any where to be found. And of the same kind were certain supposititious works, forged by some of those later sophists, and imputed to antient authors, such as the poem upon the story of Hero and Leander, said to be the work of Musæus.

The poetry of this age is almost all of this kind, and a great deal of our prose; not only what is professedly poetical, and is very properly said, by Mr. Pope, not to be poetry, but *prose run mad*, but every thing that is intended for a very fine composition. One of the most remarkable of this sort, that has been published of late years, is Hervey's Meditations: But the best by far of the kind are, the characteristics of my Lord Shaftsbury, particularly the last volume of them, which is almost wholly in this style *.

The distinguishing marks of it are, a great copiousness of words, and these the

---

* This noble author, as I have elsewhere observed, has the richest and most copious style of any writer in English; but as in this he has imitated Plato, so, I think, he has fallen under the censure which the Halicarnassian pronounces upon Plato, of being ostentatiously rich in words, and abounding too much in periphrases, and different ways of expressing the same thing—ἰσχυσται τις ἀπειροκαλις περιφρασις, ωλοτω ὑπατων ἐπι διωνυμων (leg. ἐπιδιωνυμων) κιμι ; *Epist. ad Cn. Pomp.* c. 2. He is too, as the Halicarnassian says of Plato, ib. over-abundant in epithets, which he has used with a poetical licence. He often concludes his periods with two nouns, and each its attendant epithet, which gives a kind of dancing cadence to his periods, to which one may beat time; such as, ' a man of profound craft, and ' notable dexterity;' ib. p. 112.—' divinely authorised ' instructor, and spiritual chief;' p. 114. Sometimes he has three of this kind all in a string: ' A sacred hor-
' ror, religious antipathy, and mutual discord, among ' worshippers;' ib. p. 60. But, with all these faults, I think it must be admitted, that his style is correct as to the grammatical part, and very elegant; and, if his faults of style were greater than they are, I should forgive them all, in favour of his high taste of antient literature and the fine arts, and a certain liberal air and gentleman-like manner, which runs through all his

moſt pompous and high ſounding that can be found; a great many metaphors and other tropes; abundance of epithets, antitheſes, ſimiles, and poetical deſcriptions; paronomaſias, pariſoſes, and ſuch like figures, as make the language go ſmoothly off the tongue.

And ſo much for both kinds of the highly ornamented ſtyle, the ſevere, and the gay or florid.

writings, and is, I think, a peculiar and diſtinguiſhing mark of his ſtyle.

But his matter does not pleaſe me ſo much as his ſtyle; becauſe I approve of nothing written againſt the eſtabliſhed religion of the country, whether in the way of ſerious argument, or of ridicule. The raillery, it is true, of my Lord Shaftſbury is very delicate; and he has treated the Chriſtian religion, and its profeſſors, with decency, at leaſt, and good breeding, which is more than can be ſaid of ſome later infidel writers, one of whom has told us, in ſo many words, that, before a man can believe the Bible hiſtory, the whole principles of his underſtanding muſt be ſubverted. But my Lord Shaftſbury was a high-bred man of faſhion, who had improved a natural good taſte, not only by the ſtudy of the *politeneſs of antient dialogue*, to uſe his own expreſſion, but by keeping the beſt company in the age in which he lived—a thing which I hold to be no leſs neceſſary to make a polite writer, than a well-bred gentleman.

CHAP. XV.

Of the middle style.—Examples of that style, antient and modern.

THE third and last character of style I mentioned is the middle or temperate kind, partaking of both, but shunning the extremes of either; for it is not so simple as the one, nor so much ornamented as the other. Of this kind, according to the Halicarnassian, is the style of Isocrates the orator, and of Plato the philosopher, but both bordering on the excess of gay and florid; nor was this style perfected, says he, till the time of Demosthenes*. He, in some of his orations, as we have seen, and where the nature of his subject required it, is as perfectly simple as Lysias; but, in his public orations, the style is admirably tempered by the simplicity of Lysias, the austerity of Thucydides,

* Περὶ τῆς διωτητος τε Δημοσθενος; cap. 14. 15. 16.

and the sweet and pleasurable style of Isocrates and Plato. This the Halicarnassian, in the passage above quoted, has proved by examples from all the three authors.

The Halicarnassian's own style is of this kind, plain and didactic, but with as much ornament as art or science admits. And of the same kind are the rhetorical works of Cicero, particularly his three books *de Oratore*, the most finished of his works of that kind, in which he has very successfully imitated the dialogue of Plato.

The best writers in English compose in this style; such as Milton, Lord Clarendon, Lord Bolingbroke, Dr. Atterbury; and, to come down to our own times, Dr. Armstrong and Mr. Harris, who has, like Plato and Cicero, adorned philosophy with the lights and graces of eloquence; and, like the Halicarnassian, has shewn that grammar and criticism are susceptible of the ornaments of words.

CHAP. XVI.

Of a fourth general character of style, the sublime.—It consists chiefly of the matter—Examples of it.—The counter part of the sublime, or mock-heroic.—Examples of this style, antient and modern.—Improper use of it by Mr. Fielding, in his history of Tom Jones.—Of a sixth general character of style, the ridiculous.—The meaning of the word.—The nature of the thing.—The reason of the pleasure it gives us.—General observations upon it.—Vanity and affectation the proper subjects of it.—Examples of a proper and an improper ridiculous character.—Authors antient and modern that have excelled in the ridiculous.—It does not belong to the greatest geniuses.

I Have, in the preceeding chapter, spoken of three general characters of style; I am now to treat of a fourth, which I call the *sublime*; it may also be called the *high ftyle;* but we muft diftinguifh it from what I call the *highly ornamented ftyle,* from which, I think it is very different. For it is the matter chiefly that conftitutes the fublime; and, if it be not of a nature high and exalted, whatever ornaments of diction we may beftow upon it, we fhall never attain to this character of ftyle.

What then is the matter or fubject of the fublime? I anfwer, it is God and nature; the works of God and nature; wifdom, virtue, heroic characters of men and their actions; and, in fhort, whatever we conceive to be higheft and moft exalted, whether in nature or in art.

But is the matter alone fufficient to conftitute the fublime? If it were fo, then the Phyfics and Metaphyfics of Ariftotle, or whatever elfe is well written upon fubjects of high fpeculation, muft be reckoned fublime. Something more then, in my apprehenfion, is required to entitle any compofition to that name: And what is that? It is, that the writer fhould have fentiments suitable to the subject, and that he should express those sentiments. And what are those sentiments? I answer, sentiments of high admiration, such as subjects of the kind we are speaking of ought to inspire, and will inspire, into every man of genius. If, therefore, a philosopher only teaches and explains any high theorem (and that is all that belongs to him as a philosopher), but expresses no emotion, nor any thing like rapturous or enthusiastic admiration, he is not a sublime writer, though he may have very great merit as a philosopher, and may raise such ideas in others, and perhaps feel them himself, though he do not express them; which, I believe, was the case of Aristotle, and was certainly the case of Plato.

But is there no ornament of words, no particular kind of style, required to express the sublime? I think not; only the words must not be low, nor the composition mean and abject; for these would debase the noblest thoughts. But, I think, no ornament is required; or, if any is given, it ought to be rather of the severe kind, than of the florid and pleasurable. For such figures as the parisosis, paronomasia, and like endings, would be much worse than no ornament.

Let us see how this notion of the sublime will apply to some famous passages that have been quoted as instances of the sublime; and I will begin with the words of Moses, giving an account of the creation of the world by Almighty God, a subject, no doubt, in its nature most sublime: 'And 'God said, Let there be light, and there was 'light.' The thing to be expressed here is, the act of Omnipotence creating, at once, and by a simple *fiat*, the finest and most subtile of all material things:

> Etherial, first of things, quintessence pure.
> Par. Lost. B. vii. v. 244.

Such an act, so far exceeding all human comprehension, was not easy to be properly expressed; for, as the same author says,

> Immediate are the acts of God, more swift
> Than time or motion; but to human ears,
> Cannot without process of speech be told;
> So told, as earthly notion can receive.
> Book vii. v. 176.

To endeavour to adorn with words such a thought, would be to degrade it. Moses, therefore, has expressed it in the simplest, and, at the same time, the noblest manner, by which he has told us, as well as could be told by *process of speech*, that the thing was immediately done by the word of the Almighty. And, though the words be as simple as possible, yet it may be observed, that there is a beauty and an emphasis in the repetition of the word *light*; for the thought would not have been so well expressed, if it had stood thus: 'God said, Let there be light, and it was so.' Accordingly Milton, in translating the passage into verse, has not neglected this beauty:

> Let there be *light*, said God, and forthwith *light*
> Etherial, first of things, quintessence pure,
> Sprung from the deep.   B. vii. v. 243.

And as it is thus properly expressed by Moses, it could not, I think, have been so expressed but by a man who had a just conception of so great an act of power[*].

[*] This is the opinion of Longinus, who quotes this passage as an instance of the sublime, and make Moses's conception of the power of God the foundation of the

Book IV. PROGRESS OF LANGUAGE. 293

Another instance of the sublime, quoted also by Longinus, is the prayer of Ajax in the Iliad, upon occasion of a thick darkness which covered the Grecian army, in the midst of a hot engagement. He prays to Jupiter to deliver them from the darkness; and then, says he, destroy us in the light, since that is your will. The words here are all common, ordinary words, and nowise figured in the composition *; but the sentiment is noble, and truly heroic, and that makes the sublime of the passage; for he

---

sublime of the passage. He had before quoted a passage from Homer, which, he says, is sublime, because the poet there expresses an idea of Neptune worthy of the god. In like manner, says he, the law-giver of the Jews, not a common man, having conceived such a notion of the power of God, expresses it thus: Longinus's words are—ταυτη και ὁ τῶν Ἰεδαιων θεσμοθετης, οὐχ ὁ τυχων ἀνηρ, ἐπειδη την τῦ θεῦ δυναμιν κατα την ἀξιαν Ἰχωρησεν, κᾳξηφηνε· εἰθυς ἐν τη εἰσβολη γραψας τῶν νόμων,—ειπεν ὁ θεος, φησι, τί; γενεσθω φως, και ἐγενετο· γενεσθω γη, και ἐγενετο; De subl. 9.

* Ζεῦ πατερ, ἀλλα συ ῥυσαι ὑπ' ἠερος υἱας Ἀχαιων·
Ποιησον δ' αἰθρην, δος δ' ὀφθαλμοισιν ἰδεσθαι·
Ἐν δε φαει και ὀλεσσον, ἐπει το τοι εὐαδεν ὑτως;

Il. ρ. v. 645.

does not pray to live, but to have an opportunity of dying bravely in the light. And we may obferve, in paffing, that there is a bluntnefs in defiring Jupiter to deftroy them, which fuits very well the character of Ajax; but could hardly, with propriety, have been put into the mouth of any other of the heroes.

Longinus quotes feveral other paffages from Homer as examples of the fublime, particularly his defcription of the battle of the gods, in the 22d Iliad, and the convulfion of nature upon that occafion. For thefe I refer to Longinus himfelf; and I will only add, that, when they are examined, it will be found, that the fublime of them all confifts chiefly in the thought: I fay *chiefly;* for I would not be underftood to deny that there is a language fuitable to great thoughts, and that there fhould be a certain dignity both in the words and the compofition. But over-doing in fuch cafes is very dangerous; and it is much better that the language fhould be too little, than too much ornamented.

But what shews evidently that the matter is principal in the sublime character of style is this, that, if the matter be low and trivial, and, at the same time, the sentiments heroic with language suitable, then it becomes a species of writing altogether different, and indeed opposite, and which, accordingly, bears the name of *mock-heroic*, or *burlesque*. Of this kind we have an antient poem, by some given to Homer, but, probably, the work of a sophist of later times; I mean the battle of the frogs and mice, in which we have ascribed to those little contemptible animals the sentiments and actions of the heroes of the Iliad and Odyssey; and the ridicule of the pompous language of tragedy, by making it too pompous, or what we call bombast, was frequent among the poets of the old comedy at Athens.

In modern times, there are many works of this kind, both in prose and verse; but the best of them all, in my judgment, is the Dunciad of Mr. Pope, in which, to the ridicule of the mock-heroic, is joined the keenest satire. And though, I believe, most scholars who understand the original are of opinion, that he has not translated Homer well; yet every body, I imagine, will admit that, in the Dunciad, he has parodied Virgil exceedingly well; but of this I have said enough elsewhere*.

Mr. Fielding, in his comic narrative poem, the history of Tom Jones, has mixed with his narrative a good deal of the mock-heroic; and, particularly, there is a description of a squabble in a country churchyard wholly in that style †. It is, indeed, an excellent parody of Homer's battles, and is highly ridiculous; but, in my opinion, it is not proper for such a work: *First*, because it is too great a change of style, greater than any work of a legitimate kind, which I think Fielding's is, will admit, from the simple and familiar to the heroic or mock-heroic. It is no better than a patch; and, though it be a shining one, no regular work ought to have any at all. For Horace has very properly given it as a mark of a work irregular, and of ill texture, the having such purple clouts, as he calls them;

* P. 110.   † Book iv. c. 8.

> ——Late qui splendeat unus et alter
> Assuitur pannus.——   ARS POET.

Secondly, because it destroys the probability of the narrative, which ought to be carefully studied in all works, that, like Mr. Fielding's, are imitations of real life and manners, and which, accordingly, has been very much laboured by that author. It is for the probability of the narrative chiefly that I have so much commended Gulliver's Travels. Now, I appeal to every reader, whether such a description in those Travels, as that of the battle in the church-yard, would not have intirely destroyed the credibility of them, and prevented their imposing upon any body, as it is said they did at first. This, therefore, I cannot help thinking a blemish, in a work which has otherwise a great deal of merit, and which I should have thought perfect of the kind, if it had not been for this, and another fault that I find to it, namely, the author's appearing too much in it himself, who had nothing to do in it at all *. By this the reader will underſtand that I mean his reflections, with which he begins his books, and ſometimes his chapters.

And ſo much for the mock-heroic, or burleſque, which I call a fifth general character of ſtyle.

Of kin to this, is that kind of ſtyle which we may call the *ridiculous;* a ſtyle very much practiſed, but the nature of it not underſtood by every body. I uſe the word in the claſſical meaning, to ſignify what-

---

* The fable of this piece is, I think, an extraordinary effort both of genius and art; for, though it be very complex, taking in as great a variety of matter as, I believe, any heroic fable, it is ſo ſimple as to be eaſily enough comprehended in one view. And it has this peculiar excellency, that every incident of the almoſt infinite variety which the author has contrived to introduce into it, contributes, ſome way or other, to bring on the cataſtrophe, which is ſo artfully wrought up, and brought about by a change of fortune ſo ſudden and ſurpriſing, that it gives the reader all the pleaſure of a well written tragedy or comedy. And, therefore, as I hold the invention and compoſition of the fable to be the chief beauty of every poem, I muſt be of opinion, that Mr. Fielding was one of the greateſt poetical geniuſes of his age; nor do I think that his work has hitherto met with the praiſe that it deſerves.

ever tends to excite laughter, whether person or thing. In our sense of the word, when applied to a person, it signifies one who is himself the object of laughter; whereas, in the sense the Romans used the word, it signified a person who excited laughter, without distinction, whether it was at his own expence, or at the expence of another, or without being at the expence of any body, if he presented to us images that were risible. According to the Roman use, therefore, of the word, when applied to persons, it was equivocal, signifying two characters of men very different, one whom we call ridiculous, and another that we would rather call a wit, or a merry facetious fellow *. And it had the same ambiguity when applied to the words or sayings of men, as when applied to their per-

* It was not, however, even in this sense, a respectable character among the Romans; nor did Cato mean to pay a compliment to Cicero when he said, upon hearing his jocose pleading for Muræna, in which he ridiculed the stoical philosophy professed by Cato,— 'Quem ridiculum consulem habemus!' And a professed jester was a very contemptible character, both among the Romans and Greeks. He was called *Scurra* by the former, and γελωτοποιος, or βωμολοχος, by the latter.

X 2

sons; for it denoted either what we would call a witty or pleasant saying, that is, a saying that excites laughter not at itself, but at something else *, or what we call a ridiculous saying, that is, a saying which makes us laugh at itself, and, by consequence, at the person who uses it. It is in the first of these senses that I apply the word to style, meaning a style that makes us laugh, not at itself, but presents to us other images of laughter. It is in this sense that Cicero uses the word, in his books *de Oratore*, where he lays down rules for the ridiculous, which he makes to be a considerable talent of an orator †. And it is in this sense that Horace uses the word, when he says,

>—— Ridiculum acri
>Fortius ac melius magnas plerumque secat res.

Having thus settled the meaning of the word, the question is next concerning

---

* In this sense it is used by Cicero; when speaking of an orator; He commends him for saying many things—' Non ' solum acutè, sed ridiculè et facetè ;' Lib. i. de Orat. c. 57. And, in the same sense, Julius Cæsar, relating a *bon mot* of one of his soldiers, says, ' Non irridiculè dixit;' de Bell. Gall. Lib. i. c. 42.

† De Orat. Lib. ii. c. 58.

the thing itself: What is it that excites this extraordinary commotion in us, by which not only the countenance, but the whole body is altered; and, if it goes to any excess, may be said to be convulsed? It is evidently not a mere bodily affection, but proceeds originally from the mind. What affection then, or passion of the mind, produces it? Is it joy? It is so in children, who laugh merely because they are pleased; and it may be so likewise in men, whose understandings differ little from those of children: But it is not so in men of sense; far less is it grief, anger, indignation, or any such like passion. Or what quality is it in the object, person, or thing, which excites it? It is not goodness, most certainly, fitness, or aptitude, for any purpose; neither is it malice, evil, or mischievousness; nor is it beauty, for that excites love and admiration, not laughter. But what shall we say of the contrary of beauty—deformity? Is it not the object of ridicule? And, I believe, upon inquiry, it will be found, that every thing ridiculous, I mean, what is the object of laughter and derifion, is, in fome way or other, *deformed**.

So far, therefore, we are advanced in this inquiry, as to have found out that the object of laughter is deformity: But the queftion ftill remains, What is deformity? It is the oppofite of beauty, as we have juft now faid. But what is beauty? will a man afk, who has a philofophical turn, and wants to be at the bottom of this queftion. This is a matter of no fmall inquiry, and goes deep into philofophy and the nature of things; but it will be fufficient, for our prefent purpofe, to fay, that beauty confifts of a whole, and correfponding parts, in which there is nothing defective, nothing fuperfluous or redundant, nothing that is unfuitable or foreign to the defign of the whole. Beauty, therefore, neceffarily implies fome defign, plan, or fyftem; and where that is miffed of, or where we find any thing incongruous, diffonant, or incom-

---

* 'This is the account that Cicero gives of the ridiculous: ' Locus autem, et regio quafi ridiculi, turpitudine
' et deformitate quadam continetur;' Lib. ii. de Orat. c. 58.

patible with that design, then have we the idea of deformity.

But if this be the object of ridicule, then is not only *folly*, but *vice*, ridiculous; for nothing is more discordant or incompatible with the system of a rational and social nature, and with the system of nature in general. But vice is the object of hatred and aversion; and, if it be accompanied with abilities and power, or fear and terror, not of ridicule, what shall we say then? Must we retract what we have laid down, that deformity is the subject of laughter? No; that will not be necessary; but we must add to the definition, and say that it is *the deformed without hurt or mischief**. So that whatever quality is hurtful or mis‐

---

* Arist. Ars Poet. τὸ γελοῖον ἐστιν ἁμάρτημα τι καὶ αἰσχος ἀνώδυνον, καὶ ου φθαρτικον;' cap. 5.

And Cicero, in the passage above quoted, after having said that deformity is the subject of ridicule, adds, ' Nec ' insignis improbitas, et scelere juncta, nec rursus mise‐ ' ria insignis, agitata ridetur. Facinorosos enim majore ' quâdam vi, quam ridiculi, vulnerari volunt; miseros il‐ ' ludi nolunt, nisi si se forte jactant.' And, a little after, he says, ' Quamobrem materies omnis ridiculorum est in ' istis vitiis, quæ sunt in vita hominum, neque carorum,

chievous, either to the perfon who poffeffes it, or to any other, or to both, as is often the cafe, is not *ridiculous*.

But the queftion is not yet anfwered, From what affection or difpofition of the mind this action of the mufcles of the face and agitation of the body proceeds? It is not from joy, grief, or any other of the paffions above-mentioned; it is evident likewife, that we are not indifferent with refpect to the perfon or thing at which we laugh. It remains, therefore, that it can only proceed from *contempt*; and, accordingly, we never laugh at what we value or efteem, in fo far, at leaft, as we value and efteem it. For it may happen that a perfon who, upon the whole, is valuable and eftimable, has fomething in him that is ridiculous.

But there is one thing farther that is ftill to be accounted for concerning the ridicu-

---

' neque calamitoforom, neque eorum qui ob facinos ad
' fupplicium rapiendi videntur; eaque, belle agitata, ri-
' deniur;' Lib. ii. de Orat. c. 59.

lous, and that is, how it comes to give us pleasure; for that it does give pleasure, and very high pleasure too, to certain characters of men, is a fact that cannot be disputed. And I say this pleasure proceeds from our opinion that we are free from the blemish or deformity which we laugh at in others, and therefore are so far superior to them. And hence it is, that vain and conceited men are most disposed to laugh at the vanities and follies of others; whereas men of sense and modesty are the least disposed to do so*.

---

* Aristotle, in the 11th chapter of the 1st book of his Rhetoric, gives no other reason why the ridiculous is pleasant, except that it raises laughter, and is a kind of play or diversion—ἡμῖν δὲ καὶ ἔστι ἡ παιδιὰ τῶν ἡδέων καὶ πᾶσα ἄνεσις, καὶ ὁ γέλως τῶν ἡδέων, ἀνάγκη δὲ καὶ τὰ γέλοια ἡδέα εἶναι, καὶ ἀνθρώπους καὶ λογους καὶ ἔργα. But the question returns, Why is laughing pleasant, and why does this kind of play and diversion please some persons much more than any other? For that all diversion is naturally pleasant, being an ease or remission of the mind from labour and serious thought, cannot be denied. But why should the view of deformity be so peculiarly pleasant, as to excite in us a kind of convulsion of the body? I can assign no other reason but the one I have mentioned, viz. the comparison we secretly make between the deformed object and ourselves.

If the curious reader further inquire, how it comes that this pleasure, which the ridiculous gives us, is expressed by laughing? the answer is, that every emotion or passion of the mind is denoted by some symptom or affection of the body, which by nature is made to accompany the emotion or passion of the mind, and which, therefore, may be called the language of nature, long prior to any language of human institution. Why such an action of the muscles of the face, or the corresponding agitation of the body, should be an indication of the sense of the ridiculous, is, I believe, as difficult to explain, as why blushing should be a sign of shame, paleness or redness of the face, of fear or anger. All I know of the matter is, that, in some brutes, particularly in some dogs, a similar action of their's is a sign of pleasure or joy. And, as the infants of our species in many things resemble the brutes, so, as I have already observed, they express their joy in that way; even men, when they are pleased, *smile*, which no doubt has some affinity to laughing; and, accordingly, it is expressed in Latin by a word which

denotes laughter in a small degree, *subri-
deo* *.

From this account of the ridiculous, several observations will arise that are worth attending to: The first I shall mention is connected with what I have just now said; and it is this—that men of great understanding, and sublime genius, though they perceive the ridicule of things, will not delight in it, nor dwell upon it, but will rather turn their attention from it, because truth and

---

* Homer, who, to use an expression of Shakespear's, *knew all qualities of human dealings with a learned spirit*, has well distinguished betwixt a *laugh* and a *smile*, for which last the Greeks have, I think, very properly, a distinct word, as we have in English, not as in the Latin and French, a word compounded with that which denotes laughter and the preposition. It is in that most beautiful passage, the sweetest by far and most tender in the whole Iliad, where he contrives to make Hector meet Andromache and his child in the streets of Troy. When he first met them, he stood and smiled, looking upon his child with silent joy. Ἤτοι ὅμην μειδήσεν, ἰδὼν εἰς παιδα σιωπη. Here if Hector had laughed, it would have been foolish and childish; but, when going to embrace his son, he shrunk from him into the bosom of his nurse, frightened with the nodding of the plumage of his helmet, both he and the mother very properly laughed.

Ὣς δὲ ὁ μὲν μείδησε πατὴρ τε φίλος, καὶ πότνια μήτηρ.
Iliad 6. v. 481.

beauty are their pursuit, not deformity. And accordingly we find, that none of the great writers of antiquity, such as Homer and Virgil, Plato, Aristotle, or even Demosthenes, to whom, as an orator, it might have been useful, practised it. With respect to the last mentioned, we are expressly told, by the Halicarnassian, that he had no talent for it; and I believe that to have been the case of the other great authors above mentioned: For, if we have no delight in the thing, and do not practise it, we cannot excell in it. But the Halicarnassian does not tell us the reason why Demosthenes had not this talent, which I take to be this, that he possessed much greater, and was a man of an exalted genius. The only exception almost I know to this rule is Cicero; but, though he was a great writer, he was far from being a great man; he had many weaknesses and littlenesses; and, among others, a great deal of vanity; and the necessary consequence of this was, his delighting much in the ridiculous, in which he no doubt excelled Demosthenes, as much as he fell short of him in all the great talents of an orator. ‡

Another observation is, that, though weakness and folly, not vice, be the subject of ridicule, yet it is not every weakness or folly that is properly ridiculed. For natural infirmities and defects, whether of body or mind, ought not to be laughed at; because, though they be imperfections, and therefore may be accounted deformities, yet, as the person is not to blame for them, they are not the subject of ridicule. But folly, and even misery, *si se jactat*, as Cicero has observed[*], are proper enough subjects of contempt and ridicule. Nothing, therefore, in the characters of men, is truly ridiculous, except that species of folly we call *vanity*, by which a man either pretends to valuable accomplishments which he has not, or values himself upon mean and trivial qualities deserving no praise. Such folly will make even natural infirmities and diseases ridiculous— as when a weak man, whether by nature or by disease, pretends to be strong as a Hercules, or an ugly man gives himself the airs of an Adonis, or a man naturally dull would impose himself upon us for a great wit and ge-

[*] De Orat. ubi supra.

vius. But, without vanity or affectation, no kind of defect or imperfection either of body or mind can make the person ridiculous, tho' they may be ridiculous in themselves. For, whatever is unfit to serve the purpose for which it is intended, or consists of discordant and incongruous parts, is by nature ridiculous, though the person to whom it belongs may not be so. Thus, for example, if I be dressed in the most fantastical manner that it is possible to imagine,

> Si curtatus inæquali tonsore capillo:
> Occurro,— — —
> ———— si forte subucula pexæ
> Trita subest tunicæ, vel si toga dissidet impar.
> Hor. Epist. II. in fine.

and if I at the same time think myself well dressed, I am a coxcomb and ridiculous. But, if it be only the effect of negligence, or if for any particular purpose I shall think proper to put on a fool's coat, I am not ridiculous, though such discordancies and incongruities in dress, or in any thing else, be no doubt in themselves ridiculous, because they are deformities.

Horace adds,

> ——Quid, mea cum pugnat sententia secum;
> Quod petiit, spernit; repetit quod nuper omisit;
> Æstuat, et vitæ disconvenit ordine toto;
> Diruit, ædificat, mutat quadrata rotundis?
> Insanire putas solennia me, neque rides.

And his friend was in the right for not laughing, at least not laughing at Horace, unless he was at the same time vain of what he ought to have been ashamed of. For, tho' such inconstancy and whimsicalness be in themselves ridiculous, they do not make the person so without vanity or affectation. And there is a reason for not laughing even at the things themselves, namely, that they often ruin the person's fortune, and make him lead an unquiet and miserable life—so that they are not without hurt or mischief.

In this matter, therefore, of the ridiculous, we must distinguish between things and persons. A thing is ridiculous, that is, deformed, if it be not at the same time mischievous. But a person is not ridiculous, though he may have such deformity, if it be not accompanied with vanity and affectation.

A third obfervation is, that though vice he not of itfelf a fubject of ridicule, nor a vitious perfon ridiculous, yet if to vice be joined vanity and affectation, then is fuch a character, of all others, the moft proper object of ridicule. If a man have other qualities that are good—if he be generous and humane, and do a great many good actions, though he may have vanities and follies that are very ridiculous; yet a man of fenfe and good nature will not be difpofed to laugh at him, nor delight to fee him expofed: But if to vanity and folly is joined vice, and an ill difpofition of mind, then he will laugh moft freely, and think the expofing fuch a perfon is a piece of juftice done to the public. For this reafon I think the character of the *Nabob*, in one of Mr. Foote's pieces, is one of the moft proper fubjects of ridicule that ever was exhibited on any ftage, becaufe in that character we have joined to the affectation of being a fine fpeaker and a man of tafte, the pride of wealth, the infolence of power, and great cruelty and hard-heartednefs; and, if the poet had brought him, in the conclufion of the piece, to misery and disgrace, which certainly poetical justice required, I should have thought the piece very compleat. On the other hand, as he has made his *Bankrupt* an honest man, so that he rejects with indignation all the fraudulent schemes of bankruptcy proposed to him, he should not have made him ridiculous in the end of the piece, by assenting to the opinion of every body with whom he converses, and being always of the mind of him whom he last hears.

The two great writers in antient times of the ridiculous kind were Aristophanes and Lucian, both of them excellent in their different ways; but they were neither of them, in my judgment, sublime geniuses, nor did they attempt any thing of the high kind. For it appears to have been a maxim among the antients, that no man was formed by nature to excel in ways so different. And accordingly, we do not find in all antiquity any one poet, both of tragedy or epic, and of comedy, or so much as a player that acted both tragedy and comedy. The greatest writer of this kind among us, greater I think than even his master the author of Hudibras, and the greatest of the kind perhaps that ever wrote, is Dean Swift. But, neither do I think that he was a sublime genius. And he very wisely, in my opinion, forbore to attempt either tragedy or heroic. And I should have thought even his ridicule better, if it had been more cleanly, and if he had attended to what Cicero has said of the ridiculous:—Hæc ridentur vel sola, vel maxime, quæ notant et designant turpitudinem aliquam non turpiter; Lib. 2. de Orat. c. 58.

I have only further to observe on this subject, that, as the ridiculous exposes incongruity, absurdity, and deformity, of every kind, it is of necessity satirical, and, therefore, we very properly join together satire and ridicule. There may, however, be satire that is not ridiculous. Such is the satire which has for its object crimes or enormous vices, which ought not to be laughed at. This satire we commonly distinguish from the other by the name of *invective*.

And so much for the ridiculous, which may be called a sixth general character of style.

CHAP. XVII.

Of another general character of style, viz. the witty.—Nature of wit, and the three things which it requires.—Examples of this from the laconic apophthegms—from the sayings of philosophers, and from Cicero.—Wit arises from the ambiguity of words, either single or in composition—from metaphor—simile—antithesis.

THE next character of style I shall mention is the *witty*. *Wit* and *wisdom* were formerly synonymous terms in English; but they now signify things very different; nor indeed is it easy to say what is meant by *wit*, according to the present use of the word. As it is used by some, it seems to be the same with the *ridiculous*; and certainly there is a great affinity betwixt the two. Accordingly, many of the instances of the ridiculous given by Cicero in his 2d book *de Oratore*, may be also said properly to be witty. There is no doubt, therefore, but that the same saying may be both witty and ridiculous; on the other hand, there is as little doubt that a thing said may be witty, and not in the least ridiculous; or, *vice versa*, it may be ridiculous and not witty; so that there must be a difference betwixt the two. Some likewise confound *wit* and *humour;* but the distinction there is more evident. For they are so unlike one another, that if we attempt to join the two together, the humour is commonly lost, as I shall shew when I come to define what humour is. Others again use the word in so vague a sense, applying it to every thing they think pretty or genteel in writing or discourse, that it is hardly possible to say what they mean by it. It is therefore necessary, if we have a mind to speak intelligibly, to try whether we cannot define this quality of style better, I think, than it has hitherto been defined, at least in any thing that I have seen written upon the subject: But it is to be remembered, that I do not pretend to comprehend in my definition every meaning that those who use this word may give to it. But what I propose is to distinguish it from the other general characters of style that I have mentioned, and from the next and last that I shall mention.

Of the sublime I have said, that what is principal in it is the sense or matter, and that the expression is but secondary; but of this character of style, I say that it consists equally of both; for, in the first place, sense, and a sense not very obvious, or near the surface, is absolutely required, otherwise it will not be true wit, nor indeed wit at all; and the deeper the sense is, and the further removed from common apprehension, provided it be not an absolute riddle, the better the wit. But, secondly, it is as necessary that the expression should be uncommon, and even surprising, otherwise it will not, in my apprehension, be wit, however great the sense contained in the words may be. And, lastly, the expression must be short; for wit will not bear to be diffused through many words, but must be pointed, and, as it were, darted upon us, so as to strike us at once; and hence it is commonly said of wit, that it is *piercing*.

These, I think, are the outlines of this various and multiform thing we call *wit*, such as, I think, will comprehend every species of it. But it will be neceſſary to explain it more particularly, and to illuſtrate what I have ſaid by examples.

To be convinced that the beſt ſenſe, without an uncommon turn of the expreſſion, will not make wit, we need only go through the laconic apophthegms collected by Plutarch, or the ſayings of the Greek philoſophers collected by Diogenes Laertius. In theſe there is, no doubt, a great deal of ſenſe; but it is in ſome of them only that there is wit, and theſe are ſuch of them as contain the ſenſe in few words, and with a turn of expreſſion that is uncommon and ſurpriſing. I will give a few examples, which will explain what I mean better than any words I can uſe, beginning with the laconic apophthegms.

Ageſilaus the Spartan king, was not only a great king and commander, but what the French call *un homme à bon mot*; and there are more good ſayings reported of him than

of any other Spartan. Among others, being asked why the city of Sparta was not walled? 'These,' said he, (shewing a body of Spartans armed,) ' are the walls of Spar-
' ta *.' Expressed in this way, it was both sense and wit; for it was an uncommon expression to call men the walls of a city. At the same time, it has that brevity and pungency that wit requires: But, if he had said simply and plainly, that a city was better defended by the valour of its citizens than by walls, it would have been sense and truth, but not wit; and this I think is the case of another answer which he made to the same question, and which is likewise recorded by Plutarch in the same place. ' A town,' says he, ' ought not to be fortified by stone and timber, but by the virtues of its inhabitants.' This, we may observe, has a rhetorical turn, and many such things are to be found in the Greek orators; but I would not call it wit. Again, the same Agesilaus, when he was recalled out of Asia, a considerable part of which he had con-

---

* Plutarch's Morals, edit. Froben. p. 155.

quered, to defend his own country that was attacked by the Athenians and Thebans, who had been bribed by the Perſian money, which had upon it the ſtamp of an *archer*, ſaid, when he left the country, that he was driven out of Aſia by thirty thouſand archers, ſo many pieces of that coin having been ſent to Athens and Thebes *. Now, if he had ſaid plainly, that he was driven out of Aſia by the money of the Perſian king, not by his arms, it would not have been wit, but only plain truth. And what makes the ſaying more ſurpriſing at firſt ſight, and conſequently gives it the greater poignancy, is, that an army, ſuch as his, of heavy armed men, ſhould be overcome by an army of archers.

Agis, another king of Sparta, being aſked ſeveral times by a worthleſs and impertinent fellow, who was the beſt man in Sparta? anſwered at laſt, ' He that is leaſt ' like to you †.' This is wit as well as ſatire; for it was an anſwer which the man who aſked the queſtion certainly did not expect,

---

* Plutarch, p. 155.   † Ibid, p. 169.

and surprises the reader very near as much as it did him. And, since he was urged to answer so impertinent a question, it could not be said to be ill-bred.

Antalcidas the Spartan, the same, as I suppose, that concluded the peace with the Persian king which bore his name, answered to an Athenian that called the Spartans unlearned, 'It is true indeed,' said he, 'we alone 'of all the Greeks have learned nothing ' bad from you *.' This was likewise both wit and satire, and also a great truth; for the Athenians, when they became corrupted themselves, did, by their wit and eloquence, contribute very much to corrupt the rest of Greece.

As to the sayings of the Greek philosophers, collected by Diogenes Laertius, there is more sense in them than is any where to be found in so few words; but there is wit in very few of them, because they want that uncommon turn of expression, which, as has been shown, is essential to wit. Nor

* Plutarch, p. 160.

was it to be expected that men, who were intent upon discovering the nature and truth of things, should study figures and forms of expression for the purpose only of catching the applause of the vulgar. The wittiest of all the philosophers was Aristippus the scholar of Socrates. At the same time, he was the most worthless, and, for that very reason, the wittiest; because the use he made of his philosophy was to flatter and make his court to the great and rich, in order to partake of their good things, in the enjoyment of which he made the happiness of life to consist. Now it is well known how much wit, if discreetly used, will make you a favourite of such men. And indeed flattery, without that seasoning, must soon become nauseous to a man of the least delicacy of taste.

This being the character of Aristippus, we are not to wonder, that, of all the philosophers and men of letters who frequented the court of Dionysius, he was the man who pleased the tyrant the most [*],

---

[*] Diogenes Laert. in vit. Aristippi, initio.

though it appears that, in some of his witty sayings, he used a good deal of freedom with the tyrant himself: As when Dionysius asked him, why philosophers came so much to the gates of the rich, but the rich not to their gates? because, says he, philosophers know what they want, whereas the rich do not *. But those, who, like Aristippus, make their court to the great, know very well that flattery, in order to make it palatable, requires a little zest of that kind.

Of kin to this saying was another in answer to one, who asked him the same question, why the philosophers were always to be seen at the gates of the rich? Physicians, says he, in like manner, are to be seen at the gates of the sick; but it is not, for that reason, better to be the sick man than the physician †.

Having employed an orator to plead a cause for him, and having gained it, the orator, meaning to insult philosophy and Socrates, asked him, with an air of triumph,

* Diogenes Laert. in vit. Aristippi, c. 69.
† Ibid. c. 70.

of what use now was Socrates to you? Of this, answered Aristippus, that what you said of me was true*.

A man wanted that Aristippus should take his son and instruct him, for which Aristippus demanded a price that the other thought extravagant; for, says he, I could buy a slave for that price. Do, says Aristippus, and then you will have two †. Here, I think, is true wit; for there is great sense in the saying, though not obvious to one who does not know that it is only philosophy which makes a man truly free. And, at the same time, the expression is as short and surprising as can well be.

It may be reckoned wit when an argument is cleverly turned against a man. Of this kind was what Aristippus answered to Diogenes, whom he found washing some herbs that he was preparing for his dinner. If, says the Cynic, you could dine upon herbs, you would not make court to tyrants. If you could live and converse with men,

---

* Diogenes Laert. in vit. Aristippi, c. 71.
† Ibid. 72.

replies Ariſtippus, you would not dine upon herbs *.

It is, I think, for the credit of the other Greek philoſophers, that there are but few

* Diogenes Laert. in vit. Ariſtippi, c. 68. Horace, in his epiſtle to Scæva, Lib. i. Epiſt. 17. mentions this ſaying of Ariſtippus;

Si pranderet olus patienter, regibus uti
Nollet Ariſtippus. Si ſciret regibus uti,
Faſtidiret olus, qui me notat.   v. 14.

Horace, it may be obſerved, was a little deſultory in his philoſophy, as he tells us himſelf; for ſometimes he was a rigid Stoic:

Virtutis veræ cuſtos rigiduſque ſatelles;

But he adds,

Nunc in Ariſtippi furtim præcepta relabor,
Et mihi res, non me rebus, ſubmittere conor.
    Lib. i. Ep. 1.

The meaning of which laſt line is, that, whereas the Stoics ſubmitted with reſignation to the lot which Providence had aſſigned them, and only endeavoured to act well the part which was allotted to them in the drama of human life, Ariſtippus, not contented with that lot, endeavoured to make a fortune for himſelf. And hence it is that Horace, in the ſame epiſtle to Scæva, deſcribes him, ' Tentantem majora;' but he adds, ' Fere præſentibus æquum.' And it was no doubt his character, as Laertius informs us, in the beginning of his life, that, though he aimed at the

fayings recorded of them which can be called witty; and I shall only mention one of Arcefilaus, the founder of the Middle Academy, who, being asked, why so many of

highest fortune, he could suit himself to the lowest. Although Horace, in this passage, says, that he only slipt into the precepts of Aristippus, as it were, by stealth, and imperceptibly even to himself; yet it appears to me, that, in the practice of life, he followed much more the philosophy of Aristippus than that of Epicurus, which he professed. For Epicurus, though, like Aristippus, he made happiness consist in bodily pleasure, yet he held that the greatest pleasure of that kind was to be found in temperance and sober living; therefore he lived most frugally and penuriously in his garden, without going near the great and rich; and he boasted, that he could live upon a penny a-day; whereas his friend Metrodorus required two-pence. Aristippus, on the other hand, made his happiness consist in costly and delicate living; and, in this respect, he preferred his life to that of the Cynic, who lived miserably, as he thought, upon the meanest and cheapest things:

—— Rectius hoc, et
Splendidius multo est, equus ut me portet, alat rex.

Now it is evident, not only from what Suetonius tells us in the life of Horace, but from the account which Horace gives of himself, that he did, in this respect, follow the precepts of Aristippus; for he lived very much with Mecænas, and was so often at his table, that Augustus, in a letter of his, which Suetonius has preserved to us, ' In vita Horatii,' calls him the pa-

all other sects went over to the Epicureans, but none ever came from them? answered, That men might be made eunuchs, but eunuchs never could become men*.

Cicero also has furnished us examples of witty sayings, where the wit consisted as much in the turn of expression as in the thought. There was one P. Cornelius, who was a great thief, but very brave, and a good general. He was chosen consul, for

---

rasite of Mecænas. And, indeed, in this epistle to Scæva, he very plainly declares himself a follower of Aristippus, and advises Scæva to follow him likewise. When he came, however, to be in the decline of life, he began to be of another opinion; and I am persuaded that, where he says,

Dulcis inexpertis cultura potentis amici;
Expertus metuit.———

he made the application to himself. And, in an epistle to Mecænas, answering one from him, in which he required that Horace should come to him at the time he had promised, he plainly tells him, that he could not now give him the attendance that he had formerly given him; and that, rather than do it, he would resign every thing he had got from him; Epist. vii. Lib. 1.

* Laert. in vit. Arcesilai, c. 43.

carrying on a very dangerous war, by the intereſt of C. Fabricius, his profeſſed enemy, to whom when he returned thanks for acting ſo diſintereſted a part, 'You owe me 'no thanks,' ſaid he, 'if I choſe rather to be 'robbed than ſold as a ſlave*.' This was wit, becauſe it was ſhort, pungent, and unexpected; and it is not only witty, but it has a good deal of the ridiculous in it, as it expoſed the knavery of the man, and therefore it would naturally raiſe a laugh in thoſe that heard it. Of the ſame kind was what Fabius Maximus ſaid to one Livius Salinator, who had loſt the town of Tarentum, but was of great uſe in aſſiſting Maximus to retake it. Of this ſervice Salinator putting Maximus in mind, and telling him that it was by his means he had taken the town, 'No doubt,' ſays he, 'if you had not 'loſt it, I ſhould not have taken it †.'

In all theſe, and ſuch like inſtances, it is the uncommon turn given to the thought that makes the wit of the ſaying, which

* Cicero de Orat. Lib. ii. c. 66.
† Idem, ibid. c. 67.

otherwife would be nothing but plain fenfe. In many other ways fuch turns might be given to the thought and expreffion; and, if there be fenfe at the fame time, we will call it fmart, clever, and witty. Of this kind there is a great deal in Mr. Fielding's work, which I have quoted more than once, the Hiftory of Tom Jones, in which there is no lefs wit than manners and characters. I fhall not quote inftances, becaufe they are to be found in every page of the work; but I will give one inftance more of this kind of wit from a famous faying of Lewis XI. king of France, who had received an injury from fome perfon before he was king, and while he was only Duke of Orleans, and was advifed to refent it after he became king: 'No,' fays he, 'a king of France ought not to avenge the injuries of the Duke of Orleans.' This was both fenfible and witty; but, if he had only faid, that now, when he was king, he ought not to refent the injuries that he had received when he was only Duke of Orleans, the wit of it would have been intirely loft.

There is one way of giving an uncommon and furprifing turn to the expreffion, and fo making wit, that is very well known. It is by ambiguity or double meaning, and this either of fingle words, or of a compofition of them; I mean a phrafe or fentence. The firft kind is well known by the name of a *pun*, and, when there is fenfe in it, joined with fatire or ridicule, it may be reckoned a fpecies of wit. It was not unknown among the antients, though, I believe, lefs practifed among them than among us. Cicero gives an example of it that happened in a trial where a very little man was produced as a witnefs. As it cannot be rendered into Englifh, I have given the Latin words below *. The other kind is where the ambiguity is not in a fingle word, but in feveral, making a fentence. It is diftinguifhed among us from the other by the name of *a play upon words*. This fort of wit appears to have been more practifed among the antients; and Cicero gives us

---

* Pufillus teftis proceffit. *Licet*, inquit, *rogare*, Philippus? Tum quæfitor properans, *modo breviter*. Hic ille, *non accufabis*; *perpufillum rogabo*. Cic. de Orat. lib. 2. c 60.

several instances of it*. Both the two surprise and please likewise, if there be sense in them; but they are not at all fit for grave composition. Nor does Cicero, though a great joker, and very witty, more, I think, than became a man of consular dignity, and the first senator in Rome†, use them in his orations, or in any of his philosophical works.

---

* One of them is an invitation, which a joker of those days gave to himself to sup with one Sextius, who wanted an eye. ' Cœnabo, inquit, apud te huic ' lusco familiari meob. Sextio, *sui enim locum esse video,*' where the joke turned upon the last words, which might signify, that there was place either for one guest more, or one eye. Another instance he gives is of a saying of one Nero upon a thievish slave: ' Ridiculum est illud ' Neronianum vetus in furace servo. *Solum esse cui domi* ' *nihil sit nec obsignatum nec occlusum* ;' of which the joke was, as Cicero tells us, that the words applied equally to a good or bad slave; *Ibid. c.* 61. This is said by Cicero to be *ridiculous*, and so it is as well as the other, because they allude the one to bodily deformity, and the other to knavery. But he gives an instance afterwards of a double meaning of this sort, which is only witty, but not ridiculous. ' Africano illi majori, coronam sibi ' in convivio ad caput accommodanti, cum ea sæpius ' rumperetur, P. Licinius Varus, *Noli mirari*, inquit, si ' non convenit; *caput enim magnum est*.' He adds, *Hoc* ' *laudabile et honestum*;' Ibid. That is, not ridiculous.

† There was a collection of his jokes and smart sayings made in his own time; and Dr. Middleton, in his

The next kind of wit I shall mention is that which consists in *metaphor*, a figure so much used in this kind of style, that it may be called the figure of wit; and, according to Aristotle, it constitutes chiefly what he called the το αστειον, answering to the Latin word *urbanum* or *urbanitas*, a term which comes nearer to the signification of our word *wit*, than any other that I know in Greek or Latin; but it comprehended, besides *wit*, genteel pleasantry, and likewise politeness, as is evident from many passages of antient authors, and particularly one in Horace, where he mentions, as belonging to the character of *Urbanus*, the greatest of all politeness, that of sinking or lowering yourself in company, in order that you may not offend the vanity of those with whom you converse.

life of Cicero, vol. II. 8vo. p. 294. and 334. has given us several of them. They gave great offence to many, and sometimes, I believe, did much mischief; for it is not unlikely that his pun, when speaking of Octavius, he said, that the young man was *laudandus, ornandus et tollendus*, upon the word *tollendus*, cost him his life, and the republic its liberty. And, it is certain, that while he was in Pompey's camp, before the battle of Pharsalia, his jokes were so severe, and so unseasonable, that Pompey wished him upon the other side; and then, says he, you will begin not to despise us, but to fear us.

Urbani parcentis viribus, atque
Extenuantis sese consulto. ———

It is not, however, every metaphor, as Aristotle has observed *, that makes wit,

---

* Aristotle has bestowed no less than two chapters, viz. the 10th and 11th of his 3d book of rhetoric, upon the τὰ ἀστεῖα, or the τὰ εὐδοκιμοῦντα, another word that he uses, and which, I think, comes likewise very near our word *wit*, because it signifies those sayings which procure a man praise and applause. As he is an author who has defined more and better than any other, it is from him chiefly that I have taken the definition of wit. And, first, he has required that there shall be truth and sense in the witticism, and such as does not lie too near the surface; διὸ δὴ δεῖ φαίνεσθαι τὸ λεγόμενον ἀληθὲς καὶ μὴ ἐπιπόλαιον, c. 11. And again, in c. 10. he says, ἔτι τὰ ἐπιπόλαια τῶν ἐνθυμημάτων εὐτέλεια, (ἐπιπόλαια γὰρ λέγομεν τὰ παντὶ δῆλα, καὶ ἃ μηδὲν δεῖ ζητῆσαι), ὅτι ἴσα ἡ γνώμη εὐκομψα ἐστι, ἀλλ᾽ ὅταν ἡ ἅμα κείμενα ἢ γνώσις γίνηται, καὶ εἰ μὴ πρότερον ὑπάρχει, ἢ μικρὸν ὑστερίζῃ ἡ διάνοια. There cannot, I think, be a better definition than this of what may be called the *matter* of wit, that is, the thought, independent of the expression. For, says he, it must not be upon the surface (that is the meaning of the Greek word ἐπιπόλαιον) so as to be obvious to every body, nor must it lie too deep, so as not to be understood, or, at least, not easily understood; for then it is a riddle; but it must be betwixt these two, so as to be apprehended by the mind, if not immediately, at least upon a very short reflection.

or, as he calls it, the το αστειον; for there is no trope or figure of words more common, being used, as we have seen, not only for ornament, but for necessity. But it must be a metaphor not commonly used, or, at least, not commonly applied to that subject; and it must be strong and lively, setting the thing as it were before our eyes, and at the same time conveying some important meaning; then it will have all the characters of wit above-mentioned, for it will convey sense in the shortest way possible, that is, by a single word, and at the same time in an uncommon way, and such as will both sur-

---

But, that the thought should be such, is not, according to Aristotle, sufficient. There must also be a certain turn of expression. For, says he, διαγων δι και λεξιν και ενθυμηματα ταυτα ειναι αστεια, ὁσα ποιει ἡμιν μαθησιν ταχειαν; Ib. And he particularly mentions the metaphor as one way of giving wit to the expression. But, says he, the metaphor must not be far fetched, or αλλοτρια, as he calls it, for then it is difficult to be understood. Neither must it be too common or obvious; for then it will not strike or surprise us. And, further, it ought to set the thing as it were close before our eyes, προ ομματων ποιειν, by which the expression acquires a kind of life, and what he calls ενεργεια.

prife and pleafe. Of fuch metaphors ufed in his time, Ariftotle gives fome examples *.

A fimile may be called a metaphor extended, as a metaphor is a fimile contracted; it is therefore natural that there fhould be wit likewife in a fimile. But it is not every fimile, any more than every metaphor, that is witty; for it is required that it fhould be fhort. An Homeric fimile, therefore, with a long tail, as Mr. Perault expreffes it, is not wit, but belongs to a

---

* Of this kind is what one Leptines, whom he mentions, faid concerning the deftruction of Lacedæmon, that they ought not to fuffer Greece to become *one-eyed* or *borgne*, as the French exprefs it in one word. ουκ εαν περιιδειν την Ελλαδα ετεροφθαλμον; Ibid. c. 10. meaning, as I fuppofe, that Athens and Lacedæmon were the two eyes of Greece. Another example of this is what Pericles faid of the ifland of Ægina, that it was λημη τω Πειραιως; Ibid. which may be tranflated an eye-fore of the Athenian harbour of the Piræum; a metaphor which, it feems, was not fo common in Greek as in Englifh, otherwife it would not have been quoted by Ariftotle as wit. Of this kind are two metaphors ufed in Englifh, by which we call *old age* the *evening*, and *youth* the *morning of life*. Thefe metaphors were alfo ufed in Greek, as appears from a paffage in Longinus.

style quite different. Secondly, it muſt not be common or obvious, otherwiſe it will not ſurpriſe, which all wit ought to do. And, thirdly, it muſt convey ſome important meaning; for, ſuppoſing it to have the other two requiſites, but to want this, it will be called not wit, but a quaint conceit *.

It is the great uſe which wit makes of metaphor and ſimile, that has induced Mr. Locke to make it conſiſt altogether in the reſemblance of things; but, I think, it is evident, from the examples I have given, that there may be wit, and very true wit, without metaphor, ſimile, or any thing relating to likeneſs or reſemblance; ſo that I doubt Mr. Locke has proceeded upon too narrow views of the ſubject, when he made wit conſiſt in finding out the reſemblances

---

* Neither did this kind of wit by ſimiles eſcape Ariſtotle; for he tells us, that ſimiles are witty for the ſame reaſon that metaphors are; ἐςι δὲ καὶ αἱ εἰκόνες, ὥσπερ, εἴρηται καὶ ἐν τοῖς ἄνω, αἱ εὐδοκιμοῦσαι τρόπον τινὰ μεταφοραί· ἀεὶ γὰρ ἐκ δυοῖν λέγονται ὥσπερ ἡ ἀνάλογον μεταφορά; c. 11. And, in the preceeding chapter, he gives an example of a ſimile of Pericles, in which he compares the deſtroying the youth of a city to the taking the ſpring from the year.

of things, as well as when he made judgment confift in difcovering their differences.

There is alfo another figure belonging to wit, viz. antithefis, which is a common figure, as well as metaphor and fimile; but a witty antithefis muft not be common, for it muft fet in oppofition two things that are not commonly oppofed; and it muft have this quality, belonging to all kinds of wit, of containing fome truth not common or trivial [*].

As wit neceffarily requires that there fhould be fomething uncommon, both in the thought and expreffion, Ariftotle has well obferved, that the wit is moft pungent when the meaning comes out altoge-

---

[*] It is in this *figure* belonging to the compofition, and as oppofed to *tropes*, that Ariftotle makes the wit of expreffion chiefly confift: For, after having explained the matter of wit in the paffage above quoted, he adds, Κατα δε την λεξιν τῳ μεν σχηματι και αντικειμενως λεγεται, Ib. c. 10. Then he proceeds to fpeak of the wit that confifts in the trope of metaphor, της δ' ὀνοματι εν τῃ μεταφορᾳ, &c.

ther different from what was expected in
the beginning; for then it becomes very
striking and surprising, and the mind says
to itself, 'This is the truth of the matter,
'but I was mistaken *.'

Thus I have endeavoured to define this
undefineable thing called *wit*; and I have
made it to be, ' Sense not common, shortly
' conveyed in a way not common,' whether by metaphor, simile, antithesis, words
ambiguous, or in any other way not ordinary, and therefore surprising. By this definition it is sufficiently distinguished from

---

* Ἐστι δὲ καὶ τὰ ἀστεῖα τὰ πλεῖστα διὰ μεταφορᾶς, καὶ ἐκ τᾶ πρὸς ἐξαπάτην, (l. ἐξαπατατᾶι), μᾶλλον γὰρ γίνεται δῆλον, ὅτι ἔμαθε, παρὰ τὸ ἐναντίως ἔχειν—καὶ ἔοικε λέγειν ἡ ψυχή, ὡς ἀληθῶς, ἐγὼ δ' ἡμαρτον; Ib. c. 11. And he gives an instance of a saying that was become proverbial, but was first used by Stesichorus the poet, who, speaking of the calamity that was to befal a people, of having their country laid waste by an enemy, said, that their grasshoppers would sing upon the ground; meaning that all their trees would be cut down. For the Greek word τέττιξ, or the Latin *cicada*, does not denote what we call *grasshopper*, but what the French call *cigale*, an insect which sits upon trees during the summer months in the warm countries, and really sings, or makes a musical noise, which our grasshoppers do not, any more than they sit upon trees.

Book IV. PROGRESS OF LANGUAGE. 339

the ridiculous, though they be not incompatible; and it often happens, in fact, as I have shewn, that they go together; and how it is to be diftinguifhed from humour, will appear in the next chapter.

As to the pleafure which *wit* affords us, Ariftotle, I think, has well accounted for it. He fays, that, if to learn be pleafant, as it certainly is to the rational mind, to learn eafily and quickly muft certainly be very pleafant; and this is the cafe when we learn by one, or a very few words. Now, uncommon metaphor, fhort fimiles, by which we are led to find refemblances in things that we knew nothing of before, teach us in this way, efpecially if there be, at the fame time, antithefis, becaufe every thing is beft illuftrated by its contrary. And if we at firft mifapprehend it, and then are fet right, it is thereby made evident to us, that we learn what we did not know before [*].

---

[*] Ariftotle begins his chapter (Rh. l. 3. c. 10.) upon the ϰοτιϛιϛ, by laying down the foundation that there is for the pleafure of it in nature, ἀρχὴ δ᾽ ἐϛιν ἡμιν αὕτη· τὸ γὰρ μανθανειν ῥαδιως, ἡδὺ πᾶσι φυσει ἐϛι, τα δὲ ὀνοματα σημαινει τι· ὥϛε ὅσα των ὀνοματων ποιει ἡμιν μαθησιν, ἥδιϛα.

I have been the fuller upon the subject of wit, that it is a colour of style which is predominant, more than any other, in the writings of the present age, as well as in our conversation; the reason of which is, that our taste of style is commonly formed

ὡς μὲν ἐν γλώτταις ἄριστ᾽, τὰ δὲ κυρια ἴσμεν, ἡ δὲ μεταφορα ἐστιν τουτο μαλιστα. Then he proceeds to tell us that the similes of the poets have the same effect; for a simile is a metaphor, only lengthened out, but for that reason it pleases less; ἐστι ἡ εικων, καθαπερ εἰρηται προτερον, μεταφορα, διαφερουσα προθεσει, διο ἡττον ἠδυ, ὁτι μακροτερως, και ὁ λογει ως τουτο ἐκεινο. The meaning of which last words, as he has explained it in his Poetics, *cap.* 4. is, that a metaphor is a proposition in a single word, affirming that this is that. Then he goes on to inform us, that the learning must be quick; ἀναγκη δε και λεξιν και ὑπερματα ταυτα εἰναι ἀστεια, ἱνα ποιη ἡμιν μαθησιν ταχειαν. And, in the next chapter, he further tells us that the wit is so much the greater by how much the thing is said in fewer words, and by way of antithesis or opposition; the reason of which is, that by opposition the thing is better learned, and, by few words, more quickly, ὡσῳ ἀν ἐλαττοσι και ἀντικειμενοις λεχθη, τοσωτω ἰνδεχιμι μαλλον, τὸ δ᾽ αιτιον, ὁτι ἡ μαθησις δια το μην ἀντικεισθαι, μαλλον, δια δε το ἐν ὀλιγῳ, θαττον γινεται; an expression so short, and at the same time so clear, and what we would call clever, that, if the subject were capable of wit, it might be said to be witty. It is at least a specimen of Attic brevity, and the genuine didactic style.

upon the study of such authors as Tacitus, Seneca, and the fashionable French writers of the present age, to whom I would advise an author, who affects this style, to add Portius Latro, and the other declaimers, whose clever and witty arguments Seneca the rhetorician has collected. And, however various and undefineable a thing wit is commonly reckoned to be, I am much mistaken if the three characteristical marks I have given of it will not agree to every thing which a man of sense will call wit.

CHAP. XVIII.

The difference betwixt humour and a humourist—One species of humour is the imitation of the humourist—a general definition of it—Use of it in modern comedy—incompatible with wit.

I COME now to speak of the last general character of style I shall mention, and that is, the style of *humour*. Humour, applied to the body, or to the temper of the mind, is very well understood; nor is it, even in the last sense, a word peculiar to the English language; but, applied to style, it is peculiar, and is not to be translated, by one word, into any other language that I know. In this sense, it is a word generally as little understood as the one we have endeavoured to define; I mean *wit*. And by some they are used as synonymous terms, and, by many more, there is no determinate meaning applied to either.

The easiest way, I believe, to come at the true meaning of it, will be to consider what is the meaning of the word *humourist*, which, by its sound, ought to have some connection with it. Now, the meaning of this word is pretty much settled; for I think it is agreed by all, that a humourist is a man of a character singular and odd. Are then an humourist and a man of humour the same? They certainly are not. But suppose that a man, though no humourist himself, has the faculty of imitating, in speaking or in writing, such a character, should we not say that he was a man of humour? And I think every body must agree in giving him that name.

But is he the only man of humour? or is this but one kind of humour? Suppose the person has the faculty of representing other characters, that are not whimsical or odd, is not he likewise a man of humour? If so, then humour must be the talent of imitating characters and manners in general. But, I am afraid that, as the last definition was too narrow, this is too general; for it would take in all poets, even such as, like Homer and Virgil, imitate heroic characters. But nobody ever said that Homer, Virgil, Sophocles, or Euripides had humour.

It appears, therefore, that the imitation of high characters and manners does not make what we call humour. Does humour then consist in the imitation of the characters of men in low or middle life, such as the personages in comedy are? If this were so, then we should say, that there was humour in the comedies of Terence, or in the imitations of characters, such as Lord Townly, Sir Charles Easy, or Young Bevil, in our own comedies. But this, I think, can hardly be said. It is not, therefore, the imitation of all comic characters that constitutes humour. Neither is it the imitation of heroic characters; yet it appears that humour consists in the imitation of certain characters. Of what kind then are the characters which it imitates, besides those we have already mentioned, viz. the odd and whimsical?

And I say it is all other characters that have a mixture of the ridiculous in them. This makes a great affinity betwixt ridicule and humour; but the difference is, that what is only *described* by what we have called the ridiculous style, is *imitated* by humour *.

And here we may see the reason why humour makes us laugh more perhaps than any thing else in speaking or writing. It is because it imitates the ridiculous, which is the strongest and most lively way of setting it before our eyes; for we cannot be so much moved by any description of a ridiculous person, as by having him shewn to us.

Humour, therefore, I define *the imitation of characters ridiculous;* and this definition comprehends the imitation of the character of humourists, because such characters have always a mixture, more or less,

* See the difference explained betwixt *describing* a character and *imitating* it, p. 124.

of the ridiculous. It belongs to a figure of composition, of which I have already treated under the name of the *Ethic*; and I might very properly have explained it when I was upon that subject; but I thought it was better to defer it till I came to speak of wit, with which it is commonly thought to have a great connection.

By far the greatest part of the characters of modern comedy are characters of humour; for, since comedy ceased to be the representation of the manners of common life, the odd and the ridiculous predominate in it; and it is now rather an entertainment for making us laugh, than moral and instructive as it was formerly. Nor are many of our comedies much different from an entertainment which professes nothing else but to make us laugh; I mean *farce*.

But our comedy-writers should take care not to mix wit with their humour, two things, which, though supposed to have a great connection, and by some to be the same, are quite different, and almost incompatible. For all kind of ethic writing, as I obferved before, muft be in the fimple ftyle; and, if it be witty, or anywife figured in the compofition, it will not be underftood to come from the heart, or to be the genuine reprefentation of the character of the fpeaker or writer. And this holds particularly in low characters; for, if the poet introduces them fpeaking wittily, he goes out of the character altogether, and it is evident the wit is his own, not that of the perfon who fpeaks it. An inftance of this I remember in the Beaux Stratagem, where *Scrub* (which is undoubtedly a character of humour), in defcribing his occupation in the family, is made to fay, ' On Friday I go to ' market; on Saturday I draw warrants, ' and on Sunday I draw beer,' where the affectation of wit, by the play upon the word *draw*, deftroys the native fimplicity and humour of the character.

I do not know any work in Englifh, nor indeed any work, in which there is more humour, as well as wit, than in Fielding's Hiftory of Tom Jones. All the characters in it are characters of humour, that is, of the ridiculous kind, except that of Mr. Allworthy, Jones himself, Sophia, and Blifil, who is a complete villain, and, perhaps, two or three more; but he has taken care never to mix his wit with his humour; for all the wit in the piece is from himself, or, at least he does not put it into the mouth of his characters of humour.

CHAP. XIX.

Particular characters of style.—First, the style of conversation—quite different from that of public speaking.—The epistolary style—more concise than that of conversation.—The didactic style—of two kinds. —The different manner of the two didactic poems of Virgil and Lucretius.— The historical style.—It consisted of two parts among the antients—narrative and rhetorical.—Is only narrative among the moderns—but the narrative often too rhetorical and poetical.

HITHERTO I have treated only of general characters of style, applicable to many different subjects; but I am now to consider style as suited to particular subjects and occasions. And I will begin with the first and most necessary use of language, *conversation*, which is either upon the subject of the common affairs of life, or upon matters of art and science. This method of communication was, like every other, at firſt rude and artleſs; but, in proceſs of time, it was formed into a ſtyle.

This ſtyle is very different from almoſt every other kind of compoſition, and particularly from the rhetorical ſtyle, or the ſtyle of public ſpeaking; to which, indeed, it may be ſaid to be the juſt oppoſite, both in reſpect of the tone or pronunciation, and of the whole taſte and manner of the compoſition. And, as very few perſons have ſuch extent of genius as to excell in things altogether unlike or oppoſite, it ſeldom happens that thoſe, who have great talents for public ſpeaking, and practiſe it much, excell likewiſe in the ſtyle of private converſation; but by far the greater part of orators, when they enter a little ſeriouſly into converſation, fall into the tone of an oration. And, on the other hand, thoſe who ſpeak moſt agreeably in private converſation, when they attempt public ſpeaking, take it up in a tone much too low, and which may be called *prattle*, compared with what public ſpeaking ought to be. There have been, however, in our age, and there are some still living, who are exceptious to this rule; but they are few in number.

Negatively, therefore, this style may be defined not to be the style of public speaking. But what is it positively? I say it is a style that, however much laboured it may be, ought to appear altogether unpremeditated: It should, therefore, have no studied ornaments; the words should be common and ordinary, the composition plain and simple. Periods, therefore, should be avoided in this style, as much as they are sought for in an oration; and it should not run out, even into long sentences, with parentheses, or any other figure, which tends to make the composition any wise perplexed or involved. It is not, however, without ornament belonging to it; for it admits of wit of every kind, which indeed is a more proper ornament of conversation than of more grave and serious compositions. But there ought not to be too much even of this ornament, otherwise it ceases to be simple and natural. This is the great fault of the dialogue in Congreve's comedies, which are overlaid with wit; and, in general, it is the fault of moſt of our Engliſh comedies.

But the chief ornament of converſation is what I call the *ethic*, or the expreſſion of characters and manners, whether it be the ſpeaker's own character, or that of any other perſon; and here comes in humour, which every body allows to be one of the moſt pleaſant things in converſation. It is this that makes ſtory-telling agreeable, which, without this ſeaſoning, is commonly very diſagreeable. But, among people of faſhion, the humour ought not to be of the loweſt kind, nor deſcend to downright farce.

Theſe, I think, are the principal characters of this ſtyle; nor do I know that there is any material difference whether the ſubject of converſation be the ordinary occurrences of life, or matters of art and ſcience, except that, in the laſt caſe, there ſhould be more exactneſs and accuracy in the uſe of words. And there is one kind of wit, which is tolerable and even agreeable, if not too frequent, in converfation upon ordinary fubjects, but is not at all proper upon fubjects of learning; I mean any kind of ambiguity or playing upon words. Neither is there much place for humour upon fuch fubjects.

To this ftyle is nearly related the next that I fhall mention, viz. the Epiftolary; nor do I know any difference betwixt them, except that the ftyle of the latter fhould be more concife and compreffed, and more cut into fhort fentences, or commas, as the antient critics call them; for the converfation-ftyle admits of a greater flow, and more loofenefs and prolixity of expreffion. Of this kind is the letter of Lentulus, which I before quoted from Salluft *, and Cicero's, and thofe of other antients written in good tafte. It was this concifenefs and frugality of words, which, I believe, made Ariftotle be reputed fo good a letter-writer †; for that is the diftinguifhing characteriftic of his ftyle. As to the letters of Seneca, and

* Pag. 206.
† Demetrius Phalerius, Par. 219. περι ερμηνειας.

some of Pliny the younger, they ought not to be called letters, as not being written for private use, but for the public; and indeed they are altogether things of show, and are rather epideictic orations, but in a bad taste of composition, than familiar epistles. In this they have been imitated by many moderns, who, not knowing what regular form to give to their loose disjointed thoughts, have thrown them together into a series of letters, in which I observe some of the French writers have taken occasion to shew their breeding and address, by treating their imaginary correspondents with most courtly *politesse*.

The next particular character of style I shall mention is the didactic, or the style of science. This I distinguish into two kinds; the first coincides with the style of which I have already treated, viz. the style of conversation. For it is when science is delivered by way of dialogue, the most antient way undoubtedly of teaching, or of searching and investigating, and I am persuaded the best. It appears to have been the only method practised in the most learned country, that, I believe, ever existed, I mean Egypt, and among the Pythagoreans, the most learned sect of philosophers that ever was in Greece. Socrates, as it is well known, used no other method of instruction *. And in this manner of delivering philosophy, his scholar, Plato, copied him, and so successfully, that his dialogues, so

---

* Every man who has any experience in teaching children (and all vulgar or uninstructed men are more or less children,) must know, with great certainty, that it is the best: When a child hears any thing in a continued discourse, he does not much mind it; but, if the question is asked, his attention is excited, and the answer is infixed in his memory, especially if the teacher can, by proper introductory questions, contrive it so that it is made by himself; for then he seems to be his own teacher, and what he finds out in that way he considers as a discovery of his own, which he very seldom forgets. It is in this way that Plato, in the *Meno*, makes a slave of *Meno*'s solve a problem of geometry, about which many of those who think themselves pretty good geometers might at first blunder, as much as the slave did. And, not only in teaching did the antient Greek philosophers use this method of question and answer, but also in disputation, and in the investigation of any subject. This method was at last reduced into an art, and was called *dialectic*, from the Greek word διαλεγεσθαι, signifying to *converse*; from whence the word διαλογος, and our own word *dialogue*.

far as they keep to the style of conversation, are master-pieces of the kind that never yet have been equalled, though often imitated. This is acknowledged by all the antient critics, and particularly by the Halicarnassian*, who in other respects is not a little severe upon Plato's style. This sort of didactic writing admits of all the ornaments belonging to conversation upon matters of science, and particularly the *ethic*, with which Plato's dialogues abound; and besides, he has given them a fable, with various turns and incidents, and has really made them dramatic pieces, as I shall take occasion to observe, when I come to speak of poetry.

The other kind of didactic style is that by which any art or science is delivered in continued discourse or writing, without question or answer, or introducing any personages to dispute together. This method has been almost universally practised ever since the days of Aristotle, who appears to

---

* Epist. ad Pompeium, c. 2. where he contrasts this plain, and simple, and *unmade* style, as he calls it, with that kind of forced, or *made* style, which he sometimes runs into.

me to have been among the firft, at leaft of the Socratic family, who ufed it. When it is perfect of the kind, it is of all others the moft completely fimple, fo fimple as hardly to deferve the name of ftyle or compofition; nor has it any thing that can entitle it to that appellation, except order and method, and the moft exact propriety of words. For it admits of no tropes or figures, either of fingle words or of compofition, nor of any the leaft fuperfluity of words, not even of words to explain or remove ambiguities: So that the only virtues of this ftyle are brevity and perfpicuity. The moft perfect model of this kind of writing is Euclid's Elements, in which there is not fo much as a metaphorical word to be found from beginning to end; and all mathematical writings fince his time have been of this kind. Ariftotle's works of abftrufe fcience, fuch as he calls his *Efoteric* or *Acroamatic* works, which he never intended for the ufe of the people, are of the fame kind. Thefe are his books of logic, his books of phyfics, entitled *De Phyfica Aufcultatione*, and his books of metaphyfics, in none of which is there, as far as I can recollect, a single metaphor to be found, unless perhaps some so common as to have escaped my observation.

But sciences that do not admit of such strict demonstration, and are of more popular use, will bear more ornament in the delivery, and, I think, are the better for some variety of expression, and for explanation and illustration by metaphors, comparisons, and examples. The sciences I mean are morals, government, criticism, and the popular arts of rhetoric and poetry. And accordingly, Aristotle, in his books upon those subjects, which he intended for the use of the people, does not write in a style so dry and jejune, but, on the contrary, pleasant, agreeable, and as much ornamented as he thought the style of a philosopher ought to be. And Cicero goes so far as to say, speaking, as I think he must be understood, of his popular writings, that his style was incredibly sweet and copious*.

---

* Cic. Topica ad Trebatium, c. 1. where he says a thing which could hardly be believed, if we had not so good authority for it, namely, that Aristotle's writings were not at all known to the rhetoricians,

His works of this kind are his morals to Nicomachus; his books upon government, his three books on rhetoric, and his single book on poetry, mutilated and imperfect as

and but to very few philosophers. He adds, 'Qui-
'bus eo minus ignoscendum est, quod non modo
'rebus iis, quæ ab illo dictæ et inventæ sunt, al-
'lici debuerunt; sed dicendi quoque incredibili qua-
'dam cum copia, tum etiam suavitate.' To those, who are only conversant with Aristotle's works of abstruse philosophy, this account of his style will appear very strange; but, to prove that it is true of his popular writings, I will give but one instance, from his introduction to his Book of Poetry, which is as follows:—Περι ποιητικης αυτης τε και των ειδων αυτης, ηντινα δυναμιν εκαστον εχει, και πως δει συνιστασθαι τας μυθους, ει μελλει καλως εξειν η ποιησις. ετι δε εκ ποσων και ποιων εστι μοριων. ομοιως δε και περι των αλλων οσα της αυτης εστι μεθοδου, λεγωμεν, αρξαμενοι κατα φυσιν, πρωτον απο των πρωτων. This is a period of which the composition may be said to be numerous and flowing. Of the same kind are the introductions to some even of his books of deep philosophy. I have mentioned in the text his books of Metaphysics; and I will add an example of a very good period, with which he begins one of his most abstruse works, and upon a most abstruse subject; I mean his books περι ψυχης. ' Των καλων και τιμιων την ειδησιν υπολαμβανοντες, μαλλον δ' ετερας ετερας η κατ' ακριβειαν, η τω βελτιων τε και θαυμασιωτερων ειναι, δι' αμφοτερα ταυτα την της ψυχης ιστοριαν ευλογως αν εν πρωτοις τιθειημεν.'

it is. And, besides these, there is the introduction to his Metaphysics, which is written in a very agreeable style, and is, I think, a fine piece of composition.

There are two famous didactic poems, both excellent of the kind, but written in styles very different; I mean Lucretius's poem *de rerum Natura*, and Virgil's Georgics. The first has hardly any ornament at all in the didactic part, and

—— Si prius ordine verbum
Posterius facias,——

perfect prose, and mere philosophy, translated from the books of Epicurus and his followers. But, in his introduction, and the beginnings of his books, there is as fine poetry, and language as highly ornamented, as is to be found any where. Virgil, on the other hand, is ornamented throughout, not only in his Exordium, the beginnings of his other books, and his digressions, but likewise in the didactic part, where he delivers the precepts of the art. For proof of this we need go no farther than the first Georgic, in which, after the propofition of the fubject, the invocation, and the fine compliment to Auguftus, he enters upon his fubject, by defcribing the time when the hufbandman fhould begin to plow in the fpring, in the two following beautiful lines:

> Verè novo gelidus canis cum montibus humor
> Liquitur, et zephyro putris fe gleba refolvit.

Then, in the next following, he defcribes the operation of plowing as poetically as it is poffible; for he paints it, and fets it before our eyes:

> Depreffo incipiat jam tum mihi taurus aratro
> Ingemere, et fulco attritus fplendefcere vomer.

Here is not only true poetical defcription, by the circumftances of the thing, but great beauty of numbers, and that peculiar *artifice* of verfification which diftinguifhes Virgil's poetry from every other in Latin.

Lucretius, on the other hand, after a very pompous exordium, in as fweet flowing verfe as ever was written, and after a fine compliment to his patron Memmius, begins his fubject in this manner:

> Principium hinc cujus nobis exordia sumet,
> Nullam rem e nihilo gigni divinitus unquam.
> Quippe ita formido mortales continet omnes,
> Quod multa in terris fieri, cœloque tuentur,
> Quorum operum causas nulla ratione videre
> Possunt; ac fieri divino numine rentur.
> Quas ob res, ubi viderimus nihil posse creari
> De nihilo; tum, quod sequimur, jam rectius inde
> Perspiciemus; et unde queat res quæque creari,
> Et quo quæque modo fiant opera sine divum.
> Nam si de nihilo fierent, ex omnibus rebus
> Omne genus nasci posset; nil semine egeret.

It is needless to quote more passages from the two poets; these are sufficient to shew their different style and manner. The question then is, which of the two is best? And, for my own part, I have no scruple to declare, that I think Lucretius's manner is more correct, and in better taste. For every work, whether in prose or verse, should perform in the best manner that which it promises. Now, both are didactic poems, professing the one to teach Epicurus's philosophy, and the other agriculture; and it is certain, that every art or science is better taught in plain simple language, where nothing is studied but propriety, than in a high figurative style, and pompous artificial verse. And, accordingly, there are many obscurities and ambiguities in Virgil, though he treat of a subject much better known, and less difficult to be understood, than in Lucretius, who, as he tells us himself, had even a language to invent for expressing

———— *Graiorum obscura reperta.*

At the same time, I think, every poem should be ornamented more or less, and that there should be in it both fine language and fine versification. Nor is either of these wanting in Lucretius. But the difference betwixt him and Virgil is, that he uses them where they should be; Virgil throughout, and where they should not be.

I would not, however, have it thought that Virgil did not know,

Descriptas servare vices, operumque colores.

But he complied with the fashion of the times, and made a poem more, I believe, to the taste of Augustus and his court than to his own. For at that time there was beginning in Rome a magnificence, and a kind of luxury of taste, which at last corrupted not only painting, as Pliny tells us *, but all the arts. And I not only praise the correctness of taste of Horace, but his manly firmness and resolution, in daring to write his satires and epistles in a style very suitable, indeed, to the subject, but I am persuaded not agreeable to the taste of Augustus, or of his patron Mecænas. The same complaisance to the taste of the times very probably made Dr. Armstrong, in his admirable poem upon health, imitate Virgil rather than Lucretius. For, had he delivered his precepts for preserving health in the same plain language and artless numbers that Lucretius has used in delivering his doctrines of philosophy, no body would have read him.—And so much for the didactic style.

* Pliny, Nat. Hist. Horace says the same of the theatrical music among the Romans; where, speaking of its antient simplicity, and the refinements that had been made upon it in later times, he says,

> Sic priscæ motumque et luxuriem addidet arti
> Tibicen, traxitque vagus per pulpita vestem.
> Ars Poet. v. 214.

The next style I shall mention is the historical. This style, in antient times, consisted of two parts, the narrative and the rhetorical; I mean the speeches; for as all public business was in those days carried on by speaking, an historian could not have given a full account of public transactions, without inserting speeches into his history, as well as facts and events. And accordingly Thucydides tells us, that the many speeches which he has inserted in his history were all actually spoken, at least in substance*. And besides, supposing the speeches to be feigned, as they must have been, if the author lived at any distance of time from the actions related, it was the properest way of giving an account of the motives of councils and actions, and of disputing any question about what was just or unjust, honourable or dishonourable, useful or the contrary. All this must be done in histories without speeches, by letting the story stand still to make long reflections, which *stick out*, as it were, and make, properly speaking, no part of the work. To these two parts Herodotus has added a

* Lib. I. in proëmio.

third, viz. Dialogue, and, by confequence, the imitation of characters and manners, or, as I call it, the *Ethic*, which makes his hiftory, as the Halicarnaffian obferves *, as beautiful and pleafant to read as any poem. And this is one reafon, befides the ignorance of antient cuftoms and manners, that makes the modern reader, not acquainted with this art of writing hiftory, believe the ftories in Herodotus to be no better than poetical fictions.

Our modern hiftorians, therefore, by leaving out not only dialogue but fpeeches, have eafed themfelves of very near one half of the labour which the antient hiftorians beftowed upon their works. And I believe it is well, both for their reputation and their eafe, that they do fo; for the moft of them, if they had been obliged to make fpeeches (not to mention the dialogue of Herodotus) fuch as thofe of Thucydides, Salluft, Livy, or even Herodotus, though he has not many of them, would, I am afraid, not have added to their reputation. But if they do not fhew their rhetoric in fpeeches, they

* De Thucyd. Judicium, c. 23.

have enough of it, and, I think, more than enough, in their narrative. For the narrative of an hiftorian ought, in my apprehenfion, to be plain and fimple, at leaft not rhetorical, nor adapted to move the paffions, or inflame the imagination by epithets, with which we fee the ftyle of modern hiftory is loaded, or by defcriptions fo particular as to be poetical painting, many of which we fee in fome hiftories that have a great vogue among us. Such a manner of writing hiftory makes an intelligent reader fufpect that it is little better than a novel; and, if he has curiofity enough to look into the original authors and records from which it fhould have been compiled, he will, I believe, in moft cafes, find that this fufpicion is not ill founded; and he will have this further fatisfaction for his trouble, that, by reading but one of the beft of thofe original authors, he will learn more of the facts, and, what is of greater confequence, more of the manners and opinions of the age, than by reading twenty compilements.

I would therefore advife our compilers of hiftory, if they will not ftudy the models of the historic style which the antients have left us, at least to imitate the simplicity of Dean Swift's style in his Gulliver's Travels, and to endeavour to give as much the appearance of credibility to what truth they relate as he has given to his monstrous fictions; not that I would be understood to recommend the style of those travels as a pattern for history, for which it never was intended, being indeed an excellent imitation of the narrative of a sailor, but wanting that gravity, dignity, and ornament which the historical style requires. For the subject being the great affairs of a nation, the style ought to be suitable. The words, therefore, should be well chosen, and the best in common use, and they should be put together with an agreeable composition. For history ought not to be written in short detached sentences, after the manner of Sallust or Tacitus; neither should it be rounded or constricted into periods like those of an oration; but the composition should be looser, and of a more easy and natural flow*.

* This is the description given by Demetrius Phalerius, περὶ ἑρμηνείας, of the historical period, which he places in the middle betwixt the rhetorical and that of dialogue, not being so constricted (συνεστραμμένη) as the one, nor so loose as the other.

These are the rules laid down by antient critics, by which they tell us, the ſtyle of hiſtorical narrative ſhould be framed; for, as to the ſpeeches, they belong to a different kind of compoſition, viz. the rhetorical; and there are no other rules at this day, ſo far as I know, by which we can judge of the ſtyle of hiſtory. If, therefore, we find a hiſtory, of which the ſtyle is loaded with metaphors and epithets, embelliſhed with poetical deſcriptions, the compoſition either too much rounded into periods, or altogether disjointed and unconnected, whatever praiſe or reputation ſuch hiſtories may acquire, we are ſure they are not according to the claſſical ſtandard.

The only two particular characters of ſtyle, that remain to be treated of, are the rhetorical and the poetical; but, for this, the proper time will be when I come to treat of rhetoric and poetry.

CHAP. XX.

General observations—Composition an art as well as language—The Greeks our masters both in that art and the other fine arts, such as sculpture—The Romans likewise our masters, but at second-hand—Only to be imitated in so far as they themselves imitated the Greeks—Praise of the style of Horace—Julius Cæsar—Cicero—Upon the revival of letters, the Greek writers most studied and imitated, particularly in England.

IN the preceding chapters, I have endeavoured to explain all the various immutations of single words, in respect both of sound and sense. I have also shewn the several changes they undergo by composition in both these respects. These I call the materials of which style is made; and, according to the use that is made of these materials, style assumes certain characters, general or particular, which I have also endeavoured to explain. The following chapters will contain some observations, which,

I think, naturally arife from what has gone before.

And the firſt thing to be confidered is, whether I have not made a great deal too much of this art in compoſiticn, as well as of the art of language, and whether there be really any art at all in it? This would have appeared a ſtrange doubt in antient times; but certain geniuſes have ariſen of late among us, who think they ſtand in no need of learning to aſſiſt their natural parts, and who, being confcious that they have never learned either the grammatical art, or that of compoſition, with any degree of accuracy, are willing to believe that there is no art of either; or, if there be arts of both, that, as theſe were formed without art, and have grown up from mere uſe and practice, they may be learned in the fame way. But I hope I have faid enough, in this and the preceding volume, to convince every intelligent reader that there is an art both of language and of ſtyle. That theſe arts, though they muſt at firſt have ariſen, like all other arts liberal and mechanical, from rude experience and obfervation merely, never could have been formed into arts, or practifed to any degree of perfection, except by men of fuperior genius and underftanding; and not even by them, but after a long courfe of time, and a fucceffion of ages of practice and obfervation. That the art being thus formed, and models for the practice exhibited, fuch models may be imitated even by thofe who are ignorant of the art, but not perfectly, nor without great hazard of error; and that thofe only can perform beft, and judge moft truly of the performance of others, who have both learned the rules of the art, and formed their tafte upon the ftudy of the beft models in that art; but that thofe who have done neither muft be wretched performers and very bad critics. If this be true, and I think nobody can doubt of it, whofe vanity is not concerned to maintain the contrary, it behoves all thofe who defire to excel in fpeaking or writing, or even to be good judges of thofe arts, to apply to the beft mafters, and to form their tafte upon the beft models.

The only queſtion then is, who thoſe beſt maſters are, and where the beſt models are to be found? In ſome other arts, ſuch as ſculpture and architecture, that is no queſtion; for the antients there are acknowledged maſters. Nor will any man be allowed to have a finiſhed taſte in thoſe arts, much leſs to be an able performer, if he has not carefully ſtudied the antient remains of them that are preſerved. Now, it is a fact moſt certain, that, both in Athens and Rome, the art of ſpeaking, which, as I have ſaid, is the principal and parent art*, was much more ſtudied than either of the other two. And there was a very good reaſon why it ſhould be more cultivated than any of thoſe *mute arts*, as they were called, becauſe, without eloquence, no man could riſe to any eminence in the ſtate; and even his life and fortune very often depended upon his talent of ſpeaking; ſo that every motive of glory, ambition, and even ſafety, prompted an Athenian or a Roman to apply to the ſtudy of eloquence; whereas a great ſculptor, painter, or architect could expect nothing from excelling in thoſe arts, but

* Page 2.

the reputation of a good artist, and he could fear nothing from not succeeding in them. If, therefore, the antients did not excel in an art which they practised so much, and to the study of which they had such incitements, and with the advantage too of a language so fitted, in every respect, for fine composition, it must have been great want of genius. And if we, on the other hand, with much less practice of the art, and much less incitement to the study of it, and under the disadvantages of a harsh unmusical language, have nevertheless excelled them in eloquence and fine writing, we must have a great superiority of genius; for that we exceed them in industry and application, or that we have greater advantages of education, will hardly, I think, be maintained. Now, that there is such a disparity of genius betwixt us and them, no man of sense will believe. And, if so, the conclusion seems to be, that, as there is an art of style and composition, we must go to the antient masters to learn the rules of it; and we must study and imitate the patterns for the practice of it which they have left behind them.

But, of the antients, who are to be our masters, the Greeks or the Romans? That is asking, in other words, whether we are to chuse for our masters those who were scholars themselves, or their masters? And here the parallel will likewise hold betwixt the two arts above-mentioned, particularly the art of sculpture, and this art of composition. For, though the Romans had statuaries as well as writers, who no doubt likewise formed themselves by imitation of the Greek models, it is allowed by all the connoisseurs, that none of the statues which they have produced can bear a comparison with the Greek; and a judge in that art can immediately distinguish the Greek statue, by a certain symmetry, elegance, and grace, which do not belong to the Roman.

But, of the Greek masters, whom are we to prefer, the more antient, or the later writers? This question Horace has determined; for he has told us[*], that the most

---

[*] Quia Graiorum sunt antiquissima quaeque
  Scripta vel optima.
  Lib. 2. Epist. 1. v. 28.

antient are the best. And this is undoubtedly true with respect to poetry, of which he is speaking; for Homer is certainly the best, as well as the oldest poet. And, tho' all the later poets have imitated him, none have equalled, much less exceeded him. By this I would not be understood to mean, nor was it, I am persuaded, Horace's meaning, that there were no poets in Greece before Homer (for that, I think, by the nature of things, was impossible); but that there were none before him whose poems were thought worth preserving. And it is in the same sense that Herodotus is the oldest, and, in my opinion, the best, of the Greek historians. Demosthenes, however, we must admit, is an exception from this rule; the reason of which is, that there was in his time a greater scope, and finer field for eloquence, than ever there had been at any time before in Greece. For it is only great occasions that call forth and produce great men in every art. And it was for the same reason that, in Rome, before the age of Cicero, there was no orator so great as he. But, if Demosthenes be not the oldest, he is the latest great orator of Greece; and, as I have observed elsewhere, all good writing after his

time was no more than imitation*. For
then the standard of beauty in eloquence,
and every kind of composition, was fixed,
as well as in the other fine arts. And here
likewise the comparison will hold betwixt

* After Demosthenes, or after the death of Alexander the Great, whom Demosthenes survived but
a short time, eloquence, as the Halicarnassian tells
us, *de Oratoribus antiquis, in initio,* began to decline;
and Cicero says the same thing, in his book *de Clar.
Oratoribus,* c. 9. where he tells us, that, after Demosthenes, Hyperides, Æschines, Lycurgus, Dinarchus,
and Demades, who all lived much about the same
time, a bad taste of speaking began to be introduced; and he names the man who first corrupted
what he calls ' Succus ille et sanguis incorruptus
' eloquentiæ, in qua naturalis inesset, non fucatus
' nitor.' This was Demetrius Phalereus, the scholar of the philosopher Theophrastus, who had been
trained up, not in the Forum, or in real business, but
philosophical disputations. ' Hic primus inflexit
' orationem,' says our author, ' et eam mollem tene-
' ramque reddidit; et suavis, sicut fuit, videri ma-
' luit, quàm gravis; sed suavitate eâ, quâ perfunde-
' ret animos, non quâ perfringeret; et tantum ut
' memoriam concinnitatis suæ, non (quemadmodum
' de Pericle scripsit Eupolis,) cum delectatione aculeos
' etiam relinqueret in animis eorum, a quibus esset

statuary and the writing art. For those statues that we now admire as the models of perfection, are in all probability no more

' auditus.' This corruption of eloquence, thus begun, went on so fast, that, as the Halicarnassian informs us, *dicto loco*, about his time a good taste in speaking was almost wholly extinguished; and, in place of the true Attic, and philosophical eloquence, as he calls it, a barbarous kind of it succeeded from Asia, Phrygia, or Caria — loud and impudent, without philosophy, or the assistance of any good learning. And in this way things continued till, by the patronage of some great men in Rome, a better taste began to revive. And how was this better taste restored? It was by the imitation of the great orators above-mentioned; and, in general, of all the great writers of antient Greece. This is evident from the writings of the Halicarnassian, who was himself one of the great restorers of this better taste, under the protection of some of these great men at Rome, with whom, it appears, he was connected. He wrote three books upon the subject of imitation, which are now lost; but they are mentioned in his letter to Pompey, c. 3. And, from the whole tenor of his critical writings, it is evident, he thought that a good style could no otherwise be formed than by the imitation of the great writers in the flourishing days of Greece. And, accordingly, he himself has in that way formed a style, which is, in my opinion, as I have elsewhere observed, the best that has been written since fine speaking and writing ceased to be living arts.

than copies of more antient statues, the work of artists who lived at or before the time of Demosthenes. This, at least, we are sure was the case of the Venus de Me-

It may be observed, from the letter above-mentioned to Pompey, c. 2. that he not only wrote to Pompey, but that Pompey corresponded with him upon subjects of literature. He has given us two quotations from a letter of Pompey's to him, which shew, both the great regard that Pompey had to his judgment, in matter of style and composition, and how good a judge he himself was in that matter, as well as a very elegant writer, even in Greek, in which language, it appears, he corresponded with the Halicarnassian. I take notice of this the rather, because, I think, justice has not been done to this great man's character, with regard to his learning and taste. And, as this is the only monument of the kind, as far as I know, remaining of this great man, the learned reader will not be displeased to read it here. The subject of Pompey's letter is the defence of Plato against the Halicarnassian's censure of his high style. The first quotation is in these words:—' Ει μεν γαρ τους ιερους σχημασι εφιλω αυτω μεσον τι πεποιηκοι και μιμησεως· ιν δη τη κατασκευη, το μη πεπτωκηι, παντη αποτυγχανται. διο μοι δοκει τουτοι τας αρχας με εκ των επικαινοτατων, ωδι ελασσονων, αλλ' εκ των πλειστων και ευτυχθυτων εξεταζειν.' The second quotation is as follows:—' Εγω δι, πεπιτερ εχων απολογεισθαι υπερ απαντων η των γε πλειστων, ου τολμω σοι παντα λεγειν· εν δι τουτο δυσχεριζομαι, οτι με εστι μεγαλοι πεπτυχων = ωδη τρεπη, μη τοιαυτα

dicis, which was no more than a copy of the statue of that goddess in her temple in Cnidus, made by one Diomedes an Athenian, as the inscription upon the pedestal of the statue at Florence bears. The original was the work of Praxitiles; and, as it is described by Lucian in his Imagines, cap. 6. and his Amores, cap. 13. it had a beauty which the copier has not endeavoured to imitate, nor, so far as I know, any later Greek statuary. The beauty I mean is the imitation of the eyes, which were represented as moist, and expressing something chearful and gracious. The head, I know, of the Medicean statue is thought by some connoisseurs not to be antient, but a modern addition, such as we know has been made to many antient statues. But, suppose this to be the case, I am

---

τελμνιτα και παραβαλλωσιν, ω ἧς και σφαλλισθαι μη ἀναγκαιον.' This is said by the Halicarnassian to be επιστολη ιπεσιδ.ντ.ς, and, I think, without the least flattery; for it is admirable, both for the matter and the style, being a most sensible piece of criticism, and in as good words, and as elegant composition, as the Halicarnassian himself could have used.

perſuaded the original head made by Diomedes had no ſuch expreſſion; and indeed we have hardly a conception how any ſuch can be given to marble.

But, though I thus prefer the Greek writers of every kind to the Roman, I would not have it believed that I think meanly of the latter, ſome of whom were excellent imitators, and thoſe that imitated moſt wrote beſt. Of this number is Horace, who certainly took to himſelf the advice he gives to the *Piſones*.

>   ——— Vos exemplaria Græca
>   Nocturna verſate manu, verſate diurna.

And he profeſſes his admiration of the Greek genius and eloquence in the following paſſage, where he contraſts the manners of the Greeks with thoſe of his own countrymen, and in that way accounts why they neither did nor could rival them in the fine arts.

>   Graiis ingenium, Graiis dedit ore rotundo
>   Muſa loqui, præter laudem, nullius avaris.
>   Romani pueri longis rationibus aſſem

> Difcunt in partes centum didocere. Dicat
> Filius Albini, fi de quincunce remota eft
> Uncia, quid fuperet? Poteras dixiffe, Triens! Eu!
> Rem poteris fervare tuam. Redit uncia: quid fit?
> Semis. An hæc animos ærugo et cura peculi
> Cùm femel imbuerit, fperamus carmina fingi
> Poffe linenda cedro, et levi fervanda cupreffo!
> Ars Poet. v. 323.

How far this account which Horace gives of the genius and character of the Romans in his time is applicable to our times, and whether the *cura et ærugo peculi* be not as great an enemy to fine writing, and all the fine arts, among us, as among them, I am not at prefent to inquire. But it belongs to our fubject to obferve, that Horace, in confequence of this admiration and imitation of the Greek mafters, is, in my opinion, the moft perfect of all the Roman writers in every kind of writing that he has attempted. For the fchools of declamation were beginning, about this time in Rome, to infect the ftyle of all kinds of writing; and I have ventured to affirm, that even Virgil has not entirely efcaped the infection[*].

---

[*] See what I have before faid upon this fubject, p. 260. et feq.

These schools, in the succeeding age, intirely corrupted the taste, and produced a Seneca, a Tacitus, and a Pliny the younger*.

Another great writer among the Romans was Julius Cæsar; great in letters and eloquence, as well as in arms. He spoke with the same spirit, says Quinctilian, with which he fought; and, if any of his orations had come down to us, I believe we should have admired those of Cicero less. Thus much, at least, is certain, that his Commentaries, the only work of his that remains, are most perfect of the kind: They are no more than memoirs, which, as we are told, he intended only as materials for history, not having time to give them the ornament and dress which history requires. But, in the opinion, not only of his friend Hirtius, but of Cicero, who had certainly no partiality for him, they were so elegantly and so well written in every respect, as to discourage even the ablest writers from attempting to give more orna-

* See what I have further said upon this subject in the passage above quoted.

ment to the subject*. Indeed, it is surprising with what a perspicuous brevity, very different from the obscure and affected brevity of Tacitus, and with what perfect simplicity of style, he has recorded the greatest military operations that are any where to be found in the history of mankind †.

But the greatest prose-writer among the Romans, both for the value and number of

---

* ' Hirtius, in præfatione ad librum octavum de
' bello Gallico. Cicero, de claris oratoribus, cap. 75.'
Hirtius says, that he more than others must admire those commentaries, because others only know how correctly and well they are written, but he knew how easily and quickly.

† It is, I think, entertaining to read the descriptions of our modern battles (which, with all their noise and smoke, compared with those of Julius, are little better than the battles of cranes and pigmies, or of frogs and mice); and to read at the same time Cæsar's account of his battles, which were truly heroic, battles, like those that Homer describes.

―――― ὅτι δή ῥ᾿ ἐς χῶρον ἕνα ξυνιόντες ἵκοντο,
Σύν ῥ᾿ ἔβαλον ῥινούς, σὺν δ᾿ ἔγχεα, καὶ μένε᾿ ἀνδρῶν
Χαλκεοθωρήκων· ἀτὰρ ἀσπίδες ὀμφαλόεσσαι
Ἔπληντ᾿ ἀλλήλῃσι, πολὺς δ᾿ ὀρυμαγδὸς ὀρώρει.

Iliad iv. L. 456.

his works, is Cicero. In his critical and philofophical works, the ftyle is moft beautiful; and his letters are perfect models of epiftolary writing. As to his orations, I have prefumed to criticife pretty feverely the ftyle of them, in which I have done no more than follow the judgment of the beft critics of the time in which he lived, and fome of them too his own particular friends, fuch as Brutus, who defiderated in him the *Succus et fanguis incorruptus*, to ufe Cicero's own words, of the Attic eloquence;

> Such was his firft battle with the Helvedi, where he fent away his own horfe, and the horfes of all his officers, that the danger might be equal to them all, which he judged to be fo great, that he would not venture in any of his three lines of battle two new-levied legions, but pofted them with the auxiliaries upon the top of the hill, quite out of the reach of the enemy. The battle, he fays, continued from morning to night, during all which time *no man faw the back of an enemy*. A mere modern reader would think this very flat, and expect that a great deal more would have been faid of fo obftinate a battle, that had lafted fo long. And indeed if we could fuppofe, in modern times, bodies and fpirits of men, arms and difcipline fit for fuch a conflict, what exaggeration would there not be in the defcription of it! How would the ftyle be loaded with epithets, fuch as heroic valour—unparalleled courage—irrefiftible fury, &c. &c.

and there is certainly something too florid, and what may be called bloated, in the style of his orations, when compared with that of Demosthenes, Lysias, or any other of the great orators of Athens. But, such as they are, they are very much better than the best after his time. To be convinced of this, we need only compare his encomium upon Julius Cæsar, pronounced in the senate upon occasion of that conqueror pardoning Marcus Marcellus, with Pliny's panegyric upon the Emperor Trajan, the most perfect thing of the rhetorical kind in later times. In the one we find a copious flowing eloquence, which fills the mind no less than the ears; and, in the other, but a scanty sense, frittered into little terse sentences, acute enough, but without gravity or weight. It must, however, be acknowledged, that he would have done better, if he had stuck closer to his Greek masters, and continued, as he began, to translate from Demosthenes, instead of practising so much on fictitious subjects in the schools of declamation. This, indeed, gave him a copiousness in speaking; but, at the same time, a redundancy and diffluence, to use a metaphor of his own, which pleased the people more than it did good judges *.

To conclude this criticism upon the Roman authors, as far as they imitated the Greeks, so far, and no farther, they succeeded. Sallust was the first, as I have already observed, who ventured to neglect that standard, and to strike out a new style of history

---

* That such was Cicero's style in his younger days before he went to Rhodes, is confessed by Cicero himself; for, speaking of his Greek master at Rhodes, Molo, he says, ‘ Is dedit operam, si modo id consequi ‘ potuit, ut nimis redundantes nos, et superfluentes ‘ juvenili quâdam dicendi impunitate et licentiâ, re- ‘ primeret, et quasi extra ripas diffluentes coërceret.’ Here the reader will observe, that he very modestly says, *si modo id consequi potuit*. Now the severe critics in Rome thought that he had not accomplished it, nor is it likely that, in so short a time as he was at Rhodes, he would be able to alter, altogether, a manner already formed; but by the people he was exceedingly admired, and, perhaps, more admired than if he had been more chaste and correct; for it was the people of Rome that admired him, not the people that admired Demosthenes. And to them we may apply the French proverb, ‘ Aux gens de village trompettes de bois.'

peculiar to himself. Tacitus endeavoured to improve upon the pattern he had set, but made it much worse, because still farther removed from the Greek standard; and so things went on from bad to worse, till at last the taste of writing, as well as of every other art, became quite barbarous.

Upon the revival of letters, the first scholars in Europe, and particularly in England, formed their style, as the best Roman authors did, upon the model of the Greek writers; for they did not imitate those who were no more than imitators themselves, but went to the fountain-head, without following the rivulets which the Latins had from thence derived. Among the first of these scholars was Chancellor More, whose judgment, preferring the Greek to the Roman writers, I have elsewhere quoted; and there can be no doubt that it was not his opinion singly, but that of all the learned of his age. Milton's style may be said to be as much Greek as it is possible to make English; and even his Latin style appears to me to have been formed, not from the

imitation of any Roman writer, but by the standard of the Greek, as the Romans themselves wrote. Roger Ascham, who lived a generation before, and was an excellent Greek and Latin scholar, has no doubt in this matter; and I will here transcribe what he says upon the subject. After having enumerated all the great authors that the single city of Athens had produced in philosophy, eloquence, history, and poetry, he adds, ' Now let Italian, and Latin itself,
' Spanish, French, Dutch, and English,
' bring forth their learning, and recite their
' authors, Cicero only excepted, and one or
' two more in Latin, they be all patched up
' clouts and rags, in comparison of fair
' woven broad cloths; and truly, if there
' be any good in them, it is either learned,
' borrowed, or stolen, from some of those
' worthy wits of Athens [*].'

[*] P. 235. of Ascham's English works, published at London 1771. This Roger Ascham was preceptor to Queen Elizabeth, and taught her Greek and Latin. He relates, p. 272. that for a year or two she employed herself constantly every forenoon in *double translating*, as he calls it, of Demosthenes and Isocrates, and of

The Greek writers, therefore, muſt be acknowledged to be the ſtandards for good writing, as much as their ſtatues are for good ſtatuary or painting. If, however, the young ſtudent will not give himſelf the trouble neceſſary to attain ſuch a knowledge of th

ſome part of Tully in the afternoon; by which he means, firſt tranſlating from the Greek or Latin into Engliſh, and then from the Engliſh back again into Greek or Latin; by which means, he ſays, that ſhe attained to ſuch a perfect knowledge of both languages, that there were few in both the univerſities, or elſewhere in England, to be, in that reſpect, compared with her. And, in another place, p. 222. he relates, that when he went to take leave of Lady Jane Gray, before his journey to Germany, he found her in her chamber reading the Phædo of Plato in Greek, ' and
' with as much delight as ſome gentlemen would read a
' merry tale in Boccace, while her parents, the duke
' and the ducheſs, with all their houſhold, gentlemen
' and gentlewomen, were hunting in the park.' And of this lady he ſays further, in a letter to a friend of his, one Sturmius a German, ' Hâc ſuperiore æſtate,
' cum amicos meos in agro Eboracenſi viſerem, et
' inde literis Johannis Checi in aulam, ut huc profi-
' ciſcerem accitus ſum, in via deflexi Leiceſtriam,
' ubi Jana Graja cum patre habitaret. Statim ad-
' miſſus ſum in cubiculum: inveni nobilem puel-
' lam, Dii boni! legentem Græcè Phædonem,
' quem ſic intelligit, ut mihi ipſi ſummam admira-
' tionem injiceret. Sic loquitur et ſcribit Græcè,
' ut vera referenti vix fides adhiberi poſſit. Nacta

Greek, as to enable him to read with ease and delight the Greek authors, there are Latin, such as those I have mentioned above, that are not unworthy of imitation; particularly, I recommend Cicero, as the

'est præceptorem Joannem Elinarum, utriusque linguæ 'valde peritum; propter humanitatem, prudentiam, 'usum, rectam religionem, et alia multa rectissimæ 'amicitiæ vincula, mihi conjunctissimum.' The young King Edward VI. who had Sir John Cheke for his preceptor, was also very learned, and, as Ascham says, p. 241. ' Had he lived a little longer, his 'only example had bred such a race of worthy learn-'ed gentlemen as this realm never did yet afford.' And, in the same passage, he mentions ' two noble 'primroses of nobility, the young Duke of Suffolk and 'Lord Henry Matravers, who were such two examples 'to the court for learning as our time may rather wish 'than look for again.'

If, therefore, the antient learning be, as I suppose, the only true learning, that age was certainly a more learned age than this. It does not belong to my subject, as I have said, to compare it in other respects with the present; but thus much I hope I may say without offence, that, if our kings and queens were educated as Edward VI. and Queen Elizabeth were, and if our people of fashion employed their leisure-hours, as Lady Jane Gray did, and the other persons of distinction mentioned by Ascham, neither our public nor private affairs would go the worse for it.

most copious and elegant, if not the most correct of them all. His works I would advise such a student to study day and night, as Horace advised the Pisones to study the Greek masters. And I know no better introduction to the reading of Cicero than his life, written by Dr. Middleton, who has shewn an excellent example, both of translating and imitating.

CHAP. XXI.

The necessity of forming a style by imitation— The Greek authors the best models for imitation—Next to them the Latin—Who next to the Greek and Latin?—Not the writings of the French Beaux Esprits *of this age—Examination of those French writers, both as to their matter and style— The imitation of our own authors, who have formed themselves upon the antient models, is best, next to the imitation of the Greek and Latin.*

IT may seem strange, but it is not more strange than true, that every author, however original he may think himself, or be thought by others, in point of style and composition, is no better than an imitator. The case truly is, that either there is some author whom we admire, and propose to ourselves as a model, which I believe generally happens, or we take insensibly, and without knowing it, after the style and manner of those with whom we converse, or of the books which we read; and the utmost that invention has ever done in this matter, is either to improve or heighten one style that has been formerly used, or to mix different styles together, and temper the one with the other. It is therefore of the utmost importance to every man who would form a good style, to be very careful in the choice of the authors whom he reads, or whose style he would chuse to imitate. And we have seen an example of an author who certainly had genius (I mean Tacitus), and would have written well, if, instead of imitating Sallust and the schools of declamation, he had chosen for his model some of the great authors of Greece. It was in this way, as I have elsewhere observed, that Dionysius the Halicarnassian formed so excellent a style; and, by the same means, in later times than those of Tacitus, Lucian wrote in a manner of which Athens needed not to have been ashamed, when in the height of its glory for arts and learning.

Since, therefore, we muſt of neceſſity imitate, the only queſtion is, whom ſhall we imitate? And, according to my judgment, the Greeks ought to be our maſters in the writing art, no leſs than in ſculpture and painting. Next to them are their imitators, the Latin writers. But, ſuppoſe a man underſtands neither Greek nor Latin, and yet will write, who then ſhall be his model? Shall it be the Italian authors, the French, or ſome of our own? For as to the Swediſh and German authors, I believe nobody will propoſe them as patterns of ſtyle.

As to the Italians, there was a time in England when the authors of that nation were very much in faſhion. And it appears evidently, that even the great Milton has ſtudied and imitated them a good deal. And, indeed, if we are to forſake the antient models, I do not know that we can chuſe better. For, not only ſome of the old Italian authors are excellent writers, but it appears to me, from ſome things which I have ſeen lately come from that country, that the taſte of good writing is ſtill preſerved there, as well as of ſculpture and painting. But thoſe authors, however excellent, are so much out of fashion at present, that, I believe, no man in Britain imitates them as standards of good writing.

The question, therefore, lies altogether betwixt French and English authors. And, as many now-a-days think the French writers better standards than even the Greek and Latin, and some of our most fashionable authors have imitated them, even so far as to adopt the idioms of their language, it is, I think, worth the while to examine their pretensions, and inquire, at some length, whether we ought, for them, to give up the antient authors, or even our own.

And, in the entry of this inquiry, it is proper to observe, that it is not of the French writers of the last age that I speak, nor of all of this. I think I know myself some writers at present in France, who are men of sense and modesty as well as of science, and who write sensibly and soberly. We must admit, that, in this age, natural knowledge and the discovery of this our earth owes a great deal to the labours of the learned of France; and, in former ages, it cannot be denied, that they contributed very much to the restoration of learning, and particularly of Greek learning. But the writers I speak of are late writers, distinguished in their own country by the name of *Beaux Esprits*, from the *sçavans* or learned of the nation. These gentlemen know little or nothing of the antient learning, nor indeed of any good learning of any kind, but set up for writers upon the stock of their own wit and genius merely, not knowing that the greatest natural genius, if it be not furnished with materials by the study of books, or the practice of business, and the knowledge of mankind thence arising, cannot produce any thing of value; and further, that it is not sufficient for an artist of any kind to have both genius, and materials for that genius to work upon, if he be not likewise instructed in the rules of the art, and have formed his taste by the study and imitation of the best models. These are the writers who, by the *brilliancy* of their style, as it is called, that is, in plain English, by a florid, and sometimes pert and flippant manner of expreſſion, have debauched the taſte of many of our writers, and made them reject the grave, ſober, and ſenſible ſtyle of the great antient maſters.

And, firſt, let us conſider the ſubject of theſe writings:—If it be of a philoſophical kind, it is either a ſyſtem of nature, without that which is principal in nature, I mean, *mind*; for our atheiſtical writers muſt not pretend to be originals in their ſubject, any more than in their ſtyle, but are copies of the French in both. And the French have this eminence above them, that the lively impiety of ſome of them has done much more miſchief than the dull dogmatical infidelity of our irreligious writers. And, indeed, theſe French authors have the honour, if it may be called ſuch, to have propagated, almoſt all over Europe, the diſbelief of all religion, natural as well as revealed, and, by conſequence, a general corruption of manners.—Or it is hiſtory without facts, or, at leaſt, without authorities for facts. For it is part of the ſtate aſſumed by theſe authors, that they will not deign to quote; but we muſt take every thing upon their word, even facts collected from authors, whom it is well known they do not understand; and very often they take upon them to contradict facts related by authors, both antient and modern, upon the credit of their miserable narrow systems of philosophy;—Or, lastly, it is some random incoherent thoughts thrown out upon the subject of morals or politics, without any real knowledge of human nature, and the various steps of its progression *. Such is the matter of those writings, and the style is suitable to the matter, without dignity or gravity, trifling, florid, and flashy; for it is not to be expected that such writers should have sense enough to be above *wit*, *point*, and *turn*. They write a kind of epigrammatic style, consisting all of short, smart sentences, without beauty or variety

---

* I am really diverted with the vanity and futility of these *petits maitres* writers upon the subject of men and manners. They seem to take it for granted, that the French nation is, or, at least, was, in the age of Lewis XIV. the standard of the perfection of human nature. And there is another postulatum, which they desire the reader should grant, viz. that they themselves are the first of their nation, or, at least, have a large share of this national perfection.

of compofition, and as little connection in the language as there is in the matter.

Such are the writers who have *given the tone*, to ufe an expreffion of their own, to Europe; and the queftion is, whether, for the fake of imitating them, we fhall give up the antients, and our own authors, who have fo fuccefsfully imitated the antients? If we are to forfake the antient models in other arts, as, for example, in ftatuary and painting, and make the French our models in thefe, as well as in the writing art, every connoiffeur would be fcandalized, and exclaim againft the degeneracy of our tafte; he would complain that we no longer relifhed the chafte beauties of an Italian hand, but were pleafed with the gay, florid, coxcomb manner of the French*. The fame,

---

* I have been told a ftory of a French painter, in the King of France's academy of painting at Rome, who was copying Raphael's battle of Conftantine and Maxentius, where there is a remarkable horfe. An Italian, looking over his fhoulder, obferved that the horfe he painted was not the horfe of Raphael: 'Ah, dit il, Monfieur, il faut animer la froideur de 'Raphael,' So he made a kind of coxcomb French horfe.

I am perfuaded, will be the judgment, with refpect to the writing art, of every man who has ftudied the antient authors; at leaft, I have never known any who thoroughly underftood thofe authors, and yet preferred the ftyle and compofition of the French.

I have only further to add, upon the fubject of the French learning, that, if it continue to prevail as much in Europe for the next half century as it has done for the laft, there will be an end of antient learning, of which we fhall know no more than thofe miferable disfigured fcraps of it that are to be found in French books.

But, fuppofing a man will write without the affiftance of antient learning, and yet not imitate the French, what is he to do? I will give him the fame advice that I would give to a man who would paint or practife fculpture without going to Italy, and ftudying the antient monuments of thofe arts that are to be feen there, which would be to ftudy the works of fuch painters or ftatuaries among us, as have formed their taste upon the master-pieces of art to be seen in Italy. In the same manner, I would advise a mere modern author to try to acquire a good taste of style by studying some of the best English authors, such as Milton, Clarendon, Hooker, Dr. Sprat, Bishop Wilkins, who have so successfully copied the Greek or Latin masters. When those authors wrote, there were no French writers that were thought worthy of being imitated. Tacitus was not then come into fashion; and the short, priggish cut of style, so much in use now, would not at that time have been endured. In short, no other models of style were acknowledged but the great authors of antiquity, and chiefly the Greek. The consequence of which was, that, though there were some better, some worse writers, according to the different geniuses of men, there were none in those days that wrote in a bad taste. It is, I think, much more for the honour of the nation that we should imitate those authors rather than the French; and I am sure that, by doing so, we shall form a much better style.

CHAP. XXII.

Composition not so difficult in English as in Greek and Latin—This arises from the want of rhythm and melody in our language, and the variety of structure of the antient languages—What is proper and suitable, essential in writing as well as in other arts—Art should not appear too much in composition—The practice of making different styles of the same words useful—Translation, and the use to be made of it.

FINE speaking or writing in any language, is, no doubt, a matter of great labour and difficulty. But it should be an encouragement to a British orator or writer, that it is not near so difficult in English as in Greek or Latin; the reason of which is, that it never can be so fine, let us labour it as much as we please. Now, according to the Greek proverb, 'Fine things are difficult*,' and the finer the thing the greater the difficulty.

* χαλεπα τα καλα.

A great part of the labour of antient compoſition was beſtowed upon the pleaſure of the ear. For they were not only at the greateſt pains to avoid all harſhneſs of pronunciation, and diſagreeable colliſion of ſounds, but they ſtudied ſo much the numbers even of their proſe, and what they called the melody of their language, I mean their accents, that their compoſitions may be really ſaid, without figure or exaggeration, to have been ſet to muſic; and yet, ſo greedy were their ears, as Cicero has expreſſed it, and ſo difficult to be ſatisfied, that even Demoſthenes, as he ſays, did not always fill his*. This muſical part we have nothing to do with; and, if we ſhould attempt any thing of that kind in our language, we run the hazard of making our compoſition much worſe. For, even among them,

---

* Speaking of eloquence, he ſays, ' In quo tantum abeſt ut noſtra miremur, ut uſque eo difficiles ac moroſi ſimus, ot nobis non ſatisfaciat ipſe Demoſthenes; qui quanquam unus eminet inter omnes in omni genere dicendi, tamen non ſemper implet aores meas: Ita ſunt avidæ et capaces, et ſemper aliquid immenſum infinitumque deſiderant;' Orat. ad M. Brutum, c 29.

as Cicero has obſerved, *nimium quod eſt, offendit vehementius, quàm id quod videtur parum*; *Orator. c.* 53. Then they muſt alſo have beſtowed a labour upon the various ſtructure and arrangement of their words, ſuch as our modern languages will not admit of. In ſhort, it appears that all we can do in the matter of ſtyle is to chuſe proper words, give them the figures of compoſition ſuitable to the ſubject, and vary thoſe figures as much as we can, ſo as to avoid a monotony of compoſition. But, in all this there is one thing that muſt be particularly attended to, as without it all our other pains to make our compoſitions agreeable would be loſt, and that is, the το πρεπον, as the Greek critics call it, or the *decorum*. This predominates, as the Halicarnaſſian ſhews, in all the arts, and ſets bounds to the artiſts, beyond which they muſt not paſs. And yet it is what no critic, as far as I know, antient or modern, has attempted to define; nor indeed does it appear to me poſſible to define it, as it is dependent upon ſo many circumſtances; but every body of taſte and judgment immediately feels the want of it. And, however well a thing may be said, or if it be too well said, that is, if too much labour be bestowed, and more ornament upon the composition than is suited to the subject or occasion, it will rather offend than please a good judge.

And this leads me to another observation, that, if in any art it be necessary to conceal art, it is so in speaking or writing. And this observation applies particularly to the art employed about the words; for the matter ought always to be principal, and, if too much care appear to be bestowed upon the words, it will offend every judicious hearer or reader. Nor do I know that any greater praise can be bestowed upon a composition, than that we do not attend at all to the words, but only to the matter; not but that the words please, and very much too, if they be good words and fitly put together, but it is a pleasure that is concealed from us in a good composition, like that pleasure which the Halicarnassian tells us arises from the melody and rhythms of Demosthenes, which, says he, we ought not to deny, because we do not perceive that the composition is either melodious or numerous. For the art, says he, consists in mixing the accents and the quantities, so that neither the melody nor the rhythm appears; and, if it were otherwise, it would be a fault; for then the composition would appear like a poem or a song *. For proof of the truth of this maxim, that *artis est celare artem*, I have in another place compared the style of Demosthenes and Tacitus †. The first of these has hardly any appearance at all of art, though it be the most artificial of all compositions in prose; and a man who

---

* The passage is remarkable, and the learned reader will be glad to see it in the original:—Καὶ μέ‑ δὺς ὑπολάβῃ θαυμαστὸν ἴναι τον λόγον ἡ καὶ τῆς πεζῆ λέξει ῥυθ‑ μὸν ἐμμιλίας [leg. ἐμμελίας] καὶ ἐυρύθμιας, καὶ μιτοβολὸν, ὥσπερ τας ψέας, καὶ τοις ὀργκοις, ἡ μεθοις τουτων ἀπολαμβάνεται της Δημοσθένους ἄκραν λέξεως· μηδὲ εκκέργειν ὑπολάβῃ τα [μη] πρόοντα τῇ ψιλῇ λέξει προσμαρτυρειται. ἔχει γαρ ταυτα ὁ καλως κατεσκευασμένη λέξις, καὶ μάλιστα ἡ τοῦ τε ῥήτορος· της δι συναγρις και της πωστικη των αισθεων διαλαθανιν τα μιν γαρ συγκεχυνται· τα δε συρφέρκται· τα δε αλλα του τροπω τω ακριβειας εκβεβαι της κατασκευης έστι αιτια εξαλλχθεν δεσπι τη φανση, και κατα μιδιν ἰωκεναι της ποιηματι. Περι της τε Δημοσθ. δυνάμεως, c. 48.

† See above, page 214.

was not a critic would be apt to imagine that there was nothing more in it but plain sense expressed in plain words; whereas the art of Tacitus's style is apparent to every body; but it is, I think, bad art, and a great deal of labour bestowed to write ill *. Of this kind would be the labour bestowed to make our compositions numerous and harmonious, like that of the antients; and we have some attempts of that kind in prose composition, which do not at all please me. The antient orators are not only to be excused, but praised, for studying so much the pleasure of the ear; for it would have been a fault in them, if they had neglected the opportunity which their language afforded them of making their compositions musical. But, if I may presume to advise the British orator or writer, he will not be at so much pains about the sound of his composition, and, if he can avoid shocking the ear by rough grating sounds, or cloying it by a tiresome uniformity, he will be contented. For he may

---

* This is what the Greek critics call κακοζηλια.

as well propose to build a palace of rough pebbles, as to make a numerous and flowing composition of our harsh monosyllables*.

* By what I have said here, and in the preceeding part of this chapter, I would not be understood to deny that there is a rhythm, at least, if not a melody, belonging to our language. And, indeed, there is a late very ingenious work published in London, entitled, ' An Essay towards establishing the Melody and Measure of Speech, to be expressed and perpetuated by peculiar symbols ;' which convinces me that a great deal more, in this respect, may be made of the English language than I thought was possible; but still, I think, it is a rhythm of a different kind from that of Greek or Latin; nor do I think that, by any labour, we ever can bring our language to please the ear so much by a variety of tones, and of long and short syllables, as those antient languages do, or rather *did*; for we have so little of the practice of true rhythm and melody in our own language, that no man, who is not a musician, and has not made a particular study of tones and quantity of syllables, can apply them to Greek or Latin. When I speak of *tones*, I do not mean the tones of passion or sentiment, which are common to all languages, but I mean syllabic tones, or accents, properly so called, which the Greeks and Romans had, over and above the tones of passion and sentiment, which belonged to the players art among them; whereas the other were an essential part of the grammar of the language.

Another advice I will venture to give to a young student, who is desirous to form a good style, and to acquire a correct taste in speaking or writing, is this, That, as of the same words different styles are made by different composition, he should exercise himself in making of the same words conversation or epistolary style, for example; the historic or the rhetorical; and he may try also to make of them such verse as Milton has made of plain words. All this may be done only by a different composition. He may then proceed to ornament a little by figures both of single words and of composition, and try how much ornament each of the three first mentioned styles will bear without running into the poetic, which, if the subject be suitable, will bear every kind of ornament. By this exercise he will learn to distinguish accurately different styles and manners, and will not, in his own compositions, jumble and confound them altogether, which, in my judgment, is the great fault of our modern writing.

I would also advise our young student not only to study most diligently the antient masters, but to translate from them. It was in this way that Cicero formed his style; and, after him, I think, none of us need think the practice mean and servile, or below our genius. And I would advise to make the translations at first as literal as our language will bear; then to use greater freedom, and so go on by degrees till our performance come at last to have no longer that stiff air, which translations commonly have, but the free liberal manner of an original composition, with as much, however, remaining of the antient author as is sufficient to distinguish it from the ordinary compositions of the age. For those translations, which intirely modernize the author, I condemn altogether, and consider them rather as a disguise than a proper dress for a reverend antient; for they appear to me like a bust of Alexander or Julius Cæsar with a toupée and a bag. By this exercise continued for a long time (for nothing is to be done at once in this matter) he will form a style, which will not be altogether antiquated or uncouth, but will have something of the ruſt of antiquity* ſufficient to diſtinguiſh it from the common trivial writings of the day, and will very much pleaſe a true judge of ſtyle, though it will no doubt offend the mere modern writers, who generally conſider themſelves as perfect models and ſtandards, though they may think proper to name as ſuch ſome of their contemporary writers.

* This is what the Halicarnaſſian commends in the ſtyle of Plato; ὅτι οὐκ αὕτη (λέξη τῇ Πλάτωνος) καὶ χρῦς ὁ τῆς ἀρχαιότητος; ἔρμα καὶ λελήθοτος ἐπιτρέχει; Epiſt. ad Pompeium, c. 2.

I heard a man ſay, who had ſtudied the antient ſtatues very much, that, in order to form a true taſte of beauty and grace in that art, we muſt live, in a manner, for ſome conſiderable time among thoſe ſtatues, and turn our eyes as much as poſſible from every thing modern. I believe the ſame is true of the writing art. If we would form a perfect ſtyle, we muſt for ſome time converſe only with the beſt antient authors, till we are ſo much poſſeſſed of their taſte and manner, that we may venture upon modern reading, without running much hazard of having our taſte corrupted by it.

CHAP. XXIII.

Of the sophistical style—Three several specieses of it—The pedantic—The florid—and the austere—The present style generally of the second kind—The antient authors who have written in this style—Not approved of by the first restorers of learning—The causes that produce the sophistical style—Men of business the best writers, if not deficient in genius and learning—Sir John Checke's judgment in this matter.

I HAVE observed more than once, in the course of this work, that, whatever value we may set upon the ornaments of style, it is the *matter* of every composition that should be chiefly studied by an author. And, indeed, where too much pains appears to be bestowed upon the *words*, it offends a judicious reader or hearer. This

I think an obfervation of fuch confequence, that the reader, I hope, will excufe me for returning to it, and enlarging a little more upon it.

That the matter is principal in every compofition, and that the words are only for the fake of the matter, is what no man of common fenfe will deny. The words, therefore, fhould be fuited to the matter. If the matter be high, fo ought alfo the words to be; and if again the matter be common and trivial, the words ought to be of the fame kind. But, whatever the fubject be, whether high or low, there muft be fenfe in the compofition, for the want of which no ornament of words will atone*. And the finer the words are, if there be no weight in the matter, the compofition will for that but offend the more, and, to a man of fenfe, will appear even ridiculous; for it is with the words as with the pronunciation of them.

---

* Cicero, upon this fubject, expreffes himfelf in very ftrong terms: ' Nihil tam furiofum eft, quàm verborum ' vel optimorum inanis fonitus, nulla fubjecta fententia ' aut fcientia.'

Nothing in speaking offends you more than great emphasis and vehement action accompanying words of little or no significancy.

The over-labouring of words made that fault of style, which was known in antient times by the name of the *sophistical*, because it was by the sophists of old that it was chiefly practised*. I think it may be fitly divided into three kinds. The first is, when, upon common and ordinary subjects, words are used that are not common, but

---

* There were two famous sophists in the days of Socrates, Prodicus and Hippias. These Plato has introduced into his Protagoras; and, as he was a poet as well as a philosopher, he has imitated incomparably well the style and manner of each of them; see the Protagoras, page 234. Edit. Ficini. The passage is too long to be inserted, but well deserving to be read by every scholar. I shall only observe upon it, that the style of Hippias is remarkably metaphorical and florid, and such as, by the generality of readers now-a-days, would be thought very fine; but Plato certainly judged otherwise, though he was far from being an enemy to the ornaments of style, and has laboured words more than perhaps any philosopher, even too much, according to the opinion of some critics. The style of Prodicus is sophistical in another way; for it is full of nice distinctions of the propriety of words.

are either altogether new, and made for the occaſion, or not commonly uſed. Of this kind among us are words borrowed from the learned languages, but which yet have not been naturalized by ordinary uſe. Such words are not improper upon high ſubjects, eſpecially where the writer or ſpeaker may be ſuppoſed to be much animated and heated with paſſion; and, in treating of matters of art and ſcience, if our own language does not afford words proper to expreſs our notions, we are allowed to borrow them from more learned languages; but, if ſuch words are uſed upon common or trivial ſubjects, it makes that ſpecies of the ſophiſtical ſtyle, which is well known under the name of the *pedantic.* Nor is it confined to the words only; but, if the turn of the phraſe, and the manner of expreſſion be much too elevated or refined for the ſubject, the ſtyle may ſtill be ſaid to be pedantic *.

* This ſtyle, which it ſeems was once faſhionable in France, is very well ridiculed by Moliere in his comedy of the *Precieuſes Ridicules*. I will give but one example from it. One of theſe ladies deſires a gentleman to ſit down in the following words:

The misfortune of this style is, that the more it is laboured, the worse it is, which indeed is the case of all kinds of writing, and, in general, of all the works of art that are executed in a bad taste. Such an author, therefore, never expresses himself properly and naturally, unless, perhaps, where he is careless and inattentive to his style. And this shews us how careful every man, who writes or speaks, should be to acquire a good taste of style, and a true judgment of what is proper and suitable to his subject,

'Mais de grace, Monsieur, ne soyez pas inexorable à ce fauteuil qui vous tend le bras il y a un quart d'heure, contentez un peu l'envie qu'il a de vous embrasser.'

Congreve too, in his play of *the Way of the World*, has a great deal of the same kind of language, which he has put into the mouth of Lady Wishfort, as where he makes her say, 'that she hopes Sir Rowland does not think her *prone to iteration of nuptials*.'

This style is also ridiculed by Shakespeare in the character of Pistol. It is a good description that Sir John Falstaff gives of the plain and natural style, when he desires Pistol to *speak like a man of this world.*

otherwife he may be affured that he will lofe all the labour he beftows upon his compofition, at leaft, in the opinion of real critics.

The fecond fpecies of the fophiftical ftyle is that which is not unfuitable to the fubject, but is over-laboured, and too much adorned with tropes, and figures of the pleafurable kind, fuch as the metaphor, the antithefis, and the parifofis, and where too much is given to the pleafure of the ear, and pains more than fufficient beftowed to avoid all harfh founds, and to give a fweet flow and agreeable cadence to the periods, and their feveral members. The moft ftriking examples of this ftyle are the orations of Ifocrates, and particularly his panegyric, fo called by way of eminence, for almoft all his orations may be called by that name, being of the *epideictic* kind*, that is, not intended for bufinefs or action, but to entertain and amufe

---

* This is ill tranflated into Latin by the word *demonftrative*, which does not at all exprefs the nature of this kind of eloquence. But more of this when I come to treat of rhetoric.

panegyries*, or assemblies of people met together at the games, or upon occasion of any other festival. Isocrates is said to have spent ten, some say fifteen years, in composing this oration, in which he exhorts the Greeks to join in a war against the Persians—a longer time than Alexander took to finish that war †. It is likely, I think, it would have been better, if the fourth part only of that time had been bestowed upon it; for, though such orations, chiefly calculated for shew and ostentation, as the name denotes, admit of much more ornament than those of business; yet the style of this oration is greatly too much ornamented, especially with respect to the pleasure of the ear, if it be

---

* The orations made by the sophists at those *panegyrical* meetings, were commonly in praise of some god, heroe, or man; and hence it is that in English we call praise a *panegyric*.

† Timæus the historian made this comparison, as Longinus informs us, *cap.* 4. where he thinks proper to find fault with it, and give it as an example of what he calls the *frigid* in style; but I do not think it so bad as he would make it, though it be no doubt magnifying Alexander at the expence of this sophist, as Longinus calls Isocrates, .

true what I have read somewhere, that there is not to be found in the whole of it two vowels gaping upon one another. In this kind of ſtyle Libanius and Themiſtius, ſophiſts of later times, have written. And, in general, almoſt all the writers of the later times, (I except only the philoſophers of the Alexandrian ſchool,) have more or leſs of this panegyrical ſtyle; and, particularly, there is a writer upon the ſubject of criticiſm, of great name in modern times, and who, I think, is of ſome value for the matter, I mean Longinus, but whoſe ſtyle I think much too florid for his ſubject, or indeed for any ſubject that is treated as a matter of art or ſcience. To be convinced of this, we need only compare his ſtyle of criticiſm with that of Ariſtotle, or the Halicarnaſſian, and the difference will appear ſtriking*.

* This writer, ſpeaking of famous authors, ſays τοῖς ἑαυτῶν Παραβαλων μεθοδοις τῶ αυτω, c. 1. a ſophiſtical periphraſe, with an arrangement of the words and a cadence that I hold likewiſe to be ſophiſtical. Again, ſpeaking of the uſe of the plural number inſtead of the ſingular, he ſays, τα καινοτητα μεγαλοφρωνεστερα και αυτω διαφερομενα τῳ οχλῳ τῳ αριθμῳ, c. 23. Dithyrambic words with very little

The third and last species of the sophistical style is the very reverse of this, being as far removed as possible from the pleasurable, the pompous, and the panegyrical. It gives nothing to the pleasure of the ear; or, if it has any numbers, they are harsh and austere. The words it uses are, many of them, obsolete and antiquated, none of them of the florid or poetical kind; and, as to its composition, it is varied by all the figures possible, except such as please the ear and fancy; and, as some of the figures it uses are very uncouth, and such as derange the construction and natural order of the words very much, hence it is often perplexed and obscure.

The great author of this style, the first, and, according to the Halicarnassian, the last, is Thucydides, of whom I have spoken

---

meaning. He deals much in similes too, like some of our modern critics, as where he compares Demosthenes to thunder and lightning, which consumes things at once, and Cicero to a conflagration, which spreads far and wide, and sometimes is extinguished, and then blazes again.

elsewhere *. And I shall only add here, that it was probably in emulation to Herodotus that he framed this so singular style; for it is evident, from his introduction, that he meant his work to be of a kind quite diff^erent from that of Herodotus;— whether it were that he disapproved of the style of Herodotus, or despaired of excelling, or even of equalling him in that style †.

It is true, no doubt, what the Halicarnassian says, that Thucydides, though he had his admirers among the Greeks, yet had no imitators. But there are two Roman authors who certainly imitated him; I mean Sallust and Tacitus, of whose style I have already spoken at great length; and, I think, it is true

---

* Pag. 198.

† He says, that his history he intended to be κτημα εις αει μαλλον η αγωνισμα εις το παραχρημα ακουειν; by which last words he appears to me plainly enough to insinuate, that Herodotus's history was of the panegyrical kind, (accordingly it is said to have been read by him at the Olympic games) and more calculated to gain the prize of the day, than to be a lasting monument for the instruction of posterity.

what I have there said, that they have not improved upon their original, particularly in the narrative part, which, I think, is much worse, because it is not so plain and natural as that of Thucydides.

I know no style in English which resembles that of Thucydides, unless perhaps it be the style of Milton in his prose writings; but he, like Demosthenes, has only taken what is best in Thucydides. For Demosthenes studied Thucydides very much; and accordingly we find in him a great many hyperbatons, parentheses, and artificial constructions, which run out to a great length, and make it necessary to connect words very distant from one another, with many such like figures, by which his style is diversified, and raised above common idiom, as much as that of Thucydides, but without his perplexity or obscurity.

The style that is most used at present belongs rather to the second species of the sophistical style, that which is formed for the pleasure of the fancy and ear. The distinguishing characters of it are, first, that it is very florid and poetical, and abounds with antithesis, words anfwering to words, and other pleafurable figures. Secondly, It is compofed, for the greater part, in fhort unconnected fentences, for I cannot call them periods, with a certain neatnefs and trimnefs in the turn of them, but without any flow or variety in the ryhthm or cadence, even when they are longer. This fpruce *petit-maitre* ftyle firft began, as I have obferved, in France, and has been followed by fome later writers in Britain, who had not formed their tafte upon better models.

The antient ftyle that moft refembles this, and probably that from which it was formed, is the ftyle of Seneca, Pliny the younger, Quinctilian, and, in general, of the writers of that age. It was alfo, as I have fhewn, the ftyle of the fchools of declamation in Rome, from which I derive the corruption of the Roman tafte of eloquence and writing [*].

[*] The laft of the three authors I have mentioned, I mean Quinctilian, writes, I think, better than either of the other two; but he likewife has a ftrong

The style of these authors was not, as I have observed, approved of by the first restorers of learning in Europe. Among the earliest of these was Angelus Politianus, the saint of that age. I will give but one example of him from a passage in which he has unfortunately measured himself with a much better writer, I mean Cicero, to whom indeed he refers. It is upon the subject of too great luxuriancy in the style of young men. Of this Quinctilian says, *Lib.* 2. *Institut.* ' Audeat hæc ætas plura, et Inveniat, et inventis ' gaudeat, sint licet illa non satis interim sicca et ' severa. Facile remedium est ubertatis, sterilia ' nullo labore vincuntur. Illa mihi in pueris natura ' minimum spei dabit, in qua ingenium judicio præ- ' sumitur. Materiam esse primam volo vel abundan- ' tiorem, atque ultra quàm oporteat fusam. Quod ' me de his ætatibus sentire minus mirabitur, qui ' apud Ciceronem legerit, *volo enim se efferat in* ' *adolescente fœcunditas*.' Here the sentences are short and unconnected, but trim and neatly turned. Now hear how Cicero expresses pretty much the same thought. ' Volo enim se efferat in adolescente ' fœcunditas. Nam facilius, sicut in vitibus, re- ' vocantur ea, quæ sese nimium profuderunt, quàm, ' si nihil valet materies, nova sarmenta cultura exci- ' tantur. Ita volo esse in adolescente unde aliquid ' amputem. Non enim potest in eo esse succus diu- ' turnus, quod nimis celeriter est maturitatem assecu- ' tum;' *De Oratore, lib.* 2. Here there is not the oratorical roundness or flow, neither should it be; but as the matter is connected, so are the sentences; and, though they be not so neat and so trim as those of

first elegant writer of Latin, if I am not mistaken, after the restoration of letters. He condemns the style of all the age of Pliny: 'Optaret alius ut oratorem Plinium 'saperem, quod hujus et maturitas et disci- 'plina laudatur; ego contra totum illud 'aspernari me dicam Plinii sæculum *.'

These are, if not all, at least, I think, the chief kinds of the sophistical style, a style which is not faulty through negligence or ignorance, but from overmuch study and labour. I have already given a particular reason why Thucydides bestowed so much pains to make his style worse than it would otherwise have been; and I will now endeavour to give some more general reasons for this laborious affectation.

And the first is a littleness of mind, which makes men study much what is

---

Quinctilian, there is nothing that offends the ear like the abrupt cadence of Tacitus, and there is nothing of quaintness or smartness, but the whole is simple and natural.

* Angeli Politiani epistola prima.

trifling, or lefs principal in arts, fciences, and even the common affairs of life. Senfe, fpirit, and a certain greatnefs of mind, are neceffary for fpeaking and writing well, no lefs than for acting well. A man of a philofophical mind and exalted genius will, like Socrates in Plato *, defpife the embellifhment of words, and think that time mifpent which he employs in polifhing them and fetting them in order, for the purpofe of captivating the ears and fancies of men; or, if he fhould ftoop to do it for any important public fervice, he will certainly not over-do it, but will always confider the matter as principal, and chiefly deferving his care.

Another reafon, and which, I believe, has contributed more than any other to

---

* Plato makes Socrates fay, in the beginning of his Apology, that it would not be becoming him, at his time of life, to form and fafhion words like a young man: ὁυ γαρ οι ὅπου πρεπει, ω ανδρες, τηδι τῃ ἡλικιᾳ ὡσπερ μειρακιῳ πλαττοντι λογους, εις ὑμας εισιναι. And Ariftotle has told us, that the ftyle, and every thing belonging to rhetoric, is addreffed to the opinions and fancies of men; Rhet. Lib. iii. c. i.

make men labour words with the anxious diligence of a sophist, is the want of the practice of applying speaking or writing to business, or the common affairs of life. Men of great leisure, who are very good scholars, but are ignorant of the world, and unpractised in business, are very apt to form to themselves a style, which appears to them, and may appear to others, very fine, but is intirely unfit for business, and could not be endured by assemblies of men met to deliberate upon public affairs of great importance, or by judges, who were to decide causes upon such speaking or writing. Those, on the other hand, who are in the practice of business, soon discover that it is not the ornament of words, but the weight of matter and argument, that will convince men, who hear or read, in order to be informed, and that what art there is in the composition must be concealed as much as possible. Such an orator or writer, therefore, will not use the pedantic style of the *precieuses ridicules;* neither will his style abound with the flowers of poetry, nor will be pompous and theatrical,

Book IV. Progress of Language. 429

like Isocrates, because he knows, from certain experience and observation, that such a manner tickles the ears and amuses the fancy, but does not convince or determine men to act; and far less will he labour to obscure and involve his sense, as Thucydides has done, whose manner would be as offensive to the ears of the people, as perplexing to their understanding. And, I am persuaded, the Halicarnassian is in the right when he maintains, that no orator of Greece ever spoke in that manner.

That men of business, if they are not deficient in genius or learning, make the best speakers or writers, is not only agreeable to reason, but is verified by fact and observation. The greatest orators in Greece were the two rivals, Demosthenes and Æschines, both much versant in public business, and accustomed to speak to the people; and, in Rome, the two best writers, (I mean prose-writers, for I speak not of poets, whose style is quite different from that of business and common life), as well as speakers, were Julius Cæsar and Cicero, both men eminent in business. On the other hand, Isocrates and Thucydides, among the Greeks, were neither of them men of business, nor accustomed to speak to judges, or to the people, but formed in their closets a kind of ideal eloquence, in a very different taste indeed, but both equally unfit for the affairs of life. Sallust and Tacitus too, among the Romans, the worst writers that I know of any name or reputation, do not appear to have had any practice of eloquence, unless perhaps in the schools of declamation*.

* As to Sallust, what Sir John Checke, one of the first and best scholars that ever were in England, said of him, is well worth reading, as it is reported by Roger Ascham, his scholar (whom I quoted before) in his work entitled the *School-master*, or perfect way of bringing up youth, p. 339. of the edition of his works published by James Bennet in 1771. Sir John Checke had said, that he could not recommend Sallust as a good pattern of style for young men, ' his writing being neither plain for ' the matter, nor sensible for men's understanding. ' And what is the cause thereof, Sir? quoth I. Ve- ' rily, said he, because in Sallust's writing is more ' art than nature, and more labour than art; and in ' his labour also too much toil, as it were with an ' uncontented care to write better than he could; a ' fault common to very many men. And therefore ' he doth not express the matter lively and naturally with

Even Cicero, as I have observed elsewhere, would have been a better orator, if he had not practised so much upon fictitious subjects, but had exercised himself from the

‘ common speech, as ye see Xenophon doth in Greek;
‘ but it is carried and driven forth artificially, after too
‘ learned a sort, as Thucydides doth in his orations. And
‘ how cometh it to pass, said I, that Cæsar and Cicero's
‘ talk is so natural and plain, and Sallust's writing so
‘ artificial and dark, when all the three lived in one
‘ time? I will freely tell you my fancy herein, said
‘ he. Surely Cæsar and Cicero, beside a singular
‘ prerogative of natural eloquence, given unto them
‘ by God, both two, by use of life, were daily ora-
‘ tors among the common people, and greatest counsellors
‘ in the senate-house; and therefore gave themselves to
‘ use such speech as the meanest should well understand,
‘ and the wisest best allow; following carefully that
‘ good counsel of Aristotle, *Loquendum, ut multi;*
‘ *sapiendum, ut pauci.* Sallust was no such man,
‘ neither for will to goodness, nor skill by learning,
‘ but ill given by nature, and made worse by bring-
‘ ing up, spent the most part of his youth very mis-
‘ orderly in riot and leachery, in the company of
‘ such who, never giving their mind to honest do-
‘ ing, could never inure their tongue to wise speak-
‘ ing. But, at last, coming to better years, and
‘ buying wit at the dearest hand (that is, by long
‘ experience of the hurt and shame that cometh of
‘ mischief), moved by the counsel of them that were
‘ wise, and carried by the example of such as were
‘ good, he first fell to honesty of life, and after to
‘ the love of study and learning; and so became so

beginning, as Demosthenes did, upon matters of business. In later times, when the schools of declamation became still more in fashion among the Romans, the *umbraticus*

' new a man, that Cæsar, being dictator, made him
' prætor in Numidia, where he, absent from his coun-
' try, and not inured with the common talk of Rome, but
' shot up in his study, and bent wholly upon reading,
' did write the story of the Romans. And, for the better
' accomplishing of the same, he read Cato and Piso in
' Latin, for gathering of matter and truth, and Thucy-
' dides in Greek, for the order of his story, and furnishing
' of his style.'

A little after, in p. 343. speaking of Thucydides, he says, ' that he likewise wrote his story, not at
' home in Greece, but abroad in Italy, and there-
' fore smelleth of a certain outlandish kind of talk,
' strange to them of Athens, and diverse from their
' writing that lived in Athens and Greece, and
' wrote at the same that Thucydides did, as Lysias,
' Xenophon, Plato, and Isocrates, the purest and
' plainest writers that ever wrote in any tongue, and
' best examples for any man to follow, whether he write
' Latin, Italian, French, or English. Thucydides also
' seemeth, in his writing, not so much benefited by
' nature as holpen by art, and carried forth by de-
' sire, study, labour, toil, and over-great curiosity, who
' spent twenty-seven years in writing his eight books
' of history.'

As to Tacitus, neither Sir John Checke nor Mr. Ascham does so much as mention him; nor do I believe

Book IV. Progress of Language. 4

doctor, as Petronius expresses it, *ingenia delevit*.

I do not deny, however, that exceptions to this rule may be found among the antient writers, and particularly the Halicarnaſſian may be reckoned one; for it does not appear that he ever pleaded cauſes, or was engaged in civil buſineſs of any kind. But it is to be conſidered, firſt, that he was a teacher of youth, to whom, therefore, he was obliged to ſpeak in a language eaſy and natural. Secondly, He had formed his ſtyle by the imitation of ſuch authors as Demoſthenes, who were real men of buſineſs; and this appears to me to be the only way that a mere ſcholar can form a ſtyle, which does not ſmell too much of the lamp.

I think it is unlucky for the authors of modern times, that ſo few of them have been men of buſineſs. The beſt of them, I

that any man of thoſe days conſidered him as a pattern of ſtyle — that was reſerved for later and more ignorant times.

CHAP. XXIV.

A short account of the fate of antient learning in the several periods of the world—All the learning of Europe originally from Egypt—The first great blow to learning the destruction of the colleges of the Egyptian priests—The second, the destruction of the Pythagorean colleges in Italy—The third, the loss of the liberty of Greece, and the extinction of learning and good taste there—The fourth, the loss of liberty at Rome, and the corruption of taste there—The fifth, the conquests of the Saracens and Turks—The present state of antient learning in Europe—How the taste of it is to be revived.

AS I have said so much in praise of the antient learning, in this and the preceding volumes of this work, it may not be improper, before I conclude this volume, to give some general account of the fate of this learning in the several ages of the world, as far as they are recorded.

That all, or by far the greater part of the many arts and sciences, which Europe is at present possessed of, came originally from Egypt, I hold to be an incontestible truth. All the necessary arts of life, and all other arts of use or ornament depending upon the knowledge of the hidden powers of nature, were, I believe, practised in the highest perfection in Egypt. But the liberal and elegant arts, such as fine speaking and writing, poetry, statuary, and painting, though the elements of them were likeways brought from Egypt into Greece, prospered much more in that country, and were carried to a much greater height than ever they were in Egypt. The reason of which is, that these are popular arts, and are therefore never carried far, except in popular governments, such as those in Greece. This is particularly true of eloquence, which, as early as the days of Homer and the Trojan war, was the chief instrument of government among the Greeks. And indeed it must of necessity be so, where the power is in the hands of the people, who muſt be perſuaded before they act. Now, as I have obſerved in the beginning of this volume, ſpeaking is the principal art, prior both in time and dignity to the writing art, which was only grafted on it. For, though the ſpeaking art was in very great perfection in the days of Homer, as is evident from his poems, I believe there was very little poetry committed to writing at that time, and no proſe at all. But, as to ſciences, ſuch as geometry, aſtronomy, natural philoſophy, metaphyſics and theology, I believe they were carried to a perfection in Egypt that they have never ſince exceeded.

The firſt great revolution of learning and philoſophy was the conqueſt of Egypt by the Perſians, and the deſtruction of the Egyptian colleges of prieſts. Of this I have ſpoken elſewhere *; and it was, in my opinion, the greateſt blow to ſcience that it ever received, and which it has never ſince perfectly recovered. It did, however, lift its head again, and flouriſhed for ſome time in the Pythagorean colleges in Italy; for Pythagoras went to Egypt before the Per-

* Vol. ii. p. 262.

fian conqueſt; and, as he was there no leſs than twenty-two * years, and was initiated into the prieſtly order, there can be no doubt but that he brought away with him a great deal of the Egyptian learning, at leaſt much more of it than any Greek did before or after his time. For thoſe that went before him, ſuch as Orpheus, Muſæus, and Melampus, appear to have brought away nothing with them but muſic and ſome myſtical theology; and Thales, the only philoſopher who was there before him, appears to have learned nothing there but ſome elements of geometry, and a little phyſiology. And, with regard to Plato and Eudoxus, who went to Egypt ſo long after Pythagoras, beſides that they went thither at a time when ſcience muſt have been deep in its decline, we are informed that the prieſts were not at all communicative to them †.

Theſe Pythagorean ſchools in Italy produced, while they flouriſhed, ſome of the

---

* Jamblichus in vita Pythagoræ, c. 4.

† Strabo, Lib. xvii. p. 806. where he tells us, that Plato and Eudoxus lived thirteen years with the prieſts of Heliopolis, in order to learn aſtronomy; but, though they were at great pains to perſuade the prieſts to teach them,

greateſt men that ever exiſted, in philoſophy, government, and arms. How theſe ſchools of philoſophy were deſtroyed and diſperſed, is related by the author of the life of Pythagoras, as I have elſewhere mentioned*; and this I hold to have been the ſecond fatal blow to learning and philoſophy.

Some planks were ſaved of this ſhipwreck, and diſperſed all over Europe; but they were beſt collected and preſerved by Plato and Ariſtotle in Greece, where both arts and ſciences flouriſhed very much for ſome time. But Greece, with its liberty and glory in arms, loſt alſo its taſte for the ſciences and fine arts; and, as the Halicarnaſſian tells us †, they were, ſome time before his age, become almoſt barbarous. And this I make to be the third downfal of learning.

they learned but a few theorems; the barbarians, as Strabo calls thoſe learned prieſts, concealing the greater part from them. See what I have further ſaid upon this ſubject, vol. ii. p. 243. in the note.

* Vol. ii. p. 262.

† De Antiquis Oratoribus, in initio.

It again revived, as the same author informs us*, under the patronage of some of the great men of Rome, who, by the countenance and protection they gave to such men as the Halicarnassian, introduced philosophy and the fine arts into Rome, and revived them in Greece. In Rome they were short-lived; for the violent tyranny of the Emperors, and the general corruption of manners, soon put an end to them. But they continued longer in Greece; from whence they returned again to their native land, I mean Egypt; for in Alexandria there were schools of philosophers, geometers, astronomers, grammarians, and rhetoricians, and there were good writers down even to the invasion of the Saracens, and the second destruction of the Alexandrian library. In Italy, and all over the west of Europe, learning had been before extinguished, and all fine arts, by the invasion of other barbarians, I mean the Goths and Vandals. And here we have learning again put down for the fourth time, except some small remains of it that were preserved in Constantinople.

* Ubi supra.

But science began again to dawn, and from a quarter whence it could not have been expected, I mean from the Saracens, the same mad and barbarous enthusiasts who had destroyed the Alexandrian library. But Greece a second time catched its conquerors, and the Saracens became as zealous for Greek learning as ever they had been enemies to it. From them the first rays of science enlightened the west; for we got some knowledge of physic, and of Aristotle's philosophy from them. But we may be said to have still continued barbarous till the taking of Constantinople by the Turks, the most indocile and uncultivable of all barbarians; for they are among the few people that we read of in history, who have been dissolved in luxury and effeminacy, without being first softened and mitigated by arts. From those barbarians fled the learned Greeks that yet remained in Constantinople, and, taking refuge in Rome, introduced there the Greek language, and, with it, the genuine Greek philosophy and Greek arts; and thus, by a strange revolution of human affairs, it so happened that Greece once more brought arts into Latium*, again became barbarous, and Rome and its great men (for fo I think I may call Leo X. and his cardinals) once more reſtored learning, which from thence ſpread all over Europe with a moſt rapid progreſs.

That learning is now again deep in its decline all over Europe, cannot be denied, if it be true, as I think I have ſhewn, that the Greek authors are the moſt perfect ſtandards, both of juſt thinking and elegant writing; for, in many parts of Europe, the knowledge of the Greek language is loſt, almoſt as much as it was before the taking of Conſtantinople. It is indeed the peculiar honour of England, that the Greek learning is more eſteemed, and better preſerved there than any where elſe. But, even there, it is not ſo much cultivated as formerly; nor are the Greek maſters ſo much ſtudied and imitated as the models of fine writing. And what have we got in the place of theſe? Either Latin imitators, ſome of which are certainly not good; and, if

---

* Artes intulit agreſti Latio.   Horat.

they were better, every man of genius and spirit would chuse to drink at the pure fountains rather than at the streams, often muddy, and always more or less discoloured;—or French authors, who have introduced a kind of Asiatic eloquence into Europe, more unlike the true Attic muse than any thing that ever came from Asia in antient times. I have already observed, that it would be the ruin of other arts, should we follow the florid taste of the French in them, and give over studying and copying those beautiful monuments of antient art, still to be seen in Italy; and the same must happen to the writing art, as soon as the Greek monuments of that kind cease to be studied and imitated.

But, how are Greek learning and fine writing to be revived? No other way that I know, but as they were twice revived in Rome—by the patronage and protection of the great, who have it in their power to make Greek learning as fashionable every where in Europe as it was in Britain two hundred years ago, when even ladies of the highest rank both wrote and spoke Greek, and Queens were proud of being able to read the great authors of that language in the original. For no art or science, or even virtue, will flourish in a country where it is not fashionable; and it is the example and the praise of the men of rank in a country that make every thing fashionable.

From this short history of learning, it appears, that the seeds of arts and sciences are by nature sown in the human mind, and have always grown up, flourished, and produced fruit, with proper culture and in a favourable soil and climate, till they were either swept away by inundations of barbarians, or choaked by the cares attending the acquiring of money, or, what is still more fatal to all arts and sciences, the enjoyment of it in luxury, indolence, and dissipation. These shorten our lives as well as consume our time; so that it may be truly said of us what Seneca says of times not unlike ours, *paucos annos inter studia et vitia, non æqua portione, dividimus**.

* Natur. Quæst. lib. 7. cap. 25.

CHAP. XXV.

Conclusion of this part of the work.—Two kinds of men will despise it—the avaricious and the luxurious.—Something said to the first of these, more to the last.—Leisure, which is thought so great a blessing, is the greatest source of human misery, if not well employed.—Education only can enable men to employ leisure well.—Bodily exercises formerly employed much time—These now laid aside—Arts and sciences now only remain to fill up leisure.—By these only we have any advantages over savages.—The Romans a striking example of the effect of Greek philosophy and arts—These preserved virtue among them in the most degenerate times.—Another use of antient learning is to improve our luxury, and prevent, as far as possible, the bad effects of it.—The want of it in this respect among us, and the fatal consequences of such want.

AND here I conclude this part of my work, in which I have endeavoured to explain the nature of the ornaments of speech, pointed to the fountains from whence they are to be drawn, and shewn to what subjects they are properly applied.

There are two kinds of men who, I know, will very much despise my labours on this subject. Of the first kind are those who value nothing but money; who, if they do not believe that nothing exists except money, as Mr. Fielding says of one of that character*, at least, are concerned about nothing else existing. Of the other kind are the vain and the luxurious, who do not love money for its own sake, but desire to enjoy it according to the fashionable taste of pleasure.

To those of the first kind I have nothing to say, except that I wish them much joy of the only pleasure they are capable of relishing. And thus much I will say in commendation of their taste, that it is the passion, the most constant in human nature, and which, of all others, has the least respite or intermission. For it operates almost continually, like gravitation, or any other

* History of Tom Jones.

power of nature; and, in proportion as other paſſions decreaſe, it increaſes, and never ends but with the man. Long may ſuch buſy mortals live to accumulate wealth, of which it is to be hoped, that ſome, who come after them, may make a proper uſe; and, when they die, they may, in their epitaph, inſult philoſophy and learning, in the way that Trimalchio does in Petronius, ' Here lies ſuch a man, who died worth ' half a million, *et philoſophum nunquam* ' *audivit.*'

With reſpect to the other kind of men, as they have commonly ſome taſte, of which the avaricious are intirely void, and, if that taſte were well directed, might become worthy and uſeful men, I will beſtow more words upon them, and endeavour to point out to them the right road to pleaſure.

A young man, juſt entering upon life, with an opulent fortune and high taſte of pleaſure, thinks that he has in his hands the means of being perfectly happy, and reckons it his peculiar good fortune, that he is not obliged to labour and drudge in any business or profession, but has *leisure* to be happy. But he does not consider that leisure, though the wish of all men*, is the source of the greatest misery to our species, if not rightly employed; nor do I know any vice or folly that is not to be derived from it. Even the brute animals, when tamed and domesticated, and supplied with the necessaries of life by the labour of others, are made, in some degree, unhappy by leisure. Thus a dog, when he has been long idle, is manifestly uneasy, and at a loss what to do with himself; and accordingly, when he is called forth to his employment, we see with what joy and triumph he accepts of the invitation. But the dog is happy in this respect, that he has not invented any means of filling up his leisure that is destructive to him; so that he only suffers the pains of what the French call *ennui*. But man has employed his superior sagacity in devising so many ways of conjuring this *foul fiend* (to use an expression of Shake-

---

* Otium Divos rogat in patenti
   Prensus Ægæo——
Otium bello furiosa Thrace,
Otium Medi pharetra decori.

              HORAT. Ode 16. lib. 2.

ſpeare), moſt of them ruinous both to body and mind, that unleſs he can form a taſte for ſomething better than the common amuſements, he muſt of neceſſity be an unhappy man.

This is the caſe of every man who has leiſure which he does not know how to employ properly. But it is much more the caſe of thoſe who have wealth as well as leiſure. For wealth is an incitement to every vice and folly, by readily furniſhing the means of gratifying them. And ſuch a man, if he has not formed a right taſte of pleaſure, cannot avoid being vicious and fooliſh, and by conſequence miſerable, in a very high degree.

And how is this right taſte of pleaſure to be formed? Only by a proper education, by which we are early accuſtomed to what is right and good, fair and handſome; the conſequence of which is, that we delight in thoſe things as much as others do in the contrary, and purſue them from habit, as well as from judgment and deliberate choice. It is therefore true what Ariſtotle has obſerved*, that the chief advantage of a good education is to teach us how to employ our leiſure. This obſervation will apply to men of every buſineſs or profeſſion, if they have any leiſure at all; but much more to men whoſe whole life is leiſure. And indeed the greateſt good fortune, that can befal a man who has not education, is to have no leiſure at all, but to be conſtantly employed, eſpecially in bodily labour, for which by far the greater part of mankind are only fit. So that men, not properly educated, are by nature deſtined to be ſlaves and drudges, or elſe to be miſerable †.

There was one way, by which the men of rank and opulence, of this as well as other countries of Europe, did formerly fill up their leiſure, but which is now almoſt intirely out of faſhion; I mean exerciſes. And indeed a man, who would keep his body in high athletic order, will not have

---

* Ariſtotle's Politic. lib. 7. cap. 15. and lib. 8. cap. 3.
† As ſome men are by nature incapable of a liberal education, they are thoſe, who, as Ariſtotle has told us, are by nature ſlaves. Ibid. lib. 1. cap. 5.

much time to spare. How much those exercises were practised in antient times, and how necessary a part they made of the education of the citizens of every free state, especially of the gentlemen, or men of distinction, is well known to every scholar. Among the antients, there was one people, who were eminent for nothing but athletic exercises, and the strength of body thereby acquired; and who, by that excellency alone, under the conduct of a man who by accident had the benefit of a philosophical education, attained to great power and eminence. The learned reader will know that I mean the Thebans, who, under the conduct of Epaminondas, became the leaders of Greece*. This shews us, that

---

* Plutarch, in the life of Pelopidas, informs us, that, while the Spartans were in possession of the Citadel of Thebes, and they and the Thebans exercised together in the same Palæstras, the Thebans, by the advice of Epaminondas, wrestled with the Spartans; and, finding themselves superior in that exercise, Epaminondas from thence excited them to assert their liberty, and shake off the Spartan yoke. This produced the recovery of their Citadel out of the hands of the Spartans, and the famous battles of Leuctra and Mantinæa; in which, from the account given by historians, and particularly by Diodorus Siculus, it is evident, that the Thebans con-

though the endowments of the mind certainly hold the first rank, yet the faculties of the body ought not to be neglected; and they should be so much more generally

quered, not so much by the conduct of Epaminondas, or their valour and military discipline, as by their superiority in wrestling and strength of body: for in that way must necessarily be decided all battles in which men fight in close order, and hand to hand; where all long weapons, such as spears, must soon be broken, or rendered useless, which actually happened, as Diodorus informs us, at the battle of Mantinæa. Thus it appears, that superiority in bodily strength, and gymnastic exercises, produced that great revolution in the affairs of Greece, by which the Lacedemonians, who had been so long leaders of Greece, and, after the conquest of Athens, thought themselves invincible, were stript of all their power and glory, and so humbled, that they could never afterwards lift their head.

For the rest, the Thebans were rude, brutish people, without education or learning of any kind; the consequence of which was, that, after having obtained the dominion of Greece, by the means I have mentioned, they soon lost it, almost as soon as they lost their philosophical leader Epaminondas, and, not long after that, their city and their liberty, by the folly and brutality of their then leaders. This is the judgment of Ephorus the historian, as quoted by Strabo, Lib. ix. p. 401. upon which Strabo's own reflection is worth observing: ' That ' the Romans, by laying aside their antient rudeness and ' ignorance, and acquiring arts and sciences, were enabled ' to conquer the world.'

cultivated, that for one man who is by nature fitted to excel in the qualities of the mind, there are at least a hundred that might become eminent in bodily exercises. But if the exercises were neither of use nor ornament, they are necessary for the voluptuous and luxurious, both in order to give them a true relish for their pleasures, and to prevent, as much as possible, the bad effects of them. By exercises, I mean not what is commonly called *exercise*, but which really does not deserve the name, at least it does not answer the definition of it given by Galen the Greek physician, viz. *motion that alters the breath;* but I mean strong athletic exercises, such as are absolutely necessary for working off the effects of the full table and luxurious banquet; for luxury, joined with indolence, is certain ruin both to body and mind.

Athletic exercises, however, at least such as are proper to give any great degree of strength or agility to the body, are almost intirely disused; so that a human body in *good order* * (to fpeak in the jockey ftyle) is hardly to be found.

There remain then only arts and fciences to fill up the time of the rich and idle; and thefe, if they were properly cultivated, would make fuch men lefs luxurious, and, by confequence, the fevere exercifes lefs neceffary for them. But, if thefe are alfo neglected, and if the great men of a country, who, by their birth and rank, are deftined to fill the firft offices in it, apply themfelves to no bufinefs or profeffion, nor to arts, fciences, or exercifes, it is evident that the country muft be undone, and that

---

* The antients diftinguifhed betwixt ὑγιεια, or *health*, and εὐεξία, or *good order*; the laft of which was only the effect of gymnaftic exercifes; and there was a mafter of fuch exercifes among them, called the παιδοτρίβης, who may be faid to have been a *man-groom*, for he underftood the art of forming the athletic habit in men, as well as our grooms do the putting horfes in order. And, if a man among them was not put into this kind of training, it was eafily difcovered from his look, and the appearance of his body. This explains what Socrates, in Xenophon's memorabilia, fays to one of his followers, who neglected the exercifes of the Palæftra: ὡς ἰδιωτικῶς ἔχει τὸ σῶμα, i. e. 'How like that of a vulgar, untaught ' man is the habit of your body!'

they themselves must lead a miserable and contemptible life.

Such men would be much affronted, if they were compared with savages, whom they will hardly allow to be of the same species with themselves; and yet it is a certain fact, that it is only by means of our arts and sciences that we have any advantages over savages. For they have more sagacity and better parts than we have, and likewise much greater strength of mind, by which they persevere in all their undertakings with wonderful constancy and firmness, and can endure pain, and death itself, with a patience and fortitude that is almost incredible. Besides, a savage can hunt and fish, make the instruments for these purposes, and provide himself with all the necessaries of life. He can likewise serve his country, either in council or fight. But I do not know that there is upon the face of the earth a more useless, more contemptible, and more miserable animal than a wealthy, luxurious man, without business or profession, arts, sciences, or exercises.

If examples were wanting to shew the neceſſity of arts and ſciences in a wealthy and luxurious nation, that of the Romans would alone be ſufficient. The wealth of that people, about the end of the commonwealth and the beginning of the empire, was prodigious, and almoſt exceeding belief. For the wealth of the whole world then known was centered in Rome, collected from countries very much more opulent as well as more populous, than they are now. The eſtates of ſome individuals in Britain, great as they may ſeem to us, are but mean and contemptible, compared with the eſtates of the rich citizens of Rome. I doubt whether there has hitherto been among us any eſtate of Nabob, Commiſſary, Stockjobber, or Gameſter, that has exceeded half a million. But, among the Romans, eſtates of ſeveral millions were not uncommon *. And though the crime of ſuicide in Britain be frequent enough, yet I have heard of no Britiſh man that has put himſelf to death,

---

* See Dr. Arbuthnot's account of the wealth of the Romans, in his treatiſe upon antient coins, &c.

Book IV. PROGRESS OF LANGUAGE. 457

as Apicius did, because his fortune was reduced to £80,000 sterling*. And their luxury and magnificence was in proportion to their wealth. The expence sometimes of a single supper, among them, would be equal to what we should reckon a competent fortune even in these days †. In this country, our richest men are contented with a house in town and a country-seat; and indeed it is with difficulty that their fortunes can support the expence of both. But the Roman grandees, besides their palaces in town, had magnificent villas in different parts of Italy. Cicero, who was far from being rich or expensive, had no less than eighteen of them ‡. And, as if the land was not sufficient for their buildings, they often encroached upon the sea, which they covered with their villas, sometimes to a

---

* Seneca, Confolatio ad Helviam, cap. 10.

† Seneca speaks of single suppers that consumed the whole estate of a knight: ' Quid est cœna sump-
' tuosa flagitiosius, et equestrum censum consumente !"
Seneca, Epist. 95.

‡ Middleton's Life of Cicero, vol. 2. p. 508.

VOL. III.   H h

confiderable diftance from the fhore *. Their houfes, both in town and country, were filled with flaves, who were fometimes fo numerous, and of fo many different countries, that they were divided into nations.

What was it that preferved any virtue or manhood among a people fo rich and fo luxurious? The bad effects of wealth in Britain, fmall in comparifon of theirs, upon the morals of the people, have been moft fenfibly felt and regretted. But, among the Romans, even in the times we fpeak of, there are many fhining examples to be found of the greateft virtues, the moft eminent abilities, fortitude and ftrength both of body and mind. To what is this to be afcribed? What antidote had they againft

---

* Contracta pifces æquora fentiunt,
 Jactis in altum molibus; huc frequens
  Cæmenta demittit Redemptor
   Cum famulis, dominufque terræ
 Faftidiofus.——— Hor. Ode i. lib. 3.

Cæmentis licet occupes
 Tyrrhenum omne tuis et mare Apulicum.
   Ibid. Ode xxiv. lib. 3.

that most deadly poison of the human race, more fatal in its consequences than war, famine, pestilence, or any other calamity that ever befel the kind, I mean luxury? No other that I can discover, except the Greek philosophy* and Greek arts. These were unnecessary while they continued poor, and preserved the antient severity of their manners, but became absolutely necessary when they grew rich, and the public discipline of the state was relaxed, as well as the private manners of the citizens corrupted. Philosophy, which among them was, *The knowledge of all things human and divine*, that is, of the whole of nature and the system of the universe, presented so grand a spectacle, as raised those among them, who had any natural elevation of mind, much above all human pomp and grandeur, and made them despise all the

---

* The reason which Cicero gives for instructing his countrymen in the Greek philosophy is, ' That ' he knew no way so effectual of doing good as by ' instructing the minds and reforming the morals of ' the youth, which, in the licence of those times, wanted ' every help to restrain and correct them;' De divinatione, ii. 2. De finib. i. 3.

gratifications of luxury and vanity which their fortune afforded. The Greek arts, and particularly the rhetorical, the grammatical, and critical arts, by which they formed a good style, both of speaking and writing, were studied by all the nobility of Rome. And, as they were absolutely necessary to enable a man to make a figure, and support his rank in the state*, they

---

* The author of the dialogue *De Causis corruptæ eloquentiæ*, speaking of the incitements to the study of eloquence in the later times of the common-wealth, expresses himself in this manner;

' Quanto quisque plus dicendo poterat, tanto facilius honores assequebatur; tanto magis in ipsis honoribus collegas suos anteibat, tanto plus apud principes gratiæ, plus auctoritatis apud patres, plus notitiæ ac nominis apud plebem parabat. Hi clientelis etiam exterarum nationum redundabant; hos ituri in provincias magistratus reverebantur, hos reversi colebant, hos et præturæ et consulatus vocare ultro videbantur; hi ne privati quidem sine potestate erant, cum et populum et senatum consilio et auctoritate regerent; quin immo sibi ipsi persuaserant neminem sine eloquentia aut assequi posse in civitate aut tueri conspicuum et eminentem locum.'

And, a little afterwards,

were so much studied and practised, that they alone were sufficient to employ their whole lives. And, even with respect to philosophy, there was hardly a man of any note or eminence in Rome that was not addicted to one sect or another; and the philosophy professed by the great men of those days is a part of their history as well known as any other*.

* 'Ita ad summa eloquentiæ præmia, magna etiam necessitas accedebat, et commoda. Disertum haberi pulchrum et gloriosum; sed contra mutum et elinguem videri, deforme habebatur. Ergo non minus rubore quam præmiis stimulabantur; ne clientulorum loco potius quam patronorum, numerarentur; ne traditæ a majoribus necessitudines ad alios transirent; ne tanquam inertes et non suffecturi honoribus, aut non impetrarent, aut impetratos male tuerentur;' Cap. 36. 37.

† The old man Chremes, in the beginning of the Andrian of Terence, speaking of the passions of youth at that time, says,

Quod plerique omnes faciunt adolescentuli,
Ut animum ad aliquod studium adjungant, aut equos
Alere, aut canes ad venandum, *aut ad philosophos*.
           Andrian, v. 28.

Thus it appears that, among the youth of that age, a passion for philosophy was as common as for hounds and horses.

The first hero the Romans formed upon the Greek model was Scipio Africanus the younger, and the last man of any note, produced by the manners and discipline of the state was C. Marius. After his time, there was no man eminent either as a general or a statesman, during the period I speak of, that was not a scholar.

Thus it appears, from fact and experience as well as theory, that the cultivation of arts and sciences is absolutely necessary in a wealthy and luxurious nation. But what arts and sciences? Is it the study of botany, so much in fashion at present? Is it the knowledge of shells and insects? Is it facts of natural history? or is it the science of quantity, the knowledge of the properties of lines, figures, and numbers? Of this science I have a high esteem. I know it is very useful in the arts of life, and in explaining many things in nature; but I have always held it to be no more than the handmaid of philosophy; nor do I know that it has ever formed a hero or a patriot, a man eminent in the field or in the senate. There only remains then that learning which preserved virtue so long among the Romans, and threw a splendor upon the later times of that nation, such as never illuminated the degenerate days of any other.

There is one other use of antient learning, and which perhaps to some will recommend it more than any thing I have hitherto said in praise of it; and it is this, that it best teaches the arts of luxury; by which I mean not only the elegance and magnificence with which they adorned luxury, and raised it above mere sensuality, but chiefly those arts they employed to prevent, as far as was possible, the bad effects of it both upon body and mind. For, besides their athletic exercises, which, at the same time that they whetted the appetite for such enjoyments, gave strength and vigour to the body, they used bathing, anointing, rubbing, and other arts to preserve their health; so that, though the luxury of the Romans, at the time I speak of, was very much greater than ours, yet I aver the fact to be, that there were not among them near so many diseased and deformed by luxury, and rendered incapable of all businefs, as among us. This we are well aſſured of, not only from the public hiſtories of thoſe times, but from the private memoirs of them, preſerved in that voluminous, and at the ſame time moſt valuable epiſtolary correſpondence of Cicero, which has come down to us; and alſo from the anecdotes which Suetonius has related of the lives of the firſt emperors, ſome of whom were the greateſt monſters of luxury and intemperance of every kind that we read of in hiſtory. In ſhort, our luxury, as it is managed, is little better than the ſenſuality of barbarians; nor does it differ much from the intemperance of ſavages in ſpirituous liquors, except in this, that, though that exceſs be of all others the moſt deſtructive both to mind and body, yet, by means of the ſimplicity of the reſt of their diet, the air and exerciſe which they take, and certain antient arts that they uſe, ſuch as bathing and anointing, it does not hurt them near ſo much as our luxury, which we think ſo much more refined: And there is one thing which I would have our men who pretend to taſte and elegance conſider, and that is the deformity which our conſtant intemperance

Book IV. PROGRESS OF LANGUAGE. 465

in eating and drinking produces, and which is not to be found among the barbarous nations. For men that would be thought to have a taste for *beauty*, should study it in their persons, at least as much as in their dress, and the ornaments of their houses and gardens. And there is another thing which, I think, deserves most serious consideration, and that is the great increase of the crime of suicide among us of late. This, I think, may be in a great measure stated to the account of our barbarous *unlearned luxury*, by which the body is at last so oppressed and overlaid, and the spirits so affected, that life becomes an intolerable burden. The Romans, it is true, practised this kind of death much, but it was only to avoid the stroke of the executioner; or it was from a better motive, —to save their estates for the behoof of their families, which would have been confiscated, if they had waited till sentence was pronounced against them; by which means many an estate and family were preserved, under such emperors as Tiberius and Nero. And no doubt they sometimes chose to go out of life, when they were pressed by any calamity, public or private, which they thought infupportable. But I cannot at prefent recollect one inftance of any Roman who, from a *tædium vitæ*, low fpirits, weak nerves, or whatever other name we chufe to give to the effects of intemperance, and the indulgence of pleafure without any moderation, art, or œconomy, deftroyed himfelf.

Thus I have endeavoured to recommend antient learning, not only as it directs us to the nobleft purfuits in human life, but from its meaneft ufe, the improvement of our luxury, and the making us, if not men of virtue, at leaft men of *learned luxury*. And, upon the whole, I think, I may claim fome merit with the public, by this attempt to reftore, or preferve where it is not yet loft, antient learning, as a thing not only of elegance and ornament, but, in the prefent ftate of this nation, of the greateft public utility.

END OF VOLUME THIRD.

www.ingramcontent.com/pod-product-compliance
Lightning Source LLC
Chambersburg PA
CBHW021426300426
44114CB00010B/670